The Beatles on the Charts

The Beatles on the Charts

All Group and Solo Albums and Singles Ranked by Popularity

Michael A. Ventrella

McFarland & Company, Inc., Publishers
Jefferson, North Carolina

Library of Congress Cataloguing-in-Publication Data

Names: Ventrella, Mike, author.
Title: Beatles on the charts : all group and solo albums and singles ranked by popularity / Michael A. Ventrella.
Description: Jefferson, North Carolina : McFarland & Company, Inc., Publishers, 2023. | Includes index.
Identifiers: LCCN 2023001705 | ISBN 9781476690797 (paperback : acid free paper) ∞ ISBN 9781476648484 (ebook)
Subjects: LCSH: Beatles—Discography. | LCGFT: Discographies.
Classification: LCC ML156.7.B4 V45 2023 | DDC 782.42166092/2—dc23/eng/20230113
LC record available at https://lccn.loc.gov/2023001705

British Library cataloguing data are available

ISBN (print) 978-1-4766-9079-7
ISBN (ebook) 978-1-4766-4848-4

© 2023 Michael A. Ventrella. All rights reserved

No part of this book may be reproduced or transmitted in any form or by any means, electronic or mechanical, including photocopying or recording, or by any information storage and retrieval system, without permission in writing from the publisher.

The Beatles in the 1965 film *Help!* (United Artists/Photofest)

Printed in the United States of America

McFarland & Company, Inc., Publishers
Box 611, Jefferson, North Carolina 28640
www.mcfarlandpub.com

Contents

Acknowledgments vi
Introduction 1
About The Beatles 3
About the Charts 7

Singles 13
Albums 89

Alternate Countdowns 173
The Beatles Challenge 179
The Beatles Discography 181
The Charts 189
Index 235

Acknowledgments

Thanks to those who encouraged and helped along the way,
including proofreader/editor/Beatles fanatic Janet Davis,
Gray Rabbit publisher Ian Randal Strock,
all my friends on the various Beatles Facebook pages,
and, of course, my patient wife Heidi Hooper.

Introduction

Waking up early on Sunday was a requirement when I was a teenager. I'd sit in my bed, grab a piece of three-hole-punched lined school paper and a pencil, and turn on WGOE in Richmond to hear Casey Kasem count down the American Top 40. Writing the songs down, I'd compare them to the previous week's list, cheering on the songs I liked and booing the success of the songs I did not.

The charts have continued to fascinate me, although I stopped listening to Casey Kasem by the time I started college—it was all disco and Helen Reddy and, well, let's just say that with a few exceptions (such as The Beatles' solo songs), the mid-'70s were not the greatest time for music (until "new wave" came along, which rarely made the singles charts).

As I later played in a number of bands in college and then in law school, I had fantasies about one day seeing my own songs on the charts. Alas, that never happened.

Throughout this entire time, I knew exactly who my favorite band was, and still is to this day. So even though I may not have been keeping track of every song on the charts, I still would go to the college library every week to check out the latest *Billboard* magazine and see how John, Paul, George, and Ringo were doing.

Then Harry Castleman and Walter J. Podrazik's book *All Together Now* was released. I was thrilled! There weren't a lot of Beatles books back then, and no Internet to research things easily, so this huge discography was a great find. And the best part to me was that the appendix held charts of the very type I was keeping! I got their sequel *The Beatles Again?* but it only had a few more years of charts, so I started keeping track of the songs myself on graph paper.

In the '80s, I was a subscriber to Charles Rosenay's fanzine *Good Day Sunshine*, which kept me up to date on all the latest Beatles news. (Remember: No Internet.) I decided to take all my chart information and do an article for him. I remembered that *Billboard* would do a year-end countdown by assigning points to each song based on its position in the chart, with a song at number 100 getting one point, at 99 getting two points, and so on up to number one. *Billboard* gave the number one song 100 points plus a bonus 100 points, which didn't seem fair to me, so I didn't give the bonus points for my Beatles chart.

So the higher a song got on the chart and the longer it stayed on the chart, the more points.

In any event, the article was published in 1986. I stopped keeping the charts after a while … other things in my life took over, especially as the solo Beatles albums and songs became less frequent. I eventually started writing novels and short stories, editing anthologies, and even working on a few nonfiction books. I really wanted to write a book about The Beatles, but by that time, there were thousands (it seemed), and I thought to myself, "What can I possibly write that hasn't already been published?"

Introduction

It was when I wrote a book with Mark Arnold about the Monkees' music that I started thinking about this. That book (*Long Title: Looking for the Good Times: Examining The Monkees' Songs, One by One*) had an addendum where I took all the Monkees songs and albums, placed them in an Excel chart, and had a countdown of their hits, using the same formula I had used for the *Good Day Sunshine* article.

Because of that book, I've been invited to participate in various online chats about the Monkees and The Beatles and made friends with Charles Rosenay!!! (that's how he spells his name, with the exclamation points). When I pointed out the article I had written for him all those years ago, he was surprised that we had contacted each other almost thirty years earlier and had not realized it at first.

That's when I thought about expanding that article into this book, where I could also discuss each album and song along the way.

Easier said than done.

I had to go back and recreate every chart into a form I could export into a book. My handwritten graph paper wouldn't do. And then I realized how old I am and how much there was to do. I had stopped keeping track around 1987, and because of the *All Together Now* book, I only had about ten years' worth of research on my own. Did you know that thirty-six years have gone by between 1987 and 2023?

I had a lot of surprises as I compiled the charts. Reissues would jump back on the chart, compilations did very well, and the way *Billboard* made its charts had changed tremendously. (More on this later.)

Anyway, I hope all this is as interesting to you as it is to me. I know this book has a limited audience, and I am writing it to that audience with the assumption that you already know a lot about The Beatles so I don't need to address you like a beginner.

Happy reading!

About The Beatles

Every once in a while, some wag will say, "The Beatles? What's the big deal? They were just a fad."

Well, no. Fads come and go. The real test of quality is time.

There were comedians in the early days of motion pictures whose films sometimes were more successful than the Marx Brothers' or Charlie Chaplin's, but whom do we remember now? There were artists who made lots more money than Vincent van Gogh during his time but can you name them now? Does anyone go out of their way to watch whatever films won the Best Picture Oscar instead of *Citizen Kane* or *Raiders of the Lost Ark*? Do you think there's a reason Shakespeare's plays are still staged today?

"People will still be listening to The Beatles in the year 2000," Brian Epstein said in the early '60s, as people laughed at him. In the year 2000, The Beatles' album *1* was released, containing their top singles, and ended up as the best-selling album of *the entire decade*. Who's laughing now?

And a few hundred years from now, just like Shakespeare, people will still be talking about and listening to The Beatles.

So what makes them so special?

You have to start by putting yourself in that time period. Rock and roll was new—Chuck Berry and Little Richard and Bill Haley emerged around 1955 or so, and Paul and John met a few years later when they were teens. By 1962, when The Beatles recorded "Love Me Do," rock music was still new and only listened to by the younger generation. Older folks saw it as a fad that would go away as the kids grew up and learned to listen to "real" music like jazz and Broadway and classical.

The Beatles were different from the other rock and roll acts of the time in a few major ways. First is that they were a *band*. They weren't "John Lennon and The Beatles." With a few minor exceptions, almost all performers at the time had one obvious leader. We didn't have "The Crickets," we had "Buddy Holly and the Crickets." Each member of The Beatles handled lead vocals at least once per record so that an album by them had more than one lead singer while still sounding like The Beatles. In 1964, they had 28 songs hit the singles chart, and each of The Beatles had at least one lead vocal song in the Top 20.

Second, they used their musical talent to create more than the simple three-chord rock songs that dominated the airwaves at the time. Just compare the complexities of their original songs on their very first album to the covers they did. "Twist and Shout" has tremendous energy from their performance, but underneath that, it's not a very difficult song.

The Beatles had influences other than just rock and roll, and that shows in their original work. All you have to do is look at the songs they performed live before ever getting a recording contract and you'll see old pop standards and Broadway songs mixed in with the simple "Johnny B. Goode" rock-and-rollers. A large part of that may be attributed to Paul, whose musician father introduced him to lots of different styles. This allowed them to look at songwriting from a wider variety of influences.

Even more important, The Beatles were constantly trying to top themselves from song to song and album to album. So many bands and musicians find their style and keep it, either because they are not talented enough to expand their music or too afraid they will alienate their audience if they do so. The Beatles never worried about that.

But it wasn't just the talent they had—they were incredibly lucky. They were signed by their producer George Martin, who never tried to force them into a particular style and encouraged their experimentation. He was not a rock and roll producer and didn't try to make them sound like every other group out there. (This worried the American label, which decided their albums had to be full of reverb and echoes to match what American audiences were used to.) Then they managed to get Richard Lester to direct their films, and he produced two masterpieces of cinema that allowed us to see their sense of humor in a way other rock movies couldn't accomplish.

They were also lucky in that their manager Brian Epstein may have made them all wear matching suits (that's what all bands were like in those days), but other than that, he left them alone—and they were tremendously influential on our culture because of it.

Let's start with their haircuts. I know, right? Not a big deal today, but American boys in 1964 all had crew cuts. Much of the media that didn't get the music thought their success was because of their hair!

> **REPORTER:** *"People think your haircuts are un-American."*
> **JOHN:** *"Well, that's very observant of them, because we aren't American."*

But the day after The Beatles appeared on *The Ed Sullivan Show*, boys all across the country started combing their hair forward and letting it grow in the back.

The Beatles had to deal with silly questions from reporters and were not afraid to speak their minds. Unlike other bands who were coached to be teen heartthrobs and never alienate anyone with controversial comments, The Beatles paid no attention to that. And they had such a sense of humor! Who could dislike them?

> **REPORTER:** *"What kind of girl do you like, John?"*
> **JOHN:** *"My wife."*
> **REPORTER:** *"What kind of girl do you like, George?"*
> **GEORGE:** *"John's wife."*
> **REPORTER:** *"Ringo, do you have any political views?"*
> **RINGO:** *"No. I don't even smoke."* (He then took a very long drag on the cigarette he was holding.)
> **REPORTER:** *"Will you sing for us?"*
> **JOHN:** *"We need money first."*
> **REPORTER:** *"What do you think of topless bathing suits?"*
> **PAUL:** *"We've been wearing them for years."*

This would get them in a bit of trouble early on, such as when John claimed The Beatles were "bigger than Jesus," but as time went on, they stopped apologizing for what they said and took more controversial stands (especially John).

> **REPORTER:** *"What do you think of people burning your records in protest?"*
> **PAUL:** *"They have to buy them first, right? Then we're in favor of it."*

They meant what they said. When they first came to America, they put into their contracts that they would refuse to perform in any place where the audience was segregated. They didn't have to do that, but they insisted—and many places in the South had to change their policies if they wanted that sweet Beatles money coming in. They spoke out against discrimination ("Blackbird" was Paul's song on the topic, and the jam that later became "Get Back" was originally about racist politicians in Britain who "didn't want no Pakistanis"). They had a gay Jewish manager. The only person who got credit with them on a record was Billy Preston, a gay black man. John married an Asian woman, George married a Latina, and Paul married two Jewish women (not at the same time!). Paul and Ringo still work for and contribute to various charities, with Ringo recently dedicating funds from a birthday concert to Black Lives Matter. They didn't just speak about love and understanding—they practiced what they preached. They weren't perfect; they had their faults. But they meant what they said.

But enough of being amazed at The Beatles. If you didn't know anything about them, you wouldn't be reading this book right now, would you? We don't need to go into their entire history, and this book will assume you are familiar with the basics, but if not? There are a thousand other books about The Beatles out there to fill in those gaps.

Let's talk about the charts!

About the Charts

Billboard magazine has always been the main source of information and charts for the music industry, having been founded in the late 1800s, when they covered carnivals and fairs. There were competitors over the years (*Cashbox*, for instance) but they've fallen by the wayside.

When The Beatles first appeared on the scene, the singles chart was primarily based on radio play. You see, amazingly, disc jockeys back in those days had a lot of freedom to play what they wanted to without huge corporations dictating which songs could reach the air. As a result, the charts were very eclectic, with rock and roll charting next to Broadway songs, country ballads, funky soul, novelty songs, and anything else that grabbed the attention of the DJ. They would pay attention to the request line, and popular picks would get more airplay.

Because of the reliance on airplay, *Billboard* would also list the B-side as if it was a separate record altogether. So we'll see both "We Can Work It Out" and "Day Tripper" hit the chart together despite them both being on the same piece of vinyl.

This changed in late 1969. "Something" and its B-side "Come Together" were both zooming up the chart, with the B-side sometimes outperforming the A-side. Finally, *Billboard* said, "Screw this; from now on, we're just counting records, not songs." So suddenly, on November 29, 1969, the two songs were combined as one, and together, they hit #1.

Then for a while *Billboard* would list both sides together if the B-side was getting airplay, so we'd see "The Long and Winding Road" / "For You Blue" on the chart and then later that year "My Sweet Lord" / "Isn't It a Pity." This continued on for a while but seems to have ended a few years later, when only the A-side was mentioned.

For purposes of this book, the B-sides that charted separately in the years before 1969's change are listed separately. When calculating the points for "Something" and "Come Together," I had to figure out whether to have these listed as three separate entries or just give each song the points they were assigned together, and I decided on the latter, as if they were tied on the chart.

Another reason the B-sides stopped counting as separate entries on the chart was because *Billboard* was moving to a more scientific way of calculating the data, by looking more at sales instead of just radio play. They had been contacting a random number of record stores and record companies over the years for their input and had used the information provided to make their charts, and especially their album charts. This switch meant that by the mid-'70s, songs stayed on the charts for longer periods, because people would still be buying the singles long after DJs had gotten tired of playing them.

So here's *Warning #1*: It is very hard to compare how well songs did on the charts over the years because the methodology of creating the charts has changed over time.

Tied into this is *Warning #2*: Chart performance doesn't equate to sales. Look at it this way: A #1 song could sell only one more copy than a song at #2, and perhaps less than whatever the #1 song was a week before. The charts are really only useful for comparing the song against others at the time the chart was made.

To make matters worse, the stores and the companies might not have been as reliable as they should have been when reporting sales. I mean, come on—you don't have to be an expert in the history of modern music to know about corruption in the industry and people who have a very strong interest in exaggerating the sales of something they want to reach #1.

I know, I know—kind of makes this book useless, doesn't it? Eh, it's mostly for entertainment value. The countdowns here should not be looked at as any sort of scientific absolute.

Warning #3 is obvious: Position on the chart has little to do with the quality of the song. Mediocre songs hit the top all the time while amazing works die at the bottom. But you all should know that.

Back to the charts: In the early 1990s, *Billboard* was able to start using the scanning devices at record stores to get very accurate readings of sales. This made the chart a lot more reliable and resulted in some noticeable changes. Genres that had been undercounted in the past (country and rap especially) started doing much better on the charts. Instead of albums being released and moving up the chart week by week before reaching #1, albums would debut at #1 as fans rushed out to buy them.

By 2005, *Billboard* was also including digital downloads. Within a few years, streaming and YouTube views were included to get the most accurate reading possible. (Although this seems to be a move backward, to include *plays* as opposed to just sales. Go figure.)

All this really messes up the way we expect this to work, because if you download or stream an album song by song, each song gets credit and so now artists can (and do) have a dozen new songs on the chart at the same time. Taylor Swift comes out with a new album, and the next thing you know, every single song on the album is in the Top 20 for a week at least. People are saying The Beatles' record of having that many songs in the chart at once has been broken, but come on, this is an entirely new way to count a song's popularity. The comparison isn't fair. (And note that I said "popularity," not "sales." Given that the charts these days count streaming and YouTube and other ways to enjoy a song, "sales" no longer applies.)

So before we get into *our* charts, let's discuss what surprises we find when we look at almost sixty years of The Beatles on the *Billboard* charts.

First, let's smile and acknowledge that according to *Billboard*, the #1 performing artist since their charts began has been The Beatles. No surprise there.

But look at the charts in the back of this book. I specifically had the charts cover every single week, even if there was no Beatles song or album that week, because I wanted to see how much time elapsed between appearances. In the '60s, they put out two albums a year (more in America), and then, starting around 1969, each Beatle had his own solo releases as well. So we see that from January 18, 1964, through December 15, 1979, there was always a Beatles song or album on the charts. That's an amazing

About the Charts

achievement. The longest period when there were no Beatles on the charts was from June 7, 2008, through June 27, 2009—barely more than one year.

And recently, they're constantly there on the album chart. Thanks to remastering and repackaged versions (along with more accurate ways of counting sales), you'll see sixty-year-old albums on the charts. *Abbey Road* has hardly left the charts in the past six years and is still there as of the writing of this book (at the end of 2021). And it's not just The Beatles: many classic albums from bands can be found each week, because they're still selling.

On the other hand, this new reliance on mostly sales means things can get weird. An album can appear on the chart at #1 and then disappear within a few weeks after all the fans grabbed their copies early (for example, see Paul's *Egypt Station*'s numbers). Stranger still are things like when *Magical Mystery Tour* appears in the Top 100 and then disappears completely the very next week.

Some reappearances are easy to explain. For instance, when Paul tours, his albums pop back up on the charts. Others are complete mysteries ... *magical* mysteries!

As you read the album countdown, you'll also see a few weird things, especially if you're young and only familiar with The Beatles from their CDs or albums you can download. So let's clear a few things up:

Capitol, The Beatles' American record company, took the British albums which basically included seven songs a side and said, "We can make a lot more money by putting out albums with only six or even five songs a side! And those silly British with their singles that don't appear on albums? Heck with that, we can use those to pad our albums. And the soundtrack albums from their movies? Let's cut out half of those songs and fill the rest with the background instrumentals. The kids'll buy it anyway, it's The Beatles!"

So since this book is about the American charts only, we only see the American albums, which were usually quite inferior to the British ones. And sometimes the way they sequenced the albums made little sense. *Rubber Soul* was cut from fourteen songs down to twelve, but even weirder, Capitol took two songs from *Help!* they had cut and placed them there. That had to be frustrating for The Beatles, who clearly took time to figure out sequencing for their albums only to see that completely ignored in the States.

By *Sergeant Pepper*, the albums were the same in America and Britain (well, except for *Magical Mystery Tour*, which originally was only an EP in Britain).

The Beatles then started their own record company, Apple, in 1968. Their first Beatles release was the single "Hey Jude" followed a few months later by *The Beatles* (aka the *White Album*). That didn't stop their later manager Allen Klein from acting just as bad as Capitol and releasing another patched-together album in America called *Hey Jude*.

The Beatles were contracted to Capitol even as individuals through 1976, when the contract expired. We're not going to get into the legal hassles Apple was having at the time, but you need to understand that because of that, Capitol took the incentive to put out various collections of Beatles songs on albums such as *Love Songs*, *Rock 'n' Roll Music*, *Rarities*, and *20 Greatest Hits*—despite The Beatles' objections. (You will note that now that Apple has gained control of all The Beatles' music again, none of those have been re-released.)

About the Charts

The main problem I had with compiling this list was trying to make decisions about the albums for this chart. The *Rubber Soul* that made the chart when it was first released in America is not the *Rubber Soul* that later came out on CD and made the chart again. Do I count *Let It Be* separately from *Let It Be.... Naked*? When Paul re-releases his albums as CDs with a bunch of extra tracks and they reappear on the chart, do I count them as new albums?

Generally speaking, if the albums were indeed mostly the same, I didn't list them separately. I did so with *Let It Be* and *Let It Be.... Naked* because I felt they were different enough and were listed separately by *Billboard*. Same with *Yellow Submarine* and the *Yellow Submarine Songtrack*. Otherwise, you'll see what I decided as you read through, and if you disagree with my choices—well, all the data is here in this book for you to figure out for yourself how you would make this list!

What about ties? There were a few, broken by which one got higher on the chart, then by how many weeks it was on the chart, and then if there's still a tie, just by release date.

And then I had to decide how to deal with collaborations. Paul had two hit singles with Michael Jackson, and I debated whether to count "The Girl Is Mine" since it's on a Michael Jackson album. I eventually decided to use it since the single is credited to Michael Jackson/Paul McCartney. Recently, Paul has worked with Kanye West on the singles "Only One" and "All Day," but only one single has Paul credited alongside him and Rihanna ("FourFiveSeconds"), so that's the only one counted, even though he had no lead vocals on it. Ignore it on the list if you disagree. Trust me, I struggled over whether to include it.

I included George's band the Traveling Wilburys because, come on, he played a major part in founding it, and if we're counting albums that are only credited to Wings, then certainly the Wilburys should count. As should Suzy and the Red Stripes' song "Seaside Woman," which is actually Wings in disguise and which was even performed by them live prior to its recording (and almost made it onto the Wings album *Red Rose Speedway*). I was considering the *McGear* album, which is Paul's brother Michael backed with Wings and featuring songs co-written with Paul, but it never made the chart so that's a moot point. (And neither did Paul's albums using the name "The Fireman," nor his "Percy Thrillington" album.)

I know, not everyone will agree with these decisions, but The Beatles played on so many other recordings by other artists that if I tried to count them all, this book would be twice as large. I limited my list to only those where they were credited equally with the other artist.

In any event, let's start the countdown, current as of the end of 2021 (when a few Beatles albums were still on the charts!). Just to make sure it's clear, here's how this is organized:

First, we'll count down the singles. Every song that made the Billboard Top 100 chart is listed. You'll see the name of the song followed by the artist: The Beatles, Paul McCartney, Plastic Ono Band, Wings, Traveling Wilburys—whatever the label said.

Next is the point value. Note that the first song on our list is "Sie Liebt Dich" which first appeared on the Billboard chart on June 27, 1964. It reached #97 and was only on the chart for one week. A song at #100 gets one point in our countdown, two points at #99, three points at #98, four points at #97, and so on. The longer a song stays on the chart and the higher it gets, the more points.

Following that is the date the song first appeared on the charts (even if it left the chart and reappeared later). Next is the highest position the song reached. If a song hit #1 and stayed there more than one week, then the number of weeks in which it was at top is listed in parentheses.

The countdown progresses based on the points awarded until we get to #1 in our countdown (which might be a surprise to you!).

Next, we do the same for the albums. The main difference is this: The album chart goes up to 200, so the points are greater. Further, albums can stay on the charts a very long time or fall off the charts and then reappear later, so the "chart appearance" only reflects the very first time it appeared.

So let's start our countdown!

SINGLES

162. "Sie Liebt Dich"
The Beatles
4 points
Chart appearance: 6/27/1964
Highest position: 97
Weeks on the chart: 1

To appeal to a German audience, The Beatles were encouraged to sing "She Loves You" and "I Want to Hold Your Hand" in that language. They protested but later gave in, and then vowed never to do it again, especially since for "She Loves You," they had to record the entire thing all over from scratch since the original had all been mixed down to mono and there was no way to remove just the vocal track. The two songs were released in Germany and did well.

Swan Records had the rights to "She Loves You" in America so they were able to get the tapes of that song and release it as a single. Why not? Even if it only reaches #97, you'll make some money, right?

Not surprisingly, it's at the very bottom of our list.

161. "The Inner Light"
The Beatles
5 points
Chart appearance: 3/30/1968
Highest position: 96
Weeks on the chart: 1

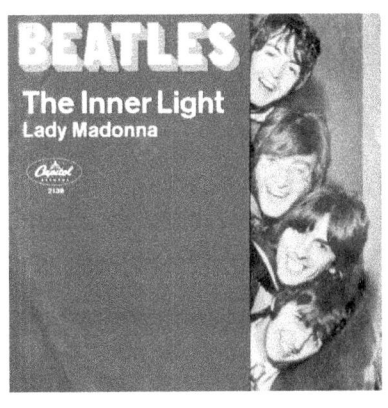

"The Inner Light" was George's first appearance as a writer on a single; in this case, the B-side to "Lady Madonna." Sitar-based Indian music might be popular on long-playing records, but Top 40 radio stations weren't interested, and so this only appeared low on the chart for one week.

This was George's third and last sitar-heavy song (after "Love You To" and "Within You Without You"). It was recorded in India using local talent around the same time George was recording the album *Wonderwall Music*. Vocals (with backing from John and Paul at the very end) were added later.

This single became quite a collector's item for a while, because "The Inner Light" never appeared on any album until *Rarities*, and not in stereo until *Past Masters Volume 2*.

160. "I'm Happy Just to Dance with You"

The Beatles
6 points
Chart appearance: 8/1/1964
Highest position: 95
Weeks on the chart: 1

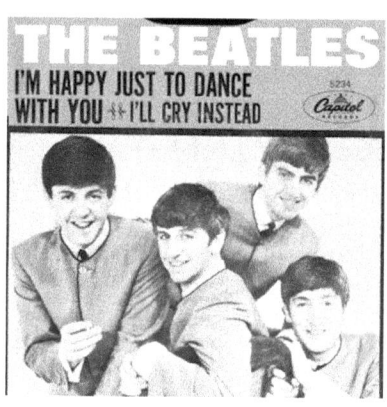

When the film *A Hard Day's Night* was released, United Artists had the rights to the soundtrack album but apparently there was a loophole that allowed Capitol to retain the rights to most of the songs. Capitol immediately went about trying to undercut United Artists by releasing three singles from the album at the same time ("A Hard Day's Night," "And I Love Her," and "I'll Cry Instead").

That was a bit much, and other than the title song, the others never reached the Top 10.

This was the B-side to "I'll Cry Instead" and was the second (and last) Lennon/McCartney song to be sung by George. Possibly due to the abundance of Beatles songs on the chart at the time, this only reached #95 for one week.

159. "Freedom"

Paul McCartney
8 points
Chart appearance: 12/15/2001
Highest position: 97
Weeks on the chart: 2

Paul's album *Driving Rain* was just about to be released when the attack on the World Trade Center changed everything. Paul was a witness to the attack, sitting in a plane at JFK airport, and he quickly wrote and recorded this song in response. It was added to the album at the last minute, but became a surprise track, since the cover had already been printed.

Paul then began organizing a fundraising concert to support the front-line rescue workers in New York City. The concert was held in October and featured Paul, The Who, David Bowie, Elton John, Eric Clapton, and many others. It ended up raising over $35 million.

"Freedom," however, did not fare as well. It appeared near the bottom of the chart for one week. It was pretty much quickly forgotten and despite being a single, has never appeared on a greatest hits album.

158. "Why"

Tony Sheridan and The Beatles
13 points
Chart appearance: 4/18/1964
Highest position: 88
Weeks on the chart: 1

Beatlemania is thriving so anything with their name is being released. This song may have The Beatles playing backup, but it's Tony singing. (Note how small Tony's name is on the single sleeve.) As expected, this did not generate much attention, except perhaps from kids buying it and then saying, "That doesn't sound much like The Beatles."

157. *Four by The Beatles* (EP)

The Beatles
17 points
Chart appearance: 6/13/1964
Highest position: 92
Weeks on the chart: 3

Extended play singles (EPs) never caught on in America. This one barely made it out of the Top 90. Two of the songs had already been released as singles prior to this ("All My Loving" and "Roll Over Beethoven"). This was probably Capitol America trying to take sales away from those singles, which were from other labels.

156. "This One"

Paul McCartney
19 points
Chart appearance: 9/9/1989
Highest position: 94
Weeks on the chart: 3

From Paul's *Flowers in the Dirt* album comes this song, which did fairly well in Britain but for some reason never hit in America. It was the follow-up single to "My Brave Face" which made the Top 40, and is one of Paul's better songs, but by the late '80s, we had gone past the time when anything a Beatle released was a hit. A very entertaining psychedelic video was made to promote it to no avail.

Despite the quality of the song (and its success in Britain), it has never appeared on any of the greatest hits collections Paul has released.

155. "There's a Place"
The Beatles
27 points
Chart appearance: 4/11/1964
Highest position: 74
Weeks on the chart: 1

Vee-Jay Records created a sub-label called Tollie and released a few Beatles singles, perhaps in an attempt to separate themselves from the Capitol lawsuits that were coming.

"There's a Place" was the B-side to "Twist and Shout" and showed up on the charts for one week, back in the days when B-sides could also rear their heads.

"There's a Place" was written with "Somewhere" from *West Side Story* in mind. John twisted it a bit by making the place in his mind, which was more than you usually heard from pop songs in 1963.

154. "Figure of Eight"
Paul McCartney
28 points
Chart appearance: 1/13/1990
Highest position: 92
Weeks on the chart: 5

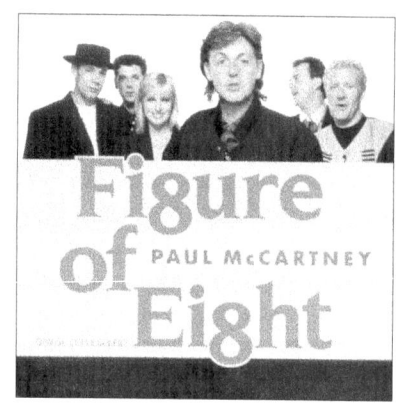

Paul's follow-up to "This One" did only slightly better. While this song is also from *Flowers in the Dirt*, the single is actually a different, new version. And unlike many singles culled from albums, this one is *longer* than the album version. It has more energy and as such, many fans consider it the superior version. Sadly, it did not do well on the charts.

153. "What Goes On"
The Beatles
32 points
Chart appearance: 3/12/1966
Highest position: 81
Weeks on the chart: 2

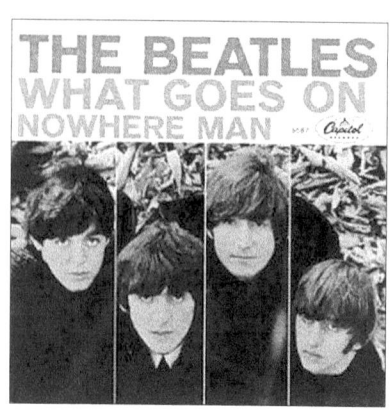

"What Goes On" was on the British *Rubber Soul*, but Capitol cut it and "Nowhere Man" and instead released them both as a single. This would be the last of The Beatles' "rockabilly" songs that Ringo sang so well.

The song was originally written by John back in the Quarryman days, but he and Paul added a middle eight. It's the only Beatles song credited to Lennon/McCartney/Starkey and is clearly written for Ringo to sing. Ringo has admitted that his contribution is mainly a few lyrics.

152. "Beaucoups of Blues"

Ringo Starr
41 points
Chart appearance: 11/7/1970
Highest position: 87
Weeks on the chart: 5

The Beatles may have stopped recording rockabilly or country-flavored songs, but that didn't stop Ringo, whose second album was recorded in Nashville. This single from the album of the same name sold mostly because it was Ringo.

The B-side was not on the album and is a country song written by Ringo called "Coochy-Coochy." Ringo has stated that he only knows three chords, but this song only has one, and goes on for almost five minutes.

151. "Sergeant Pepper's Lonely Hearts Club Band"

Paul McCartney and U2
53 points
Chart appearance: 7/23/2005
Highest position: 48
Weeks on the chart: 1

The Live 8 Concert on July 2, 2005, to raise funds for Africa featured a live version of this classic song performed by Paul and U2. It was released as a downloadable single on iTunes a few days later and hit the charts for one week before disappearing. However, it set a record for the fastest-selling online single at the time.

150. "Hey Baby"

Ringo Starr
59 points
Chart appearance: 1/29/1977
Highest position: 74
Weeks on the chart: 3

The second single from *Ringo's Rotogravure* is a very good remake of the old rock and roll standard, and, after all, Ringo had a big hit with his last rock and roll cover ("Only You"). This only stayed on the chart for a few weeks, however, and is largely forgotten now.

149. "Dance Tonight"
Paul McCartney
61 points
Chart appearance: 7/7/2007
Highest position: 69
Weeks on the chart: 2

A mandolin-led song from the *Memory Almost Full* album, "Dance Tonight" is a simple melody that was Paul's first Top 100 single in six years and his last one as a solo artist as well (unless you count the old song "Wonderful Christmastime" which tends to show up on the chart around holiday time). It did grab him a Grammy nomination for Best Male Vocalist, however. A very clever video was made to promote it, featuring Natalie Portman as a ghost. Don't ask why, just watch it and enjoy.

148. "Stranglehold"
Paul McCartney
68 points
Chart appearance: 11/15/1986
Highest position: 81
Weeks on the chart: 6

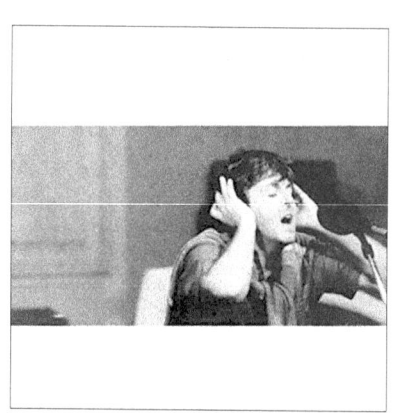

The second single (and the opening track) from Paul's *Press to Play* album did not do as well as the first single "Press," which didn't do that well, either. It's not clear why; earlier that same year, he had hit the Top 10, so it's not like Paul was suddenly unpopular. This song was written by Paul and 10cc's Eric Stewart.

147. "Jealous Guy"
John Lennon
68 points
Chart appearance: 10/15/1988
Highest position: 80
Weeks on the chart: 4

In October of 1988, to promote the movie and album *Imagine: John Lennon*, this single was released. This song originally appeared on the *Imagine* album in 1971 and had it been released at that time as a follow-up to "Imagine," it probably would have been a hit, as it is one of John's best. Here, many years later, as a song all John fans knew, it didn't attract too much attention. It only reached #80 on the charts and only stayed around for a month.

146. "Baby It's You"
The Beatles
70 points
Chart appearance: 4/22/1995
Highest position: 67
Weeks on the chart: 4

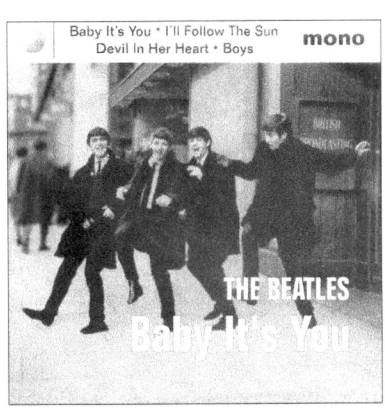

To promote the album *Beatles at the BBC*, this EP was released with their live version of the Bacharach tune "Baby It's You," originally recorded by The Shirelles. It rose up the chart to #67 and stayed for four weeks. Not bad for a thirty-year-old recording!

The other songs on this EP ("I'll Follow the Sun," "Boys," and "Devil in Her Heart") were not on *Beatles at the BBC*. This certainly made this a collector's item and probably helped its chart appearance. *On Air—Live at the BBC* later included two of them, but not "Devil in Her Heart." So if you want that song, you need this.

145. "Hope of Deliverance"
Paul McCartney
88 points
Chart appearance: 2/20/1993
Highest position: 83
Weeks on the chart: 6

Off the Ground was a well-reviewed album, but this single didn't get any higher than #83 in America, although it performed much better in the rest of the world. It's a nice, jangly acoustic number with an optimistic viewpoint that probably should have done better.

On the other hand, it had been six years since Paul had hit the Top 10, and the kids of the '90s who bought singles just weren't into "oldies" music like The Beatles. No matter how good the songs they were producing, they just weren't current Top 40 material.

The CD single had three extra songs that were not on the album: "Big Boys Bickering," "Long Leather Coat," and "Kicked Around No More."

144. *Four by The Beatles*

The Beatles
92 points
Chart appearance: 3/27/1965
Highest position: 68
Weeks on the chart: 5

Capitol tried again to get American record buyers to grab EPs to no success. It contained three covers ("Honey Don't," "Mister Moonlight," and "Everybody's Trying to Be My Baby") and one original ("I'm a Loser").

It stayed on the chart longer than the previous EP and reached higher, but still fell short of the Top 40. This one featured four songs from the *Beatles '65* album.

143. "Roll Over Beethoven"

The Beatles
104 points
Chart appearance: 3/21/1964
Highest position: 68
Weeks on the chart: 4

"Roll Over Beethoven" was never a single in America. So what's it doing on the American charts? Well, it was a single in Canada, and in March of 1964, radio play meant more than the fact that many Americans could not even buy this as an import in most stores. Given the difficulty in finding it in the States, it's not surprising that it only hit #68. Then again, it was the height of Beatlemania, and with literally ten Beatles songs in the Top 100, there might have been enough already! (Also, most fans already had these songs by that time.)

142. "Happy Xmas (War Is Over)"

John Lennon and Yoko Ono and The Plastic Ono Band with The Harlem Community Choir
115 points
Chart appearance: 12/22/2018
Highest position: 42
Weeks on the chart: 2

This holiday song was performed with a children's choir, making it perfect for the season. It was originally released late in 1971 but didn't make the chart. Part of the reason is that for years, despite this song being heard every holiday season, *Billboard*

had a separate "Christmas chart" where this would make an appearance instead of the regular Top 100 chart. (It did make the Christmas chart that year, reaching #3.)

Then, more recently, the Top 100 chart started keeping track of downloads, streams, and YouTube listens, and started counting everything. So now, every Christmas, holiday songs appear going all the way back to Bing Crosby's crooning. For a few weeks a year, the charts are dominated by Mariah Carey and Roy Rogers, Chuck Berry and Andy Williams. So "Happy Xmas" appeared on this chart in 2018 for a few weeks, along with Paul's "Wonderful Christmastime."

Why "Happy Xmas" has not appeared since that time is a mystery, given how often one can hear it being played each December.

The original single was actually printed on green vinyl.

141. "Sergeant Pepper's Lonely Hearts Club Band/With a Little Help from My Friends"

The Beatles
135 points
Chart appearance: 9/16/1978
Highest position: 71
Weeks on the chart: 8

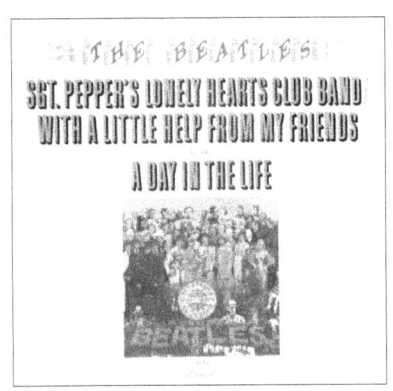

So it's 1978 and there's this new film called *Sergeant Pepper's Lonely Hearts Club Band* starring the current disco kings The Bee Gees. The Beatles' album is back on the charts and Capitol releases the first two songs as a medley single, because who wouldn't rather hear the original version? And with "A Day in the Life" as the B-side!

Well, as an old song that almost everyone already had, it did well enough, but never reached higher than #71. Many Beatles fans are not even aware this was released, which could help you win trivia contests about whether any singles were ever released from the *Sergeant Pepper* album.

140. "I Should Have Known Better"

The Beatles
151 points
Chart appearance: 7/25/1964
Highest position: 53
Weeks on the chart: 4

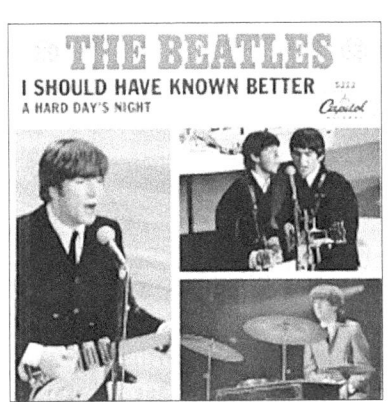

The B-side to "A Hard Day's Night" is one of John's last harmonica songs, which had become somewhat of a Beatles trademark ever since "Love Me Do." It would appear again in "Rocky Raccoon" and a bit in "All Together Now," but that's about it.

This song was one of the highlights of *A Hard Day's Night*, where The Beatles are singing this on a train (which was actually just a trailer that stagehands rocked back and forth to simulate a train's movement).

139. "I Am the Walrus"

The Beatles
152 points
Chart appearance: 12/9/1967
Highest position: 56
Weeks on the chart: 4

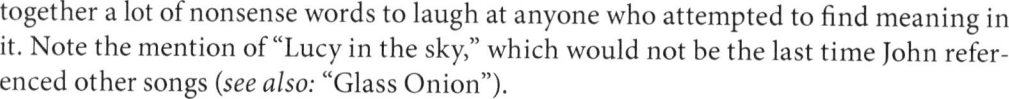

One of The Beatles' weirdest, most creative, and most interesting songs was just too strange for Top 40 radio, so only reached #56. It was the B-side to "Hello Goodbye" which hit #1.

John was frustrated that people kept analyzing his songs in ways he never meant, so he strung together a lot of nonsense words to laugh at anyone who attempted to find meaning in it. Note the mention of "Lucy in the sky," which would not be the last time John referenced other songs (*see also:* "Glass Onion").

This is the only song from the *Magical Mystery Tour* movie to be released on a single (unless you count the "fade out" of "Hello Goodbye"). It was mixed into mono back in the days when the mono versions were the "official" versions. The stereo version on *Magical Mystery Tour* switches to a fake mono when it gets to the "Sitting in an English Garden" part because they added the radio production of *King Lear* after the mono mix, and in order to do a proper stereo mix, that would be lost. However, for the *Love* album, they were able to fake it somehow, and now if you get that version, the song is in true stereo (with some sound effects added).

138. "I'm Stepping Out"

John Lennon
160 points
Chart appearance: 3/31/1983
Highest position: 55
Weeks on the chart: 6

"Nobody Told Me" sold well as the first single from *Milk and Honey*, but this follow-up couldn't make the Top 40. This is a simple song that feels like it's a practice version (which it really was). This was the last original John song that was released as a single (not counting "Jealous Guy" being released years later. See #147).

137. "Seaside Woman"
Suzy and the Red Stripes
168 points
Chart appearance: 6/11/1977
Highest position: 59
Weeks on the chart: 5

"Seaside Woman" was recorded by Wings partially to counter critics who said Linda couldn't write a song or sing. It was released under the name "Suzy and the Red Stripes" but the secret that it was really Wings wasn't well kept. An animated film was later made from the song and the single was re-released, this time giving credit to Linda. The B-side to "Seaside" is a song called "B-side to Seaside."

136. "Wake Up My Love"
George Harrison
171 points
Chart appearance: 11/20/1982
Highest position: 53
Weeks on the chart: 5

In an attempt to please his record label Warner Brothers, George recorded this very dated-sounding single, full of '80s synthesizers and drum sounds. Then, dissatisfied with the result, George refused to promote it.

The single and album it came from (*Gone Troppo*) did poorly, and it was another four years before George would once more venture into the studio.

135. "Woman Is the Nigger of the World"
John Lennon/Plastic Ono Band
175 points
Chart appearance: 5/20/1972
Highest position: 57
Weeks on the chart: 5

Is it any wonder many radio stations refused to play a song with a title like this, even though it came from a Beatle? For a song with little to no radio play, it still sold fairly well, but it ends up as John's lowest ranked single in his lifetime. It's a great John tune, and the point he's making about women's rights is valid (and pre-dated other similarly themed songs), but a better metaphor could have helped.

The single sleeve says "Nova" in big letters over John and Yoko's head, which was a complete mystery to many who bought the single, unaware that this was a picture from a magazine called that.

134. "You Can't Do That"
The Beatles
176 points
Chart appearance: 4/4/1964
Highest position: 48
Weeks on the chart: 4

This great tune was originally planned as The Beatles' next single until Paul came up with "Can't Buy Me Love." Instead, it appears on the B-side.

It's a wonderful rocker with (according to John himself) "a cowbell going four in the bar and the chord going chatoong!" The lyrics are pretty misogynistic, but hey, John learned over the years (see #135 above).

The song was not included on the American album of *A Hard Day's Night*, so you'd think it would have gotten a bit more radio play as something extra and thus performed better on the chart. On the other hand, the week it was released literally had another dozen Beatles songs to compete against.

133. "Yes It Is"
The Beatles
176 points
Chart appearance: 5/1/1965
Highest position: 46
Weeks on the chart: 4

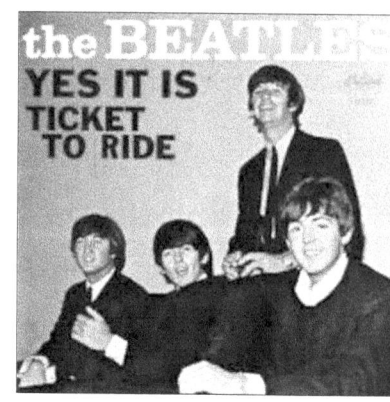

This B-side to "Ticket to Ride" appeared on the American album *Beatles VI* but never appeared on any British album until *Past Masters*.

It's a John tune with complicated harmonies, in which he admitted he was trying to write another "This Boy." George gets to play with his new volume-control pedal, which also appears on his own "I Need You" and then thankfully never again.

132. "End of the Line"
Traveling Wilburys
223 points
Chart appearance: 2/11/1989
Highest position: 63
Weeks on the chart: 9

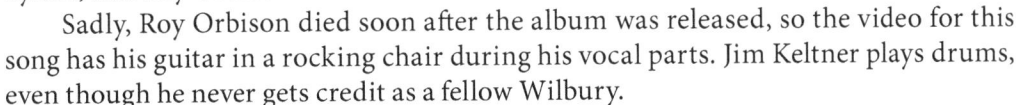

This second single from the first *Traveling Wilburys* album was written by George but all the songs on the Wilburys albums are credited to everyone.

All of the Wilburys share vocals except for Bob Dylan: Tom Petty sings the verses while George, Jeff Lynne, and Roy Orbison share the chorus.

Sadly, Roy Orbison died soon after the album was released, so the video for this song has his guitar in a rocking chair during his vocal parts. Jim Keltner plays drums, even though he never gets credit as a fellow Wilbury.

Although the album was a huge hit, the singles never caught on, neither of them reaching the Top 40 despite radio play and the video being fairly well seen.

131. "Tug of War"
Paul McCartney
231 points
Chart appearance: 10/2/1982
Highest position: 53
Weeks on the chart: 8

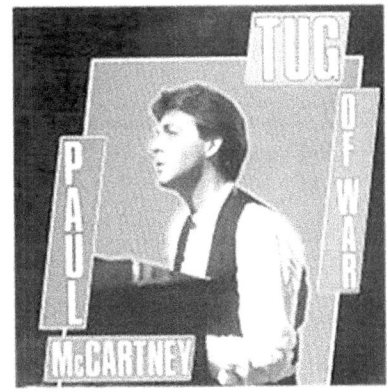

The third single from Paul's successful *Tug of War* album never hit the Top 40. It's a well-produced song by George Martin. Many think Paul is talking about the back-and-forth he experienced with John, especially since this is the first song on the first album Paul released after John's death. Then again, perhaps it's just about the struggle we all go through in life.

130. "From Me to You"
The Beatles
246 points
Chart appearance: 3/7/1964
Highest position: 41
Weeks on the chart: 6

In America, this appeared as the B-side to Vee-Jay's release of "Please Please Me." It had been a huge hit in England the previous year but here, it fell just short of the Top 40. Then again, there were half a dozen Beatles songs on the chart already, and more would be added in the following weeks.

129. "Don't Let Me Down"
The Beatles and Billy Preston
251 points
Chart appearance: 5/10/1969
Highest position: 35
Weeks on the chart: 4

The B-side to the huge hit "Get Back" didn't fare as well as the A-side. While it's an emotional John tune with some clever time signatures and counter-melodies, it really isn't a standard pop song. It was recorded during the same sessions but was left off the *Let It Be* album (having appeared a few months earlier on *Hey Jude*). This meant John only had one new song on that album ("Dig a Pony") since "Across the Universe" had been recorded a year earlier and "One After 909" was an old song originally performed with the Quarrymen!

This single is the only time The Beatles shared credit with someone else on a record (not counting Tony Sheridan sharing his with them).

128. "The World Tonight"
Paul McCartney
255 points
Chart appearance: 5/24/1997
Highest position: 64
Weeks on the chart: 10

The first single from the excellent *Flaming Pie* album didn't grab a ton of attention. In Britain, "Young Boy" and later "Wonderful Night" were released as singles instead.

A promotional documentary called "In the World Tonight" was made about the creation of the *Flaming Pie* album, and shown on VH1. Perhaps the title of the documentary encouraged the single's release.

127. "Ob-La-Di, Ob-La-Da"
The Beatles
260 points
Chart appearance: 11/20/1976
Highest position: 49
Weeks on the chart: 7

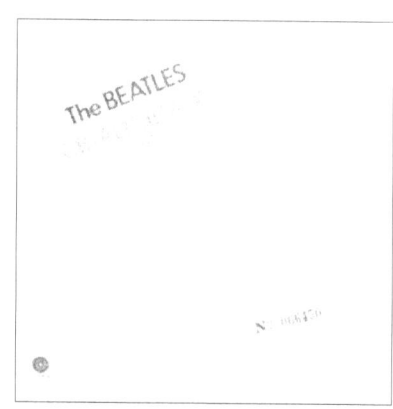

Capitol Records was doing everything they could to capitalize on The Beatles name while lawsuits kept Apple from having much control, and this single from 1976 (eight years after its original release on *The Beatles*) was another attempt. It lasted seven weeks on the chart but barely broke the Top 50. Their last collection *Rock 'n' Roll Music* was still on the chart, but this song wasn't part of that collection, so its release is kind of out of left field.

You would never tell from the recording that the other three really didn't like Paul's song, which he had hoped to release as a single. Many different outtakes are available to show that they spent an inordinate amount of time on this one song (well, inordinate for 1968—these days it seems that bands spend months on just one song). George even showed his contempt for it in "Savoy Truffle" where he sings, "We all know Ob-la-di-bla-da" in a snide voice.

But instead, this song sounds tremendously happy, with joking asides going on throughout. For instance, when Paul sings, "Desmond lets the children lend a hand," you can hear George say "arm!" and then John answer "leg!" And it ends with laughter.

The single itself was released with a sleeve to match the *White Album* cover, with "Julia" as the B-side.

126. "Mother"
John Lennon
273 points
Chart appearance: 1/9/1971
Highest position: 43
Weeks on the chart: 6

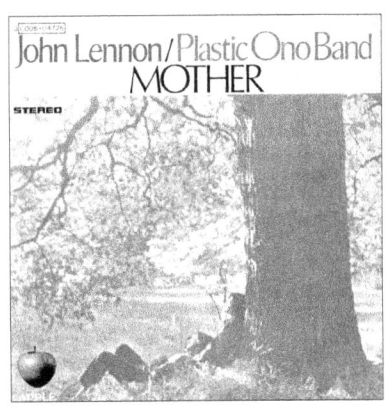

John's only single from his first musical album *Plastic Ono Band* was angry and emotional and not at all what you'd hear on Top 40 radio—so you didn't. The single edits out the bells at the start and fades it early to make it more palatable to disc jockeys, but it still fell short of the Top 40.

Both John and Paul had lost their mothers while still young. Paul addressed his memories in "Let It Be," but as John's mother had left him to be raised with his aunt, John's pain was more personal. "Mother, you had me, but I never had you."

125. "All My Loving"
The Beatles
275 points
Chart appearance: 3/28/1964
Highest position: 45
Weeks on the chart: 6

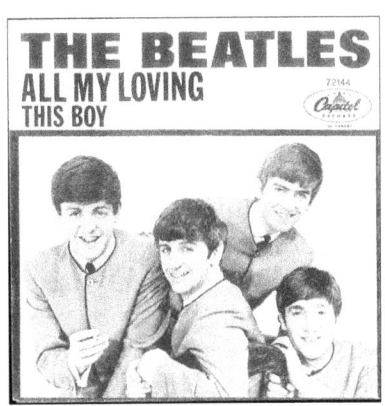

This excellent song was never released in America, but Capitol in Canada put it out. Enough copies made it over the border and into the hands of disc jockeys that it made the chart. It's still considered one of their best, appears often on greatest hits collections, and was often a featured song in their live shows.

It debuted on the charts the week before The Beatles had the top five songs on the Top 100, and reached #45. For an import single, that's a fairly impressive achievement, also given that the song was available on their first American album *Meet The Beatles!*

This was Paul's first song that proved he could write as well as John, who had dominated their partnership previously. And what a great song it is! There's the catchy verse with the descending bassline propelling it along, assisted by John's frantic rhythm guitar work. Then there's a short catchy lead using chords completely different from the main song, and then a second verse with harmonies building the song to an exciting conclusion.

If this had been released as a single in America, it would have done a lot better on the chart.

124. "Baby You're a Rich Man"

The Beatles
287 points
Chart appearance: 7/29/1967
Highest position: 34
Weeks on the chart: 5

This is a true Lennon/McCartney tune, with John providing the verses and Paul the chorus.

The point of the song, John explained, is that we're all rich in our own way. We all have value. We can all be one of the beautiful people.

As the B-side to "All You Need Is Love," both provided the perfect soundtrack for the hippies' "Summer of Love."

The beginning of the song appears in a segment in the *Yellow Submarine* film, and was remixed wonderfully in the *Yellow Submarine Songtrack*.

123. "I Don't Want to Spoil the Party"

The Beatles
292 points
Chart appearance: 2/20/1965
Highest position: 39
Weeks on the chart: 6

Although this appeared on *Beatles for Sale* in the UK, its first appearance in America was as the B-side to "Eight Days a Week." It later appeared on *Beatles VI*. (These Capitol executives had such clever names for albums.) It has a very distinctive country feel to it, which is perhaps why it didn't do better on the pop charts. Some country music historians consider this one of the first "country-rock" songs.

122. "Letting Go"

Wings
294 points
Chart appearance: 10/4/1975
Highest position: 39
Weeks on the chart: 6

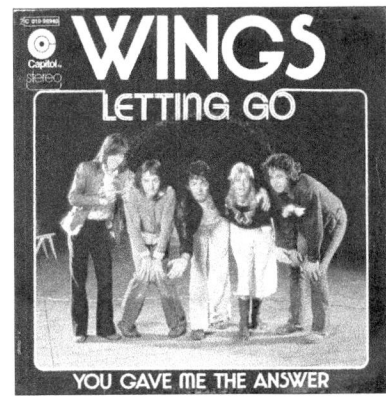

The follow-up to the #1 hit "Listen to What the Man Said" from *Venus and Mars* barely made the Top 40, which is sad because it's a great tune. The single version is actually a remixed version from the album, with a more prominent organ and a shorter run time. The vocals are also more up-front, with less echo.

The lyrics are Paul's thoughts about his relationship with his wife Linda and how he needs to not be so possessive.

121. "Ding Dong; Ding Dong"

George Harrison
297 points
Chart appearance: 1/11/1975
Highest position: 36
Weeks on the chart: 6

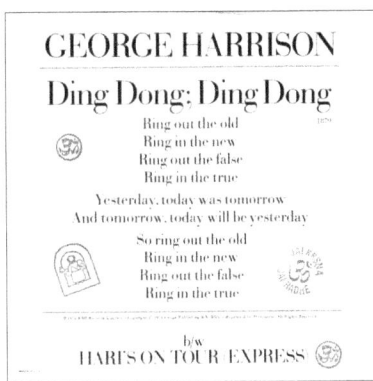

George's celebration of the new year was released too late to really take advantage of it. By the time it hit the Top 40, it was already February. "Yesterday, today was tomorrow / And tomorrow, today will be yesterday."

This song has not reappeared on holiday charts like "Happy Xmas" and "Wonderful Christmastime" have, but then again, Ringo recorded an entire Christmas album full of originals, and neither it nor its singles have appeared on any charts.

George tries for a real Phil Spector sound here, with two drummers (one of whom is Ringo) and lots of overdubs. The real treat is the clever video he made promoting it (his first) in which he performs dressed as himself from various points in his Beatles career. Oh, and a pirate.

120. "Wonderful Christmastime"

Paul McCartney
298 points
Chart appearance: 12/29/2018
Highest position: 28
Weeks on the chart: 5

Speaking of holiday songs, here's Paul's sappy contribution.

It took this 1980 song—recorded during the *McCartney II* period—almost forty years to hit the

Top 100 chart, thanks to Christmas songs only being eligible recently. It's shown up three seasons now, staying on the chart for a few weeks each time, and was on the charts at the end of 2021 as this book was completed.

That's why musicians like doing Christmas songs—they get replayed every holiday season, which keeps the royalties rolling in.

119. "Act Naturally"
The Beatles
300 points
Chart appearance: 9/25/1965
Highest position: 47
Weeks on the chart: 7

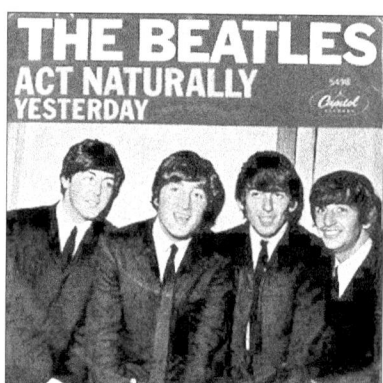

The Beatles' last cover song was a perfect fit for Ringo (who in some ways was the star of both *A Hard Day's Night* and *Help!*). In his solo career, Ringo did a duo of this song with the original singer Buck Owens.

It was left off the American *Help!* album and found itself as the B-side to "Yesterday" which wasn't even released as a single in Britain. Despite the A-side reaching #1, "Act Naturally" never hit the Top 40.

118. "If I Fell"
The Beatles
321 points
Chart appearance: 8/1/1964
Highest position: 53
Weeks on the chart: 9

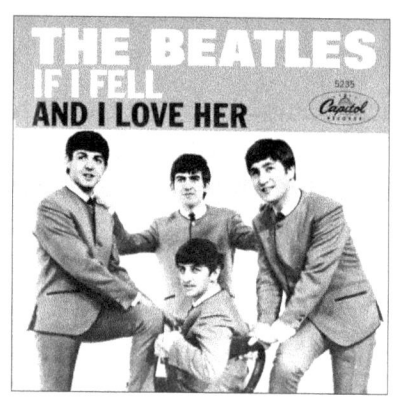

"If I Fell" is one of The Beatles' most beautiful and complicated slow love songs. It has an opening that is not repeated and then just before the verse actually begins, John changes keys to really build anticipation. Paul and John share vocals to the point where there really is no lead vocal at that part, because both parts are essential to the melody. (Ignore Paul's voice cracking on the second "was in vain.")

This was the B-side of the single "And I Love Her" from *A Hard Day's Night*, but with three singles from that album being released at the same time (along with B-sides getting airplay), it had a lot of competition and couldn't make it to the Top 40.

117. "My Bonnie"

The Beatles
344 points
Chart appearance: 2/15/1964
Highest position: 26
Weeks on the chart: 6

"It has The Beatles on it, so we must buy it" was the mantra of teens in February of 1964, where even cover bands doing Beatles songs found themselves in the record stores. Although this was recorded in 1961 (with Pete Best as the drummer) it was rushed out in 1964 like "Why" with Tony Sheridan's name in tiny print. At least John is singing on this one.

116. "(It's All Down to) Goodnight Vienna"

Ringo Starr
347 points
Chart appearance: 6/14/1975
Highest position: 31
Weeks on the chart: 7

On Ringo's album *Goodnight Vienna*, this song (written by John, who plays piano on it) opens the album and has a reprise at the very end. The single version combines the two, losing John's "With gusto, boys, with gusto!" comment. You can still hear John do the count off at the beginning, however.

Despite Ringo's seven previous singles all making the Top 10, this one never even got into the Top 30.

115. "London Town"

Wings
356 points
Chart appearance: 9/9/1978
Highest position: 39
Weeks on the chart: 8

After the success of "With a Little Luck," the following singles from *London Town* did not do well, including this third one, the title song, which barely made the Top 40. It slowly inched up the chart, stayed at #39 for two weeks, dropped to #89, and then disappeared.

114. "Thank You Girl"
The Beatles
357 points
Chart appearance: 4/4/1964
Highest position: 35
Weeks on the chart: 7

Another Vee-Jay release done to cash in on Beatlemania as much as possible, "Thank You Girl" was Paul and John's literal message to all their female fans. As the B-side to "Do You Want to Know a Secret?" it did quite well for a non–Capitol B-side.

113. "Slow Down"
The Beatles
363 points
Chart appearance: 9/5/1964
Highest position: 25
Weeks on the chart: 7

The Beatles were very clear that they wanted to write their own singles, and every single in Britain was either a Lennon/McCartney original or (later) a Harrison original. Not so in America, where the goal was making as much money as quickly as possible before The Beatles fad disappeared. This was released without The Beatles' approval (obviously) and did quite well, considering. Then again, it was at a point where anything by The Beatles would have made the chart (and did).

112. "Real Love"
The Beatles
377 points
Chart appearance: 3/23/1996
Highest position: 11
Weeks on the chart: 7

As part of the *Anthology* project, Paul, George, and Ringo took a poor cassette tape of songs John was working on and, with the help of producer Jeff Lynne, finished them with that Beatles touch. It was a difficult project to get the sound quality needed from a cheap tape full of hiss and hums, but they did a great job (although you can still tell John's vocals aren't that clear).

The resulting songs were a huge success musically, delighting Beatles fans, but surprisingly not that successful on the charts.

This was the second song from the project and its failure to reach the top of the charts may have discouraged the remaining Beatles from doing a third, as per the original plan.

It debuted at #11 but fell steadily from there. It was the last Beatles song to make the Top 40.

111. "Mary Had a Little Lamb"
Wings
391 points
Chart appearance: 6/17/1972
Highest position: 28
Weeks on the chart: 7

Mary Had A Little Lamb

Wild Life didn't impress many. The single "Give Ireland Back to the Irish" also didn't sell that well. So what does Paul do? He records his version of a nursery rhyme as a children's song, full of "la la's" and cute harmonies.

As you may have guessed, it did not do well with radio stations or listeners, and hasn't appeared on any of his greatest hits collections.

It's a nice enough song, written for his daughter Mary (named after Paul's mother who speaks words of wisdom), so Paul may not have really cared whether it was a hit.

110. "I'll Cry Instead"
The Beatles
443 points
Chart appearance: 8/1/1964
Highest position: 25
Weeks on the chart: 7

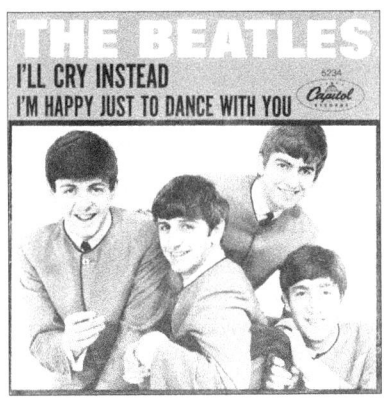

Another Capitol single from *A Hard Day's Night*, "I'll Cry Instead" is either 2:04 or 1:44 depending on whether you're listening to the mono single or the UK stereo version (which is the most common one most of us are used to). That's made the longer American version more of a collector's item, of course.

109. "Girls School"
Wings
451 points
Chart appearance: 11/19/1977
Highest position: 33
Weeks on the chart: 10

In the UK, Paul had his biggest hit with "Mull of Kintyre." Here in America, however, the record company assumed the very Scottish song would not do well and so promoted this B-side rocker instead. "Girls School" is a B-side about those sleazy sexploitation B movies. "Head nurse is Sister Scarla / Now she's a Spanish doll / She runs a full body outcall massage parlor from the teacher's hall."

108. "Rain"
The Beatles
460 points
Chart appearance: 6/11/1966
Highest position: 23
Weeks on the chart: 7

One of the greatest Beatles B-sides with some of Ringo's best drumming … but it's not really the kind of pop you would hear on the radio on those days. John even has his voice going backward at the end (the first time The Beatles had done such a thing) which also separated it from standard radio fare. As such, it didn't get as much airplay as it deserved. It was ahead of its time.

107. "Arrow Through Me"
Wings
465 points
Chart appearance: 8/5/1979
Highest position: 29
Weeks on the chart: 10

This second single from the *Back to the Egg* album (after "Getting Closer") struggled to get to #29, and fell off soon thereafter, which was very disappointing to Paul's new label Columbia, whose contract with Paul had made him the highest paid performer up to that time. Still, it's a favorite of many Paul fans.

106. "Bangla Desh"
George Harrison
465 points
Chart appearance: 8/14/1971
Highest position: 23
Weeks on the chart: 7

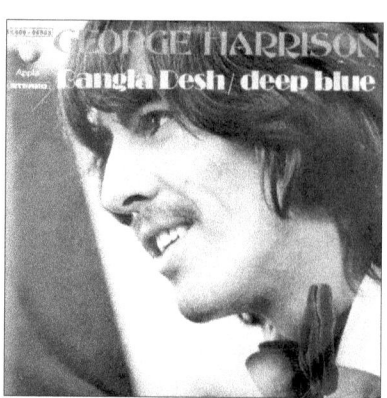

Released just days before the Concert for Bangla Desh, this single grabbed attention for its worthy cause but not for the song itself, which failed to hit the Top 20. (A live version also appears on the *Concert for Bangla Desh* album.) Then again, it's not exactly the kind of happy song that people want to play over and over again, and instead makes one sad, although willing to help.

The B-side was the acoustic "Deep Blue," another sad song, this one about George watching his mother dying of cancer.

105. "Free as a Bird"
The Beatles
470 points
Chart appearance: 12/30/1995
Highest position: 6
Weeks on the chart: 11

The first song recorded and released from the *Anthology* sessions jumped to #6 in its second week and then immediately fell away, despite a great promotional push and a wonderful video that was a kind of scavenger hunt for Beatles fans to find all the song references in the images.

The song won the 1997 Grammy Award for Best Pop Performance by a Duo or Group with Vocal, so there's that. While John sings the basic song, Paul and George take over the verses, ignoring Ringo's vocals completely. There's a bit of a coda with a ukulele and John's backward voice saying, "Turned out nice again," but when played backward it sounds like "Made for John Lennon." Turn me on, dead man!

104. "Wrack My Brain"
Ringo Starr
487 points
Chart appearance: 11/7/1981
Highest position: 38
Weeks on the chart: 11

And here's Ringo with the last song of his to hit the charts. It only reached #38 but it stayed on the charts for an impressive eleven weeks.

"Wrack My Brain" was written by George to explain his frustration with the music industry and the pressure to produce hits. ("There's no way I can see coming up with something you'd enjoy as much as TV," say the lyrics.) George produced the song as well, which was included on Ringo's album *Stop and Smell the Roses*.

103. "Give Ireland Back to the Irish"
Wings
492 points
Chart appearance: 3/11/1972
Highest position: 21
Weeks on the chart: 8

A few days after British soldiers killed Irish protesters, Paul went into the studio with his new band Wings and produced this single. The BBC immediately banned it. The B-side is just an instrumental version, because Paul thought DJs who didn't like the politics would perhaps play the instrumental version instead and then at least be forced to say the title on the air.

And to make sure his point was made, the lyrics are all on the sleeve.

102. "Handle with Care"
Traveling Wilburys
525 points
Chart appearance: 10/29/1988
Highest position: 45
Weeks on the chart: 14

This was originally meant as a George B-side. Everyone (including the record company) agreed the resulting song was too good for a B-side, and thus The Wilburys were formed.

The resulting album was a huge success but the single never made the Top 40, although it hung around for fourteen weeks.

101. "Matchbox"
The Beatles
525 points
Chart appearance: 9/5/1964
Highest position: 17
Weeks on the chart: 8

The A-side to "Slow Down" (#113) did well at a time when anything with The Beatles' name would sell, as the record label knew. As one of their standard songs from their early days in Hamburg, they could record it in just a few takes. Although originally a showcase for Pete Best, Ringo took over and rocked through it. It hit the Top 20 and stayed on the charts for two months.

100. "Venus and Mars Rock Show"
Wings
528 points
Chart appearance: 11/1/1975
Highest position: 12
Weeks on the chart: 9

After the failure of "Letting Go" to become a hit, this third single from the *Venus and Mars* album did much better, almost making the Top 10.

The single is heavily edited from the album. "Rock Show" is over five minutes long on its own, and when you add the introductory "Venus and Mars" section, the medley lasts almost seven minutes. The record label left "Venus and Mars" intact but managed to cut "Rock Show" in more than half for the single, eliminating an entire verse and fading way too early, ignoring the entire coda.

The song itself is clearly meant as a powerful opener for live shows, and mentions Amsterdam's Concertgebouw, Madison Square Garden, and the Hollywood Bowl—not to mention Jimmy Page and scoring weed. New Orleans pianist Allen Toussaint joins Wings for this one song.

99. "Stand by Me"
John Lennon
533 points
Chart appearance: 3/15/1975
Highest position: 20
Weeks on the chart: 9

After dealing with the problems with Phil Spector, John contractually had to finish his *Rock 'n' Roll* album, and ended up producing the rest himself, including this single. The single itself is slightly different from the album version, in that John decided to add strings.

This version of the old Ben E. King song reached #20 on the charts, and was the last John single for five years until "(Just Like) Starting Over." It was written by King along with Jerry Leiber and Mike Stoller who, for some reason, together used the pseudonym "Glick."

The B-side is a Lennon original that never appeared on any of his albums. It's called "Move Over Ms. L" and was originally planned for *Walls and Bridges* but got pulled at the last minute. It does, however, seem to fit with the rock and roll feel of *Rock 'n' Roll* instead.

98. "Ain't She Sweet"
The Beatles
555 points
Chart appearance: 7/18/1964
Highest position: 19
Weeks on the chart: 9

This old song from the roaring '20s (no, the 1920s, not the 2020s) was regularly a part of The Beatles' live set. This version was recorded during the Tony Sheridan sessions but this time, John was allowed to have lead vocals. Pete Best is on the drums, and George still has a way to go to become a great guitarist, but all of that didn't matter when Beatlemania hit in America, and this reached the Top 20.

ATCO somehow got the song and released it, although they clearly didn't have the rights to The Beatles' image (based on this sleeve).

97. "My Brave Face"
Paul McCartney
556 points
Chart appearance: 5/27/1989
Highest position: 25
Weeks on the chart: 10

Paul's collaborations with Elvis Costello produced some of his best work during the late '80s. Both had met when Elvis was using Beatles engineer Geoff Emerick as producer for his *Imperial Bedroom* album. (Elvis, by the way, spent most of his youth and his college years in Liverpool, so there's that connection as well.)

This excellent single should have performed better than merely getting to #25. It was the lead single from the album *Flowers in the Dirt*, and the other singles from that album never even made the Top 80.

Sadly, Paul and Elvis found themselves arguing a bit and while they produced some great songs together, their relationship did not last.

It probably didn't help Paul's ego to find that one of their collaborations ("Veronica") performed by Elvis got to #19 around the same time Paul was struggling to beat #25. On the other hand, unlike Paul, Elvis has never had a Top 10 hit, and "Veronica" ended up being Elvis' best performing song ever on the charts, so there's that.

96. "I've Had Enough"

Wings
560 points
Chart appearance: 6/17/1978
Highest position: 25
Weeks on the chart: 11

The second single from *London Town* inched its way up to #25 and then fell off the charts, which had to be a bit of a disappointment after the success of the #1 hit "With a Little Luck."

It's a simple little laid-back rock song that has mostly disappeared from Paul's catalog, never appearing on greatest hits releases and never played live in concert. Paul didn't seem to have put too much effort into the words, especially when he says he has had enough and then says, "You know sometimes you get a little weary / But if it ever happens honey / You just come along to me / Because you know I've had enough."

95. "Eleanor Rigby"

The Beatles
576 points
Chart appearance: 9/27/1966
Highest position: 11
Weeks on the chart: 8

Surprisingly, neither "Eleanor Rigby" nor its A-side "Yellow Submarine" hit #1 at a time when both sides of a single could make the chart. Then again, both of these were not traditional Beatles songs that listeners expected. Then again, "Eleanor," like "Yesterday," has only strings, with no Beatles on any instruments, and "Yesterday" was a huge hit. Perhaps it was the topic that made the difference, as "Eleanor Rigby" lyric-wise is about as far from a radio-friendly love song as you can get.

Although credited to Lennon/McCartney, this is mainly Paul's work with Ringo suggesting a few lines and George contributing to the "All the lonely people" section. Like "Yesterday," Paul had some nonsense words while he was coming up with the melody ("Ola Na Tungee / Blowing his mind in the dark / With a pipe full of clay / No one can say").

Paul chose the name "Eleanor Rigby" and then later learned that there is a graveyard in Liverpool at the church where he and John met which has a grave for an Eleanor Rigby, and not too far away is a McKenzie. So maybe it was hidden in the back of his mind the whole time.

94. "Getting Closer"
Wings
590 points
Chart appearance: 6/16/1979
Highest position: 20
Weeks on the chart: 10

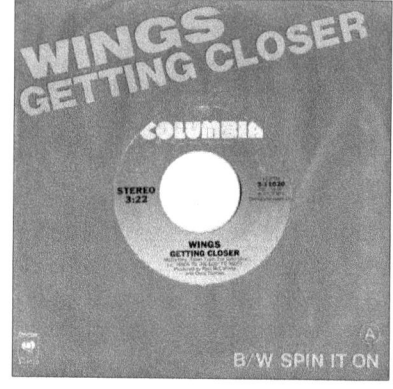

Paul's previous single "Goodnight Tonight" had hit the Top 10, but its follow-up, from the *Back to the Egg* album, barely made the Top 20. It was well produced by Chris Thomas and is one of Paul's catchier tunes.

Many thought this song showed Paul's influence from many "new wave" bands at the time (who, of course, had been influenced by The Beatles). This is especially apparent if you listen to the rocking B-side "Spin It On."

93. "You"
George Harrison
594 points
Chart appearance: 9/20/1975
Highest position: 20
Weeks on the chart: 10

George originally wrote this Motown-inspired song for Ronnie Spector, who was to have an album on Apple, but that never came to be. Her single "Try Some Buy Some" written by George had not done well, and this proposed follow-up was cancelled. George then resurrected the original backing tracks (as he had done with "Try Some Buy Some," which appeared on *Living in the Material World*) and included "You" on his *Extra Texture* album as the opening.

It received great reviews (especially after the disappointing songs from the *Dark Horse* album). The lyrics are almost as simple as The Beatles' first song "Love Me Do," but it works. It rose to the Top 20, but then dropped off quickly.

92. "P.S. I Love You"
The Beatles
601 points
Chart appearance: 5/9/1964
Highest position: 10
Weeks on the chart: 8

The B-side to their American single "Please Please Me" was another Tollie release from Vee-Jay's *Introducing The Beatles* album. Since George Martin didn't think Pete Best's drumming was good enough, he hired a drummer for the session, unaware that the band had canned Pete by then and brought in Ringo. Poor Ringo was left playing maracas for the song.

In England, this had been the B-side to their first single "Love Me Do" and was considered for the A-side until their publisher Dick James said they shouldn't do that because there was already a song with that title. Of course, now if you ask someone about a song called "P.S. I Love You," we all know which one they'd name.

91. "A Dose of Rock 'n' Roll"
Ringo Starr
605 points
Chart appearance: 9/25/1976
Highest position: 26
Weeks on the chart: 10

Ringo had huge successes in the early '70s and when his Apple contract expired, he was grabbed up by Polydor (with Atlantic distributing in America). Despite the album *Ringo's Rotogravure* containing songs written by Paul, George, and John, Ringo decided to release a song by unknown Carl Groszmann. Musicians on this song included Peter Frampton, Dr. John, Klaus Voormann, and Jesse Ed Davis.

It was heavily promoted but did poorly, as did his own Ring O'Records label, which started at the same time and died soon thereafter.

90. "And I Love Her"
The Beatles
615 points
Chart appearance: 7/25/1964
Highest position: 12
Weeks on the chart: 9

This third single in the trio released at the same time from *A Hard Day's Night* reached #12. The B-side was "If I Fell."

It's a Paul classic (with John helping on the bridge) with some interesting chord progressions and a key change just before the lead, which is something you rarely heard from pop songs in the early '60s.

89. "When We Was Fab"

George Harrison
617 points
Chart appearance: 2/6/1988
Highest position: 23
Weeks on the chart: 11

"When We Was Fab" is a great song about being a Beatle, excellently produced to sound like a psychedelic Beatles song by Jeff Lynne (who is listed as a co-writer). It contains some of George's best humorous lyrics, including "Back when income tax was all we had" and "(Fab!) Like this pullover you sent me." Just to make sure the reference is clear, the single sleeve contains the Klaus Voormann drawing of George from *Revolver*.

It was promoted with a clever video featuring Ringo and Jeff Lynne and even Elton John for a short bit (who drops a coin in George's cup). George appears in his *Sergeant Pepper* suit for a few seconds, and one part features a left-handed bassist dressed as a walrus playing a Rickenbacker. The video was produced by 10cc's Godley and Creme, but the single sadly never reached the Top 20.

88. "This Song"

George Harrison
642 points
Chart appearance: 11/20/1976
Highest position: 25
Weeks on the chart: 11

Speaking of clever videos, the promotional one for this fits the song perfectly, as George sings about his "My Sweet Lord" lawsuit. Sitting in a courtroom, he explains that *this* song has nothing "bright" about it ("Bright Tunes" being the company that sued him). It even features Eric Idle giving Python-like commentary about whether the song is actually "Sugar Pie Honey Bunch" ("No, sounds more like 'Rescue Me!'"). In the video, one of the Python-ish women is played by The Rolling Stones' Ronnie Wood, and the judge is drummer Jim Keltner. George's soon-to-be wife Olivia is one of the jurors.

Sadly, despite being one of George's most clever combinations of lyrics and music, it failed to reach the Top 20.

87. "Power to the People"

John Lennon / Plastic Ono Band
648 points
Chart appearance: 4/3/1971
Highest position: 11
Weeks on the chart: 9

Hoping to create another chant song to rival "Give Peace a Chance," John came up with this rocker. It's a simple song, made easy so anyone could sing it or chant it during protests, but other than that, there's not much to it. "It's a quickie," John later explained—written quick to get released quick. Unlike the mid-1960s John who would spend weeks in the studio to get the song just right, the later John wanted to record and release as fast as possible. (For instance: "Instant Karma" and "The Ballad of John and Yoko.")

"Power to the People" worked its way up the chart, banging to get admitted into the Top 10 for two weeks, and then fell away, having missed its goal.

John later claimed he was embarrassed by the song. It was renewed years later for Bernie Sanders' campaigns.

86. "Give Peace a Chance"

Plastic Ono Band
654 points
Chart appearance: 7/26/1969
Highest position: 14
Weeks on the chart: 9

John's first single was still credited to Lennon/McCartney even though clearly Paul had nothing to do with it. It was recorded live at a hotel in Canada where John and Yoko were doing a protest called the Bed-In for Peace. Background singers include Timothy Leary, Tommy Smothers, and Allen Ginsberg!

It became the chant song that gets repeated at various rallies, just like John wanted, although all anyone sings there is the chorus and not John's fun-filled descriptions of what "everybody's talking about."

The sound quality was such that many stations wouldn't play it, but as the first single from a solo Beatle, it did well, considering.

85. "Dark Horse"
George Harrison
656 points
Chart appearance: 11/23/1974
Highest position: 15
Weeks on the chart: 10

George decided to call himself the Dark Horse and even name his record company that in response to the success he had experienced after leaving The Beatles despite never being seen as the front-runner. Ironically, this single was not a success. After #1 singles from *All Things Must Pass* and *Living in the Material World*, the poor reception of this was a disappointing surprise. It peaked at #15 and was gone two weeks later.

The single came in a sleeve with hard-to-read lyrics and a big blue dot, for some reason. The personal lyrics are about the rumors that surrounded George's life, and were his way to reacting to them.

The throw-away B-side "I Don't Care Anymore" starts with George saying, "Okay, here we go ... we got a B-side to make, ladies and gentlemen." It just has George on acoustic guitar and sounds like a practice session of an unfinished song. Given that the song is not mentioned at all in George's book *I Me Mine* and was never made available on an album until the *Apple Years 1968–75* collection in 2014, it appears George wanted to pretend it never existed.

84. "Press"
Paul McCartney
658 points
Chart appearance: 8/2/1986
Highest position: 21
Weeks on the chart: 11

The first single from the *Press to Play* album is a creative, action-filled song that has that '80s drum sound that makes it a bit dated, but doesn't that mean it should have been a bigger hit? It crawled up the charts and then slowly made its way back down again. It was the first time in years that a Paul single didn't even make the Top 20. The promotional video has Paul wandering around the London subway system, meeting fans.

The B-side "It's Not True" is more commercial, but does not appear on the album.

83. "Strawberry Fields Forever"

The Beatles
660 points
Chart appearance: 2/25/1967
Highest position: 8
Weeks on the chart: 9

This song is so far ahead of anything else on the radio in early 1967 that it took everyone by surprise. The trippy music, the orchestration, the backward drums, the fade-out that comes back in ... there was nothing like it. Even with all that (which would normally keep such a song off the radio), it reached the Top 10 as the B-side to "Penny Lane."

Strawberry Field was actually the name of an orphanage where young John would pass by each day. With "Penny Lane" as the A-side, we got a themed Beatles single about Liverpool.

This is actually two different versions spliced together in an interesting way. The Beatles had recorded one version with their own instruments and then there was a second version done with lots of strings and backward drums and effects. John wanted to use the guitar/Mellotron version for the first verse and then use the string-and-horns version for the rest, but the problem was that they were in two different keys. George Martin solved this by speeding up one and slowing down the other until the keys matched, which gave John a more otherworldly voice. He loved it. You can hear the splice at around a minute into the song.

Even years later, when John would disavow many Beatles songs, he remained proud of this one. After his death, an area of Central Park near his home was renamed Strawberry Fields.

82. "Cold Turkey"

Plastic Ono Band
680 points
Chart appearance: 11/15/1969
Highest position: 30
Weeks on the chart: 12

John's follow-up to "Give Peace a Chance" was brought to The Beatles as they worked on *Abbey Road* but was rejected by the others, so John recorded his own version soon thereafter.

It's an angry song about John's feelings after going cold turkey off heroin, full of emotion but not exactly the kind of song that makes a hit record. Unlike John on heroin, it didn't get very high—but it stayed on the charts a long time.

This is the first song John wrote that was not credited to "Lennon/McCartney." Even "Give Peace a Chance" had that.

Soon after this was released, John returned his MBE award to Buckingham Palace, saying, "I am returning this MBE in protest against Britain's involvement in the Nigeria-Biafra thing, against our support of America in Vietnam, and against 'Cold Turkey' slipping down the charts."

81. "What Is Life"

George Harrison
693 points
Chart appearance: 2/27/1971
Highest position: 10
Weeks on the chart: 9

George's follow-up to the hugely successful "My Sweet Lord" zoomed up the charts, hit the Top 10, and then zoomed back down again, despite being one of George's best-known singles. In fact, with this song, George became the first Beatle to have two Top 10 hit singles.

The song itself has that muddy Phil Spector "Wall of Sound" but that catchy riff stays with you long after the song has ended.

George had written this originally for Billy Preston but held onto it when he realized it didn't fit Billy as well as it would fit him. As one of the many songs he had been holding over the years for The Beatles that were not accepted, he was more than willing to place it on *All Things Must Pass*.

The picture sleeve shows George playing from a balcony in his home.

80. "Crackerbox Palace"

George Harrison
701 points
Chart appearance: 1/29/1977
Highest position: 19
Weeks on the chart: 11

The second single from the *Thirty Three & ⅓* album did better than the first single "This Song."

It's a catchy song with another clever video, this one directed by Eric Idle (who has a brief cameo). It was recorded at George's estate. The video is clearly Monty Python-inspired, as we can see some of the characters that had appeared on their show. Neil Innes (from the Bonzo Dog Band, Sir Robin's bard from "Monty Python and the Holy Grail," and later the Rutles) appears as George's nanny and a few other characters.

George wrote the song after meeting a Mr. Greif who took him to comedian Lord Buckley's home, which Buckley called "Crackerbox Palace." And here you thought the line "I met a Mr. Greif" was just an easy way to rhyme "life" in the previous line. Nope, real person.

At one point in the song, George says "It's twoo, it's twoo" in reference to Madeline Kahn's lines from the film *Young Frankenstein*!

79. "Back Off Boogaloo"
Ringo Starr
721 points
Chart appearance: 4/1/1972
Highest position: 9
Weeks on the chart: 10

Inspired by T. Rex's Mark Bolan, Ringo wrote this song with George (who did not get writing credit until after his death). George produced it and his signature slide guitar is prominent. Despite some fans claiming that the song is about Paul, Ringo has consistently denied that. The lyrics that say "Don't pretend that you are dead" might imply otherwise, as it had not been that long since the "Paul is dead" rumors were prominent.

John later referred to this song when he wrote "I'm the Greatest" for *Ringo*, which contains the line "I'm only thirty-two and all I want to do is boogaloo."

Ringo liked the song so much, he recorded new versions for his albums *Stop and Smell the Roses* and *Give More Love*.

78. "The Ballad of John and Yoko"
The Beatles
729 points
Chart appearance: 6/14/1969
Highest position: 8
Weeks on the chart: 9

Here's an interesting entry: A Beatles song about a Beatle, with only half the band performing. Paul plays bass, piano, tambourine, and drums, and John handles the guitar parts. John wanted this released as soon as possible and didn't want to wait for George and Ringo to be available. It appeared only a few weeks after "Get Back" hit the charts, and replaced it in the Top 10.

Even though there were serious arguments in The Beatles camp at this time, with Paul frustrated at the other three hiring Allen Klein over his objections, Paul saw how much John wanted this done and released and went along for his childhood friend.

Many radio stations refused to play it because of the reference to Christ, and that probably prevented it from reaching any higher than #8.

This is where John started writing almost all autobiographical songs, which kind of limited their appeal and the ability or desire for others to do cover versions.

77. "She's a Woman"
The Beatles
738 points
Chart appearance: 12/5/1964
Highest position: 4
Weeks on the chart: 9

The B-side to "I Feel Fine" is a catchy tune with some uninspiring lyrics ("I know that she's no peasant") that indicate that this was a rushed job needed to fill a record. Indeed, both Paul and John admitted that this was mostly written in the studio and recorded the same day, without George (who came in later to record his lead).

Beatlemania was still going strong after a year (despite what some had predicted) and this got plenty of airplay and good sales, becoming the most successful charting B-side of their career (unless you count "Come Together" and "Something"). Despite its performance on the chart, you never see this on any greatest hits collections.

John's choppy guitar work propels the song along, and both he and Paul chuckled like naughty schoolboys as they included the line "Turn me on when I get lonely," in reference to marijuana.

76. "I Saw Her Standing There"
The Beatles
739 points
Chart appearance: 2/8/1964
Highest position: 14
Weeks on the chart: 11

The B-side to "I Want to Hold Your Hand" might have performed better except there were a dozen other Beatles songs on the chart at the same time. Over the years, it's held up as one of their most famous songs nonetheless.

As the opening from their first album, it starts with a count-off that is usually cut from final records. George Martin wanted to keep that in to start the record, to capture the live feel he was aiming for. Of course, in America, this appeared on *Meet The Beatles!* as the second song, but no American fans complained.

Paul's original lines had been "She was just seventeen and never been a beauty queen," but John suggested "You know what I mean," which works much better. Paul's distinctive bass line was lifted entirely from a Chuck Berry song.

75. "Movie Medley"

The Beatles
756 points
Chart appearance: 3/27/1982
Highest position: 12
Weeks on the chart: 11

A Dutch single by a group called Stars on 45 had hit #1 in America, containing a medley of Beatles songs (along with "Sugar Sugar" and "Venus" for some reason), and Capitol said, "Hey! We can profit from this idea!" and quickly produced a similar medley from their recent *Reel Music* album.

The medley includes "Magical Mystery Tour," "All You Need Is Love," "You've Got to Hide Your Love Away," "I Should Have Known Better," "A Hard Day's Night," "Ticket to Ride," and "Get Back." The medley itself is not as smooth as the Stars on 45 single, which was played and recorded as a medley instead of as a patched-together mix of previously recorded performances.

The single did quite well considering these were all old songs. It reached #12 on the chart and remained in the Top 100 for eleven weeks.

The Beatles were pissed at the hacking away of their songs, and that's why you will never see this released again.

74. "Day Tripper"

The Beatles
769 points
Chart appearance: 12/18/1965
Highest position: 5
Weeks on the chart: 10

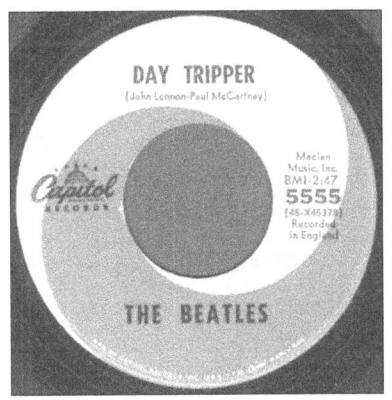

"We Can Work It Out" was released by Capitol as a "double A-side" with this song. In America, "We Can Work It Out" became the song that hit the top, but in England, it was "Day Tripper."

John liked to base songs on catchy riffs ("I Feel Fine," "Hey Bulldog") that are the kinds of hooks all pop songwriters want to create. And John did it so well.

The song is about a "weekend hippie" who was not fully committed to the "sex and drugs" lifestyle (unlike The Beatles, according to John and Paul). The "trip" refers not just to tourists on a day trip but also to a drug user tripping.

The original version has an edit that is very noticeable in the stereo mix but is hidden in the back in the mono version. It comes in the third verse, after the line "tried to please her." More recent versions since the *1* album have "fixed" the error.

73. "Yellow Submarine"
The Beatles
779 points
Chart appearance: 8/20/1966
Highest position: 2
Weeks on the chart: 9

This simple song was Ringo's only A-side. Paul admitted it was an attempt to write a children's song and as such, was a big departure for the band.

It was still fairly progressive for the time, including sound effects, a brass band for a few measures, and (originally) a fantasy storytelling intro that was wisely removed before *Revolver* was completed.

However, because it was so different from previous Beatles songs (and other songs on the radio), it didn't reach #1. It was kept from the top spot by The Supremes' "You Can't Hurry Love."

This was, of course, the inspiration for the animated *Yellow Submarine* film, which has helped to make the song more famous and popular than it may have ended up being otherwise.

72. "Hi Hi Hi"
Wings
790 points
Chart appearance: 12/16/1972
Highest position: 10
Weeks on the chart: 11

This is a great Paul rocker which followed in the tradition of getting banned from BBC just like "Give Ireland Back to the Irish." It's not subtle; it really is about getting high and having sex. The BBC objected not only to the idea that it promoted drugs but also didn't like the line "Lie on the bed and get ready for my body gun." Paul claimed this was a mistake and the proper word was "polygon," but we all knew what he meant anyway.

Because of the ban, the B-side "C Moon" was promoted in England instead and that's why you find it on certain greatest hits collections. "C Moon" was meant to counter the '60s slang of saying things were "L7"—meaning square (get it?). C Moon was a circle and thus cool.

In America, this was the first Wings single to hit the Top 10.

Even though contracts kept Paul with Apple, he made sure during this time that none of the records used the Apple logo.

71. "Blow Away"
George Harrison
794 points
Chart appearance: 3/3/1979
Highest position: 16
Weeks on the chart: 14

"Blow Away" never reached any higher than #16 on the charts, but it stayed around for fourteen weeks. It's from the album *George Harrison*.

George admits it was written as he attempted to be optimistic about bad things that happened to him, including having a major roof leak at his house—hence all the references to clouds. He then realized that in the scheme of life, this was a minor problem.

This song later appeared in the film *Nuns on the Run* with George's friend Eric Idle.

70. "So Bad"
Paul McCartney
797 points
Chart appearance: 12/24/1983
Highest position: 23
Weeks on the chart: 14

Paul admits that the lyrics were "corny" and maybe listeners did, too, as this single from the *Pipes of Peace* album never reached the Top 20 (although it had a healthy run on the charts). Critics were frustrated by Paul's "silly love songs" and were not impressed by the single. After the huge hit of "Say Say Say," this song's chart performance had to be a disappointment. Its performance was so bad.

Despite that, he redid the song for the *Give My Regards to Broad Street* film and album.

69. "Nowhere Man"
The Beatles
806 points
Chart appearance: 3/5/1966
Highest position: 3
Weeks on the chart: 9

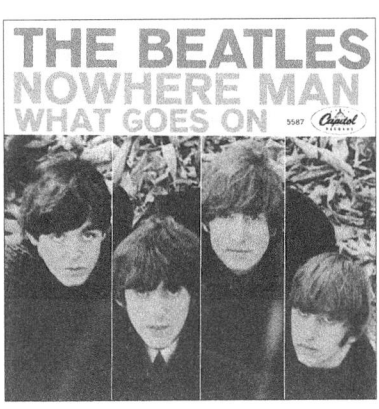

While the Brits had enjoyed this song on their version of *Rubber Soul*, we Americans only got to hear it months later when Capitol released it as a single. It later appeared on the American *Yesterday and Today* album.

This was the first major release from The Beatles not to reach #1, ending up behind The Rolling Stones' "19th Nervous Breakdown" and the awful "Ballad of the Green Berets."

It's also one of the first Beatles songs not to be about love or relationships (the first probably being "Help!").

It's the oldest song to appear in the *Yellow Submarine* film, where it was remixed, to later appear on the *Yellow Submarine Songtrack*, with the vocals surrounding you. It's a huge improvement, and is surely how The Beatles would have produced it had the technology been available at the time.

68. "Penny Lane"

The Beatles
815 points
Chart appearance: 2/25/1967
Highest position: 1
Weeks on the chart: 11

Here's the first song on our countdown to reach #1. "Penny Lane" zoomed up the charts, hit the top, and zoomed back down again, which was not uncommon to see in those days. Had it remained on the charts a bit longer, it surely would be higher in our countdown.

Originally this and "Strawberry Fields Forever" were planned for the *Sergeant Pepper* album, but when the record company demanded a single to follow "Yellow Submarine," George Martin gave them these, which he later regretted. Both songs are about John and Paul's youth and places they would visit in Liverpool.

Earlier versions can be heard on the *Anthology* album and the extended version of *Sergeant Pepper*. The piccolo trumpet solo was added at the last minute after Paul saw David Mason play one on TV during a classical performance and decided that was what was needed. The original promo single sent to radio stations had a little extra piccolo trumpet fill at the very end that was cut from the final version. That was later found on the American *Rarities* album.

It is sometimes important to remind yourself of how far musically The Beatles had come in such a short amount of time. Only four years earlier, they were singing "She Loves You, Yeah Yeah Yeah."

67. "Imagine"

John Lennon
821 points
Chart appearance: 10/23/1971
Highest position: 3
Weeks on the chart: 9

John's most famous solo song debuted on the charts at an amazing #20 and then was in the Top 10 the next week, clearly heading for #1. Then, for some reason, it never got past #3. (It was stopped by

"Theme from 'Shaft'" and Cher's song "Gypsys, Tramps & Thieves.") It fell off the Top 10 a few weeks later, then fell to #23, and then disappeared, having spent just slightly more than two months on the chart.

This was not released as a single in England until 1975, done to promote John's *Shaved Fish* greatest hits collection.

But look at it now: It shows up on many "greatest rock songs of all time" lists and is played every year in Times Square on New Year's Eve as a call for peace. Religious people sing it, unaware or uncaring that John wants everyone to imagine no religion. There are hundreds of cover versions that have been recorded. "Imagine" has certainly earned its place in Beatles history greater than the position on our countdown would indicate.

66. "Mind Games"

John Lennon
833 points
Chart appearance: 11/10/1973
Highest position: 18
Weeks on the chart: 13

Two years after "Imagine," John's single "Mind Games" barely hit the Top 20, but stayed on the charts for a more reasonable amount of time and thus just barely beats "Imagine" in our countdown. Perhaps the poor reception to *Sometime in New York City* made people hesitant to get a new Lennon single, despite the fact that the *Mind Games* album is one of his most accessible pop records.

The first version of this song was written years earlier at a time when it was called "Make Love, Not War" (which you can hear John sing during the fade-out) but was a kind of a hippie cliche by 1973 and John knew that. However, he strongly felt that the ideology of the '60s should not end simply because the '60s had ended.

65. "#9 Dream"

John Lennon
845 points
Chart appearance: 12/21/1974
Highest position: 9
Weeks on the chart: 12

You have to wonder if the people at *Billboard* knew the charts weren't scientific certainties when they made sure this peaked at #9.

John never released a second single off an album, but after the success of "Whatever Gets You Thru the Night" from *Walls and Bridges*, it was a good idea to risk it. As such, it makes this the only John album with two Top 10 singles.

Although the song is almost five minutes long, radio stations tended to play an edited version that was slightly less than three minutes. To make sure the stations weren't scared away, the record company published the nonsense words "Ah! böwakawa poussé, poussé" in all the promotional materials. "See?" they said. "John's not saying 'pussy.' You can play this on the radio."

May Pang, John's partner at the time, provided the whispering mention of John's name (played backward the second go-around).

64. "Eight Days a Week"
The Beatles
854 points
Chart appearance: 2/20/1965
Highest position: 1 (2 weeks)
Weeks on the chart: 10

This is another single that was only released in America. It had appeared on *Beatles for Sale* in December of 1964 but you couldn't get it in America for another two months. DJs with the import album had already started playing it here, which encouraged Capitol to release it as a single. It wasn't until *Beatles VI* that it appeared on an album here.

John originally wrote this when the film *Help!* was originally going to be called "Eight Arms to Hold You" and he wanted to use the "eight" imaging. The title came from either Paul's chauffeur or Ringo (Paul's told different versions), who said he had been working "eight days a week." Paul brought it to John, who pulled out the basics of the tune.

It was the first time a single started with a fade-in, which may have frustrated deejays who turned up the volume during the intro only to find the actual song blasting loudly.

63. "Paperback Writer"
The Beatles
885 points
Chart appearance: 6/11/1966
Highest position: 1 (2 weeks)
Weeks on the chart: 10

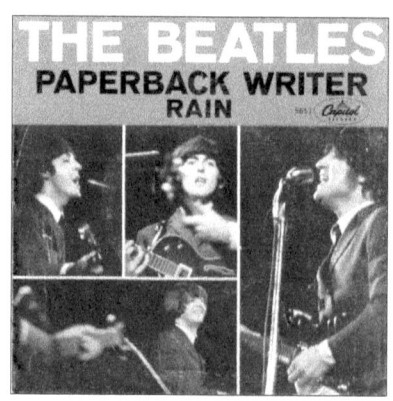

Another #1 that would be higher in our countdown had it stayed on the charts longer than ten weeks, this song features a guitar riff hook, similar to "Day Tripper" and "I Feel Fine." The two weeks it spent at #1 were not consecutive, interrupted by a Frank Sinatra song (of all things). Unlike the other riff songs, this one is Paul's, who plays the lead guitar, leaving George on rhythm and John on tambourine.

This was the first Beatles song to really emphasize Paul's bass, thanks to advanced technology allowing it to be mixed forward in a way that didn't make the needle skip. The bass pushes the song along, especially since most of it is just one chord. The song also has that distinctive guitar sound that was later prominent on *Revolver*. (In fact, in some digital computer mixes now possible in the studio, you can get that guitar sound by using the "Revolver" option.)

This is also the first Beatles single with neither side being a love song (the B-side being "Rain").

62. "Do You Want to Know a Secret?"
The Beatles
888 points
Chart appearance: 3/28/1964
Highest position: 2
Weeks on the chart: 11

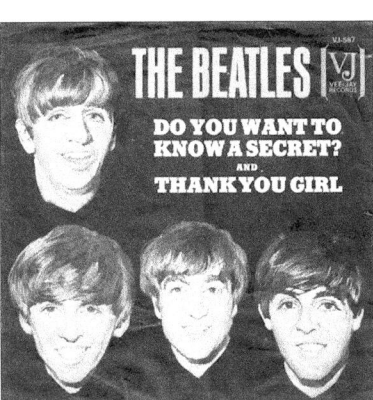

Vee-Jay is milking the dozen or so Beatles songs they think they have the rights to, so we find this single almost hitting #1, stopped by Louis Armstrong's "Hello, Dolly!"

John wrote it based on a Disney song from *Snow White and the Seven Dwarfs*. He gave it to George to sing. The Beatles never planned on having this released as a single, and you won't find George on an A-side again until "Something" five years later.

Despite almost hitting #1 in America, you never see this song on any greatest hits collections.

61. "The Long and Winding Road"
The Beatles
894 points
Chart appearance: 5/23/1970
Highest position: 1 (2 weeks)
Weeks on the chart: 10

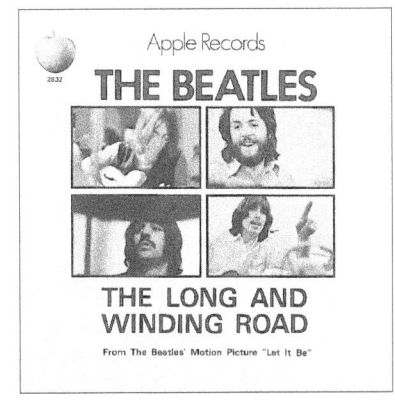

The Beatles' last released single during their time was recorded more than a year earlier during the "Get Back" sessions that became the *Let It Be* album. It was recorded live like all the songs on *Let It Be*, so rather than having Paul overdub his bass, John plays bass. You can tell.

Paul was furious when he heard the Spectorization of his song, with the orchestra and female chorus and harps. That didn't help with the discord he was already having with the rest of the group and Allen Klein, and certainly led to his announcement that he was leaving soon thereafter. He wrote a letter to Klein demanding that the song be changed, saying, "In future no one will be allowed to add to or subtract from a recording of one of my songs without my permission. I had considered orchestrating 'The Long and Winding Road' but I had decided against it. I therefore want it altered to these specifications: 1. Strings, horns, voices and all added noises to be reduced in volume; 2. Vocal and Beatle instrumentation to be brought up in volume; 3. Harp to be removed completely at the end of the song and original piano notes to be substituted; 4. Don't ever do it again." (A copy of this letter can be found in the *Anthology* book.)

Paul was ignored, and the song became the third #1 single off *Let It Be*, something no other Beatles album can claim.

60. "Can't Buy Me Love"
The Beatles
779 points
Chart appearance: 3/28/1964
Highest position: 1 (5 weeks)
Weeks on the chart: 10

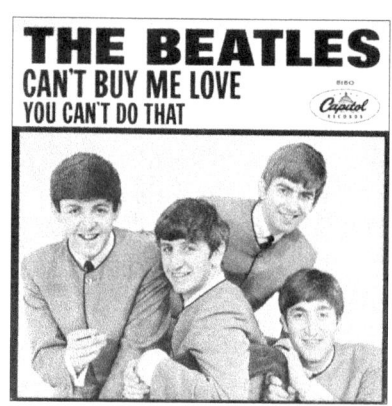

Look at this: "Can't Buy Me Love" spent half its time on the charts at #1! It debuted at #27 and the very next week, it was #1. That was the height of Beatlemania, and the week in which The Beatles had the top five positions on the chart, which no other artist has repeated (until they started counting downloads recently, meaning every song on an album now can make the Top 100 chart).

In fact, this song replaced the previous #1 song "She Loves You" which had replaced the previous #1 song "I Want to Hold Your Hand." By the time "Can't Buy Me Love" had fallen from #1, the band had spent fourteen weeks at the toppermost of the poppermost.

The pressure was on to top or at least match their previous hits, and Paul came through. It was George Martin's idea to start with the chorus hook in the same way he suggested for "She Loves You." Smart man.

59. "Revolution"
The Beatles
901 points
Chart appearance: 9/14/1968
Highest position: 12
Weeks on the chart: 11

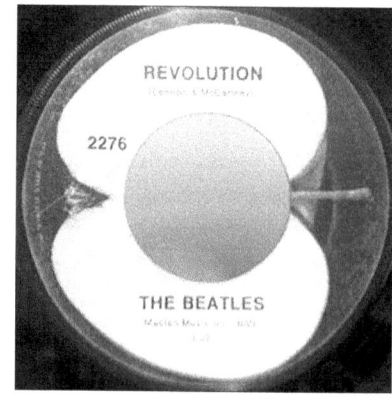

While John had previously dipped his toe into current politics with "All You Need Is Love" and "The Word," by 1968, he was diving in head first.

"Revolution" was the second recording of the song, after John decided the version that eventually ended up on *The Beatles* (White Album) was too calm. He insisted on having the guitar completely distorted, which frustrated his engineers who said, "You can't have it up that loud," but it paid off.

While many radio stations didn't like the politics of it, the song gathered attention for being the B-side to The Beatles' biggest hit "Hey Jude," which dominated the fall of 1968. Despite this, it never hit the Top 10.

58. "All You Need Is Love"

The Beatles
915 points
Chart appearance: 7/22/1967
Highest position: 1
Weeks on the chart: 11

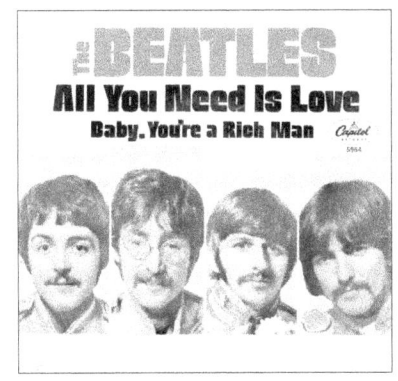

On June 25 of 1967, the first live TV show broadcast around the world to promote peace and brotherhood was aired, and The Beatles are the only thing people remember about it fifty years later. *Sergeant Pepper* had just been released, was a gigantic hit, and here they were, with a brand new song. A few weeks later, it was released as a single, where it hit #1.

Their performance was recorded live to a basic backing track, and the background chorus included Jane Asher, Pattie Boyd, Eric Clapton, Marianne Faithfull, Mick Jagger, Mike McGear, Keith Moon, Graham Nash, and Keith Richards. Paul's bass was recorded live, and you can hear a mistake at one point which, if you watch the film, happens when someone walks in front of him with a placard and hits him by mistake. Later, John redid his vocals in the studio, a few more touches were added, and the theme song for the "Summer of Love" was done.

57. "Nobody Told Me"

John Lennon
928 points
Chart appearance: 1/27/1984
Highest position: 5
Weeks on the chart: 13

John had planned to give this song to Ringo for his upcoming album *Stop and Smell the Roses*. After John's death, Ringo decided not to record it, and so Yoko had the song finished for *Milk and Honey*, released three years later.

John and Yoko had declared that they had seen a UFO over New York City in August of 1974 and so this song proclaims, "There's UFOs over New York, and I ain't too surprised."

As the first (and last) new John song, it got plenty of airplay and reached the Top 5. It was his third single to hit the Top 5 posthumously, and his last single to hit the Top 40.

56. "Maybe I'm Amazed"
Wings
929 points
Chart appearance: 2/12/1977
Highest position: 10
Weeks on the chart: 13

"Maybe I'm Amazed" was one of Paul's best-known solo songs even though it had never been released on a single. It appeared on *McCartney*, and many radio stations played it at the time as if it was a single.

The song is about Linda and how she encouraged him to keep writing and recording after The Beatles split, when Paul was so depressed he wasn't accomplishing anything. It's an inspirational song in that regard.

Wings performed it live during the *Wings Over America* tour, and this is the version that hit the Top 10. Still, if you find the song on one of Paul's greatest hits collections, it's always the studio version.

55. "Ticket to Ride"
The Beatles
933 points
Chart appearance: 4/24/1965
Highest position: 1
Weeks on the chart: 11

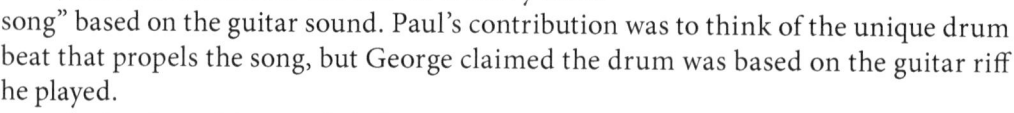

John wrote this for the *Help!* film, but the title hadn't been settled by that time, so the single proclaims it as being from the upcoming film "Eight Arms to Hold You." (See, The Beatles have eight arms total and so did the big idol in the movie…)

John later claimed it was the "first heavy metal song" based on the guitar sound. Paul's contribution was to think of the unique drum beat that propels the song, but George claimed the drum was based on the guitar riff he played.

At the time, this was their longest song, running over three minutes in length! That didn't stop radio stations from playing it, and it easily hit #1. Also of note is the coda as it fades out, which was the first time they did something completely new for that part (and which Paul would later use in "Hello Goodbye" and take it to its extreme with "Hey Jude").

The meaning of the song is unclear, and Paul and John haven't helped this, both telling contradicting versions: Paul said it was a play on taking a train to the British town of Ryde, but John claimed that when they played Hamburg, a visit to a prostitute was called a "ride" and the "ticket" was her certificate of a clean bill of health. Interesting, but neither explanation seems to fit with the lyrics at all.

54. "Helen Wheels"
Paul McCartney and Wings
948 points
Chart appearance: 11/24/1973
Highest position: 10
Weeks on the chart: 13

This was recorded during the *Band on the Run* sessions when Wings was down to Paul, Linda, and Denny Laine. Paul plays bass, drums, and lead guitar, and is having a great time. The song was named after Paul and Linda's all-terrain vehicle they had at their farm, which they had named Hell on Wheels. But the pun title is better, you have to admit, and the song is funny ("Say bye bye!").

Paul had only intended for this to be released as a single, but after it hit the Top 10 in America, it was decided to add it to the upcoming *Band on the Run* album, but only in America—so if you have an original British version of that album, you won't find it. By adding it to the American album, this gives *Band on the Run* the distinction of being the only Paul album with three Top 10 songs.

It moved up the chart slowly, hit its peak, and then took its time dropping off the chart.

It was an interesting time, because also on the chart at the same time was John's "Mind Games" and Ringo's "Photograph" (written and performed with George) and of the three, no one would have predicted that only Ringo's would hit #1.

53. "Only You (And You Alone)"
Ringo Starr
954 points
Chart appearance: 11/16/1974
Highest position: 6
Weeks on the chart: 14

Speaking of Ringo, there was a period of about a year where it seemed he could do no wrong, and every single he released hit the Top 10. "Only You (And You Alone)" was the first single from *Goodnight Vienna* and peaked at #6.

This song was originally a hit for The Platters in 1954 and Ringo recorded it at the suggestion of John, who plays acoustic guitar on the track. Ringo's pal Harry Nilsson provided the backing vocals. Nilsson also appears in the promotional video, where the UFO on the cover of the album lands on top of the Capitol Records building in Los Angeles.

52. "Lady Madonna"

The Beatles
954 points
Chart appearance: 3/23/1968
Highest position: 4
Weeks on the chart: 11

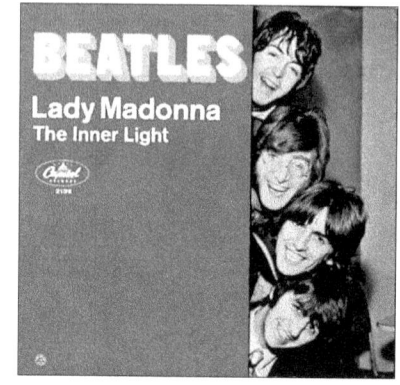

Recorded just before The Beatles left for their time in India with the Maharishi, "Lady Madonna" is a short little rock tune with Paul doing his Fats Domino impersonation. It was a definite switch from the psychedelic work that had dominated their sound for the previous few years (although the B-side "The Inner Light" fit that mold, while also being George's last Indian-inspired sitar song). Originally, John's "Across the Universe" (recorded around the same time) was to be the B-side, but John was dissatisfied with the performance and pulled it, only to give it to a charity album soon thereafter (before it was resurrected by Phil Spector and remixed to appear on *Let It Be*).

With double-tracked drums, kazoo-like solos, and a hefty sax solo, this song rocks along and stops before it gets too repetitive.

For all its catchiness, "Lady Madonna" didn't make #1, however, reaching only #4 and staying there for three weeks. But that's okay, The Beatles made it up with their next single "Hey Jude."

This was the last Beatles record on Capitol, as Apple would soon take over.

51. "Yesterday"

The Beatles
961 points
Chart appearance: 9/25/1965
Highest position: 1 (4 weeks)
Weeks on the chart: 11

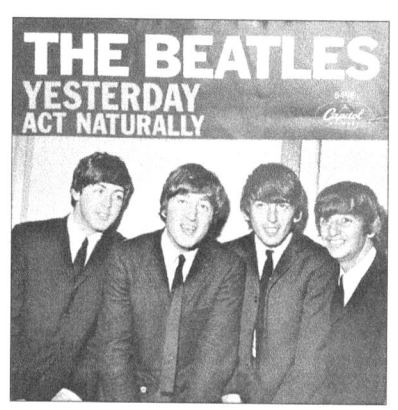

"Yesterday" was the first Beatles song to feature strings, which The Beatles were hesitant to agree to at first, especially since it was the first Beatles song to not feature all of the members. It was on the British *Help!* album, and was so different from what The Beatles had done before that they vetoed the idea of releasing it as a single.

Capitol in America never cared what The Beatles wanted, so they took it off *Help!* and released it as a single, where it zoomed up to #1 and stayed there for a month. It then zoomed back down again, which was common for records at the time. Obviously, it should be higher on our list but for the way charts were done back then.

Paul has often told the story of how the song came to him unbidden, so for quite some time, he was convinced it was an already-existing song he had heard. Upon finally being convinced it was his, he next had to find some words for it, because "Scrambled eggs / Baby how I love your legs" just wouldn't do it.

It has since been called the most-covered song in history, guaranteeing that Paul would have been a multi-millionaire even if this was the only thing he had ever done in his life.

50. "Another Day"

Paul McCartney
978 points
Chart appearance: 3/6/1971
Highest position: 5
Weeks on the chart: 12

Paul's first single was recorded during the *Ram* sessions, but didn't appear on that album. He had presented an earlier version of it to The Beatles during the *White Album* sessions.

At the time, many people were in an anti–Paul mood, still blaming him for the break-up of The Beatles, and so this was unfairly dismissed by the critics. That didn't seem to hurt sales too much, as it reached #5 and remained on the charts for twelve weeks.

Still, John sang his displeasure at Paul in his song "How Do You Sleep?" with the lines "The only thing you done was 'Yesterday' and since you're gone you're just 'Another Day.'"

49. "Hello Goodbye"

The Beatles
997 points
Chart appearance: 12/2/1967
Highest position: 1 (3 weeks)
Weeks on the chart: 11

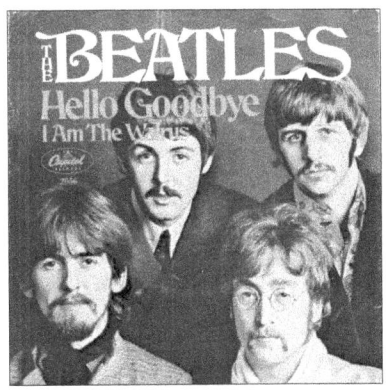

"Hello Goodbye" was a simple Paul tune, but can you imagine what would have happened if John had his way and "I Am the Walrus" had been the A-side instead? Radio stations would have felt obligated to play it since it was the new Beatles single and who knows how that would have changed the radio and music in general? Instead, they settled for the more commercial song, and while business-wise, it was a good choice, one has to still imagine what might have been otherwise.

"Hello Goodbye" stayed at #1 for three weeks, the most a Beatles song had spent at the top since "We Can Work It Out" two years earlier.

Paul claimed the song was about duality and being positive in the face of adversity ("You say stop, I say go…"). But really, the lyrics are pretty basic and simple and not very deep. The coda at the end was John's favorite part of the song, and was featured at the very end of the *Magical Mystery Tour* film.

48. "I Feel Fine"
The Beatles
1000 points
Chart appearance: 12/5/1964
Highest position: 1 (3 weeks)
Weeks on the chart: 11

John had a great riff that became a great song that topped the chart for three weeks in early 1965. However, when discussing the song in later years, he was most proud of being the first pop band to use feedback in a song. Seriously, this is important because even at this early stage of their career, they were starting to think about how to use the studio and expand the possibilities of simple pop songs.

This was recorded during the *Beatles for Sale* sessions. Originally, The Beatles had wanted "Eight Days a Week" to be their next single, but after this was completed, "Eight Days" was regulated to an album cut instead—at least, in England. In America, *Beatles for Sale* was kind of turned into *Beatles '65* and "Eight Days" disappeared and "I Feel Fine" took its place.

47. "No No Song"
Ringo Starr
1001 points
Chart appearance: 2/8/1975
Highest position: 3
Weeks on the chart: 14

The second single from *Goodnight Vienna* was a humorous song by Hoyt Axton, perfect for Ringo. It performed better than the previous "Only You (And You Alone)," reaching #3. It took nine weeks to get there, so longevity on the charts helped to push it to #47 on our countdown. Backing vocals are by Ringo's friend Harry Nilsson.

Ringo promoted it well, including an appearance on the Smothers Brothers show, and then later on the Hoyt Axton Show—where a huge crowd joined them, including Harry Nilsson, Micky Dolenz, Paul Williams, Kris Kristofferson, and Buffy St. Marie (among others).

The song is ironic in hindsight. Ringo claims in the song that he won't touch drugs or alcohol while at the time, he was having serious problems in that department. In the late '80s, he cleaned himself up, went on a vegetarian diet, and has continued to live a long and healthy life, looking much younger than his actual age.

46. "Watching the Wheels"

John Lennon
1023 points
Chart appearance: 3/28/1981
Highest position: 10
Weeks on the chart: 17

The third single off the *Double Fantasy* album only reached #10, but stayed on the chart for seventeen weeks. This was, of course, just a few months after John's death, so his music was still being played constantly and he was still on everyone's mind.

The song is another autobiographical song from John—because at this point in his career, that's pretty much all he ever wrote. It's his answer to all the people who wondered what he was doing for the five years between *Rock 'n' Roll* and *Double Fantasy*, when he was raising his son and relaxing from the contractual duties that had kept him working his entire adult life.

45. "Jet"

Paul McCartney and Wings
1027 points
Chart appearance: 2/9/1974
Highest position: 7
Weeks on the chart: 14

Paul's second song about one of his dogs (after "Martha My Dear") was the second single off *Band on the Run*. Or is it about a dog after all? Paul once told a long story about one of his dogs and her puppies, and then years later, said it was about a pony named Jet. Or was it about Paul meeting Linda's father for the first time, which is also what he's said it's about?

Maybe we should just realize that sometimes Paul writes lyrics that sound interesting and then he figures out later what the song's about. For instance, he has said, "I make up so much stuff. It means something to me when I do it, and it means something to the record buyer, but if I'm asked to analyze it, I can't really explain what it is. 'Suffragette' was crazy enough to work. It sounded silly, so I liked it."

"Jet" did better than the previous single "Helen Wheels," making it to #7 and staying on the charts for fourteen weeks. It is one of Paul's best rockers, and always impresses during concerts.

44. "Please Please Me"
The Beatles
1035 points
Chart appearance: 2/1/1964
Highest position: 3
Weeks on the chart: 13

Their first British single "Love Me Do" had done well, but not great, and George Martin was looking for a hit for a follow-up. He gave them "How Do You Do It?" and the band reluctantly recorded it but wanted to have their own songs as singles.

"Come up with something better," Martin said. John came back with this. Originally, it was a much slower Roy Orbison–type of song, but Martin had them speed it up, which added energy and excitement. "You've got your first #1," he said to them afterward, and he was right!

The Beatles' first big hit single in the UK was released here in the United States by Vee-Jay Records in February of 1963, but it didn't make the chart. The United States was not quite ready for Beatlemania. Once Capitol took over their contract and The Beatles were suddenly the Next Big Thing here, Vee-Jay re-released it and saw it rise to #3. It would have made #1 had it not been for "I Want to Hold Your Hand" and "She Loves You" taking the top two spots.

43. "It Don't Come Easy"
Ringo Starr
1043 points
Chart appearance: 5/1/1971
Highest position: 4
Weeks on the chart: 12

Ringo's first pop single was produced by George and probably co-written by George as well, even though only Ringo was credited on the record. George's original version for Ringo included "Hare Krishna" chants, which were later wisely removed at Ringo's insistence.

The lyrics seem to be Ringo comforting himself over The Beatles' break-up while noting his early childhood hardship while he had to "pay the dues." He also admitted that he was trying to break the image of just being "the drummer," and wanting to be accepted as a performer, but he knew it wouldn't come easy.

It was a smash hit, reaching #4, which, at the time, was better than Paul had achieved as a solo artist, and only slightly less than John's "Instant Karma," which had peaked at #3.

The B-side is "Early 1970," where Ringo sings about his three friends who he knows will want to play with him, with a verse each for Paul, John, and George.

42. "Oh My My"

Ringo Starr
1049 points
Chart appearance: 3/9/1974
Highest position: 5
Weeks on the chart: 14

The third single from the *Ringo* album reached #5, making Ringo the only Beatle to have three songs from one album all hit the Top 5. With the exception of "Sentimental Journey," all of Ringo's singles at that time had hit the Top 10, spurring John to send Ringo a telegram: "Congratulations. How dare you? And please write me a hit song."

The single version of this song is about thirty second shorter than the album version, but it's not really noticeable; it just fades out earlier. The song itself features Billy Preston, Tom Scott, and Klaus Voormann, and is written by Ringo and Vini Poncia, who worked with Ringo a lot at the time and later produced records for Kiss.

41. "Take It Away"

Paul McCartney
1052 points
Chart appearance: 7/10/1982
Highest position: 10
Weeks on the chart: 16

The second single from *Tug of War* (following the huge success of "Ebony and Ivory") stayed on the charts for sixteen weeks, five of them at #10, never reaching any higher!

On the album, the song fades in as the title track ends, but the single cuts out that overlap and also fades out earlier than on the album.

Ringo, Eric Stewart, and producer George Martin all play on the track and all appear in the clever video as well, which acts out the lyrics, with actor John Hurt playing the "important impresario" who watches the band and then gives a contract to Linda only. Go figure.

Paul has admitted that the song is actually about The Beatles, with the impresario being Brian Epstein, hearing about them and then going to see them live to decide for himself.

40. "Whatever Gets You Through the Night"

John Lennon
1053 points
Chart appearance: 9/28/1974
Highest position: 1
Weeks on the chart: 15

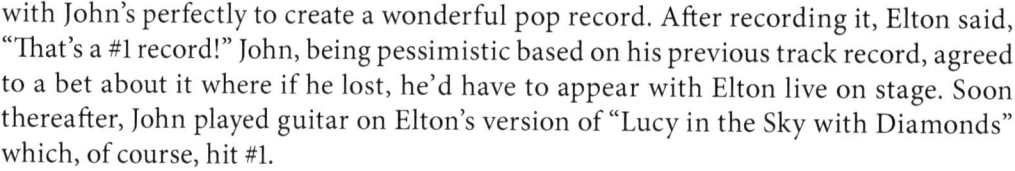

After seeing his former bandmates all reach #1, John finally hit the top with this song from *Walls and Bridges*.

It features Elton John on harmony vocals and piano at Elton's peak popularity, and his voice melds with John's perfectly to create a wonderful pop record. After recording it, Elton said, "That's a #1 record!" John, being pessimistic based on his previous track record, agreed to a bet about it where if he lost, he'd have to appear with Elton live on stage. Soon thereafter, John played guitar on Elton's version of "Lucy in the Sky with Diamonds" which, of course, hit #1.

And then, to John's surprise, so did "Whatever Gets You Thru the Night."

And so, a few months later, there was John joining Elton at Madison Square Garden to perform the song, along with "I Saw Her Standing There."

39. "We Can Work It Out"

The Beatles
1064 points
Chart appearance: 12/18/1965
Highest position: 1 (3 weeks)
Weeks on the chart: 12

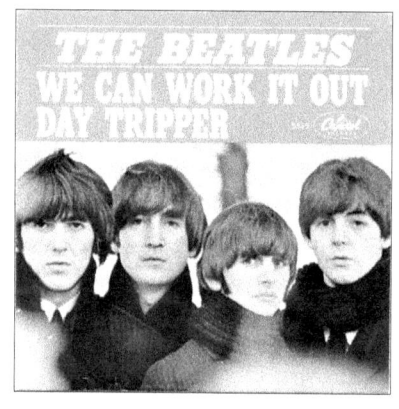

Recorded during the *Rubber Soul* sessions, this is one of the few true Lennon/McCartney equal collaborations, with Paul writing the verses ("Try to see it my way") and John the chorus ("Life is very short"). The idea of switching to three-quarters time at the end of each line in the chorus was George's.

It's interesting to note that this is a much more adult song. Instead of singing "I love you" to some "girl," Paul and John are having a conversation about a relationship. Instead of "baby" or "honey," you have "friend."

As for the single, they didn't work it out. Paul and Brian Epstein felt this was the more commercial song, but John fought for his "Day Tripper." Instead, this was released as a "double A side." In England, "Day Tripper" rose higher on the chart, but in America, "Day Tripper" stalled at #5 (see #74 on our countdown), whereas "We Can Work It Out" hit #1 for two weeks, fell back to #2 for Simon and Garfunkel's "The Sound of Silence," and then went back to #1 for an additional week.

This complicated song was never performed live by the band, but a promotional video was made where they lip-synced.

38. "Love Me Do"

The Beatles
1076 points
Chart appearance: 4/11/1964
Highest position: 1
Weeks on the chart: 14

Paul had written the basics for this simple song pre–Beatles. John later added some bits and it ended up as their first single in Britain, where it reached #17. A little over a year later, Beatlemania captured America and Tollie released it to have it reach #1 for a week. "Can't Buy Me Love" had fallen off the charts and "A Hard Day's Night" wouldn't be released for another month or so, and radio stations were dying for a new Beatles single, so Tollie (Vee-Jay) lucked out.

Originally, they had recorded this with their drummer Pete Best. Producer George Martin said Pete wasn't good enough (and, honestly, he really wasn't—just check the songs he played on *Anthology* and then compare them to the energy and power Ringo later brought to the band). So The Beatles replaced Pete with Ringo. They brought Ringo to the next session, unaware that George Martin had hired session drummer Andy White instead.

So there are three versions of this song: The original with Pete Best (on *Anthology*), the Andy White one where Ringo played tambourine (on *Please Please Me*), and a version with Ringo playing (on *Past Masters*).

37. "Instant Karma (We All Shine On)"

John Ono Lennon
1101 points
Chart appearance: 2/28/1970
Highest position: 3
Weeks on the chart: 13

John had already announced his departure to his fellow Beatles but not publicly, so the public thought this was just a side project like "Give Peace a Chance" and John would be back with his mates soon enough. The only other Beatle appearing on this single, however, was George on guitar. Phil Spector produced, throwing his layers of echo on the vocals and drums, and other musicians included Billy Preston and Klaus Voormann. John and George were impressed, and asked Spector to take over the abandoned *Get Back* tapes.

This was written and recorded in one day and was in the record stores a little more than a week later. ("Wrote it for breakfast, recorded it for lunch, and we're putting it out for dinner," John told the press.) It hit #3, where it stayed for three weeks, and remained in the Top 10 for eight of its thirteen weeks. It missed hitting #1 because of Simon and Garfunkel's "Bridge Over Troubled Water" and The Beatles' own "Let It Be."

36. "Got to Get You Into My Life"
The Beatles
1113 points
Chart appearance: 6/12/1976
Highest position: 7
Weeks on the chart: 16

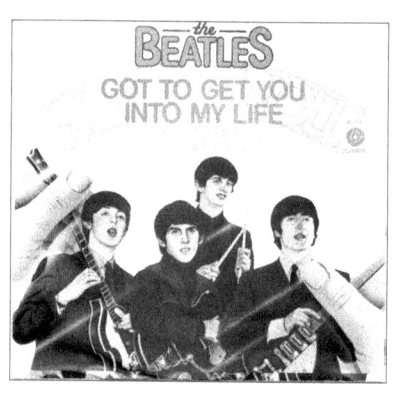

How about that. Ten years after its initial release on *Revolver*, this song gets placed on a single by Capitol to promote its *Rock 'n' Roll Music* collection and it hits the Top 10.

Paul later said the song was about marijuana. "It's actually an ode to pot, like someone else might write an ode to chocolate or a good claret," he said. Given how much Paul loves his weed (even to the point of going to jail in Japan over it), that's certainly believable. ("Every single day of my life…")

At the time, there was a made-for-TV film about the Charles Manson murders called *Helter Skelter* and the song "Helter Skelter" was getting some airplay, so Capitol almost released that as a single but then wisely decided that would be in really poor taste. So for once, they decided not to capitalize on their Beatles catalog. They did stick it on the B-side, however….

35. "Uncle Albert / Admiral Halsey"
Paul and Linda McCartney
1121 points
Chart appearance: 8/14/1971
Highest position: 1
Weeks on the chart: 13

Paul loved to do medleys (for example, "You Never Give Me Your Money" and most of side two of *Abbey Road*) and this is another example. A tremendously catchy song from the *Ram* album, it was Paul's second solo single and first #1. It jumped up the charts, going from #12 to #1 within a week, and stayed in the Top 10 for seven of its thirteen weeks.

Originally, Paul wasn't going to have any singles off *Ram*. "Another Day" had been recorded during the same sessions, but it was left off. Three months after *Ram* was released, he relented and released this single. A wise choice—it helped keep *Ram* in the Top 10 for a very long time.

Paul and John had often said that they didn't like buying a single that was already on an album. It seemed like a rip-off to them, so that attitude carried over into their solo albums. Americans had no such attitude, and the American record companies knew that a strong single was like a sampler for the album that would increase album sales. Fortunately, in this case, Paul agreed.

The song isn't really about anything. Paul does have an Uncle Albert but said that the song was not directed at him. It is not known what his position is on butter pie.

The orchestra was arranged and conducted by George Martin, who did not get the credit for it on the single or album.

It won a Grammy award for Best Arrangement Accompanying Vocalists and set a new record (for the time) for Paul for most consecutive years performing on a #1 hit.

34. "Give Me Love (Give Me Peace on Earth)"

George Harrison
1122 points
Chart appearance: 5/19/1973
Highest position: 1
Weeks on the chart: 14

After *All Things Must Pass*, George had the *Concert for Bangla Desh* and then the next year, his second non-concert and non-experimental solo album *Living in the Material World* was released. In fact, Apple Records held off releasing the album and song because of The Beatles' *1962–1966* and *1967–1970* albums and then Paul's *Red Rose Speedway*. It was a busy and exciting time for Beatles fans—a few months later, we'd get *Band on the Run*, *Ringo*, and *Mind Games*!

The song itself continues George's connection to religious spirituality and longing for a peaceful society, but is free from the "Wall of Sound" that Phil Spector had previously placed on his work.

It became George's second #1 single. Interestingly, it knocked "My Love" out of the top spot—and "My Love" was Paul's second #1 single. Neither John nor Ringo had hit #1 at that point.

The B-side is a cute little song called "Miss O'Dell" which features George cracking up while singing about The Beatles' insider Chris O'Dell, and then he gives Paul's old Liverpool phone number at the end!

33. "Listen to What the Man Said"

Wings
1126 points
Chart appearance: 5/31/1975
Highest position: 1
Weeks on the chart: 14

Paul's first single off *Venus and Mars* jumped to #1, spending seven weeks in the Top 10.

This was recorded during the band's sessions in New Orleans. Paul later stated that the song just wasn't working until they called up Tom Scott who added the saxophone bit in one take, transforming the song into a hit.

On the album, the song starts with Paul doing his New Orleans impersonation: "All right, Okay ... very good to see you down in New Orleans, man, yeah, yeah. Reet, yeah, yeah…." The song ends with an orchestral piece that leads into the next song, but on the single, it fades out.

This appears on most of Paul's greatest hits collections but not *Wings Greatest* for some reason.

32. "Get Back"
The Beatles with Billy Preston
1130 points
Chart appearance: 5/10/1969
Highest position: 1 (5 weeks)
Weeks on the chart: 12

Following their biggest hit "Hey Jude" was a fairly simple rock song that evolved from a jam during their sessions for what was eventually to become the *Let It Be* album and movie. Since this was all recorded (and can be seen in more detail in the *Get Back* movie), we can see the evolution of the song. It started out as a protest song against right-wing British anti-immigration politicians: "Dirty Enoch Powell don't want no Pakistanis…." It later turned into a jam about the "Commonwealth," with Paul singing "I'd join the Commonwealth but it's much too wealthy for me," which leads to John singing "Much too common for me"—resulting in Paul's laughter and acceptance of the new version. However, it wasn't long before Paul came up with Sweet Loretta Modern, our happy trans, and Jojo, who moved to California for the pot.

There are many versions of this song, and the single (which was released an entire year before the album) has a fade-out. However, Phil Spector's version on the *Let It Be* album tends to be the one people remember more, which does away with the fade-out and has John saying, "I hope we passed the audition."

John plays lead in this one, and Billy Preston is on keyboards (and is the only person ever to share credit on an official Beatles release). Billy was already contracted to Apple Records, so that certainly helped to avoid certain legal problems.

31. "Help!"
The Beatles
1136 points
Chart appearance: 8/7/1965
Highest position: 1 (3 weeks)
Weeks on the chart: 13

Upon being told their film "Eight Arms to Hold You" was now called *Help!*, John decided to write what he was feeling, overwhelmed with years of constant touring, filmmaking, and recording. It was his most personal song to date. At the same time, the exuberance of the performance transforms what could be a sad song into one where you don't realize the lyrics contradict the melody.

Paul says that he came up with the countermelody vocals behind the lead vocals, but other than that, it was John's song completely.

It spent three weeks at #1. Interestingly, "I'm Down" was the first Beatles B-side not to make the chart at all, despite being an excellent and exciting rocker.

The American *Help!* album starts off with a short little James Bond orchestral flourish before the song begins, and for some reason, when *1962–1966* was released, that remained, although uncredited.

30. "Live and Let Die"
Wings
1141 points
Chart appearance: 7/7/1973
Highest position: 2
Weeks on the chart: 14

Speaking of James Bond, Paul's theme for *Live and Let Die* certainly has that Bond feel to it, lushly produced by George Martin. Paul had just enjoyed his biggest hit so far ("My Love") and there was a new actor playing James Bond, so the combination of the two was a winner. Ironically, the movie studio loved the song but assumed they'd get a woman to sing it, since that had always been done with Bond movies. They were finally convinced that, you know, having a Beatle sing the theme song might actually be good for publicity. Duh!

Unfortunately, it never reached #1 but instead stayed at #2 for three weeks, held back by three separate songs jumping over Paul to take the #1 spot. ("The Morning After" by Maureen McGovern, "Touch Me in the Morning" by Diana Ross, and "Brother Louie" by Stories.) It was nominated for a Best Original Song Oscar but lost to Barbra Streisand's "The Way We Were."

Paul's feud with Allen Klein was over by this time, so this is the first Paul record to once again have a green apple label.

The B-side ("I Lie Around") is a wonderful song left off the *Red Rose Speedway* album, and sung (mostly) by Denny Laine—which is probably why it hasn't received more attention or appeared on any greatest hits collections.

29. "All Those Years Ago"
George Harrison
1145 points
Chart appearance: 5/23/1981
Highest position: 2
Weeks on the chart: 16

George had already recorded the music for this song with Ringo as his drummer, and it was planned for a Ringo solo album. When Ringo declined it, George took it back, and after John's death, decided to write all new lyrics. Paul was then invited to sing backup, making this the only song about John featuring the other three and in fact the first song these three had made since "I Me Mine." Then again, unlike "I Me Mine," they weren't all in the recording studio at the same time.

The lyrics mention John's songs "Imagine" and "All You Need Is Love."

It hit #2, where it stayed for three weeks, unable to unseat Kim Carnes' "Bette Davis Eyes," and stayed on the chart for an impressive sixteen weeks.

28. "A Hard Day's Night"
The Beatles
1157 points
Chart appearance: 7/18/1964
Highest position: 1 (2 weeks)
Weeks on the chart: 13

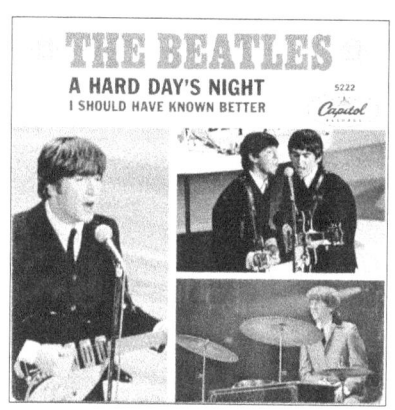

Imagine being back in 1964 and The Beatles are quite big, and unlike other pop bands of the time, they just keep on getting better and better. *A Hard Day's Night* was their first film and while pop stars had made quick little cash-in films before, none had ever had one as unique, original, and funny as this one. Even their harshest critics had to admit The Beatles had fun personalities that made watching the film a delight.

And then there was the music: This single burst into the public's consciousness with that amazing first chord, letting you know you were about to hear something good.

The title, of course, comes from Ringo saying, "It's been a hard day's..." and then upon walking outside and realizing how late it was, finishing with "night!" John used the phrase in one of his books, and then they thought it would be a great film title (certainly better than the original "Beatlemania"), so John went to work writing the song.

The song stayed in the Top 10 for two months, an amazing feat. However, in those days, songs tended to fall off the charts quickly, else this would be higher in our countdown.

27. "Spies Like Us"
Paul McCartney
1177 points
Chart appearance: 11/23/1985
Highest position: 7
Weeks on the chart: 17

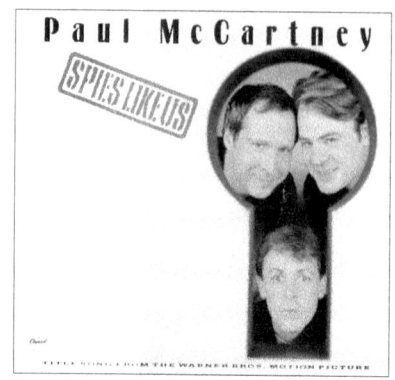

Here's a song Paul tossed off for a comedy film. It slowly crawled up the charts, reaching #7 in its twelfth week, before slowly crawling back down. Its longevity on the chart helped place it in our countdown's Top 30. It's also Paul's last song to hit the Top 10 (unless you count a certain collaboration coming up later in our countdown).

Paul plays all the instruments in this one except for a synthesizer added in later by Eddie Rayner from Split Enz. A number of people sing backup, but despite the promotional video implying otherwise, none of them are Chevy Chase or Dan Ackroyd.

26. "Let 'Em In"

Wings
1187 points
Chart appearance: 7/4/1976
Highest position: 3
Weeks on the chart: 16

This second single from the *Wings at the Speed of Sound* album spent a month at #3. It was held back by Elton John and Kiki Dee's "Don't Go Breaking My Heart" and The Bee Gees' "You Should Be Dancing."

Paul mentions all the people knocking at his door that he'll let in, including his own Auntie Gin, his brother Michael, Linda's brother John, Phil and Don (The Everly Brothers), and Martin Luther, who famously posted his thesis on the church door. The song starts off with a doorbell playing the "Ding Dong; Ding Dong" notes, but George doesn't get any credit. (That's a joke.)

Years later, on his album *Ringo Rama*, Ringo sang a few lines from this as his song "English Garden" was fading out. And speaking of fading out, "Let 'Em In" has a bit of a fake fade-out in that just when you think the song is disappearing, the last two notes pop back in at full volume to surprise you.

25. "Photograph"

Ringo Starr
1206 points
Chart appearance: 10/6/1973
Highest position: 1
Weeks on the chart: 16

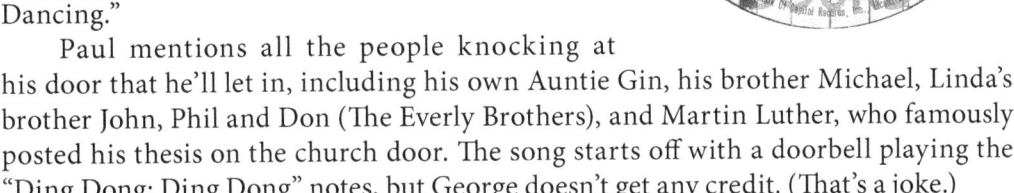

And now we have an unusual tie. The first single from the hugely successful *Ringo* album crawled up the charts and eventually hit #1 in its eighth week. This was Ringo's first #1 single.

The song was written by Ringo and George, although Ringo has admitted that he "only knows three chords," so George may have provided the rest.

The lyrics feature Ringo lamenting that all he has to remember someone by is a photograph. Underneath the bright melody is quite a sad song. "Now you're expecting me to live without you / That's not something that I'm looking forward to."

The album was produced by Richard Perry but this particular song seems to have been recorded with Phil Spector in mind, as it is extremely dense with instrumentation, including strings, a chorus, horns, and lots of percussion.

The B-side is "Down and Out," a simple three-chord song from Ringo that could be the faster sister to "Back Off Boogaloo," featuring George's slide guitar. It's not on the album but has been included in re-releases.

24. "You're Sixteen"
Ringo Starr
1206 points
Chart appearance: 12/15/1973
Highest position: 1
Weeks on the chart: 15

Weeks after "Photograph" hit #1 came this second single which, amazingly enough, has the exact same number of points in our countdown, despite having a completely different trajectory on the charts. So while Paul and George took a few years between their two #1 hits at this time, Ringo met their standard within a few months' time.

"You're Sixteen" is a 1960 song written by The Sherman Brothers (who wrote the songs for *Mary Poppins*, among other things). Paul appears, but only to play a kazoo-sounding solo! Backing vocals are all from the amazing Harry Nilsson. As it fades out, you can hear Ringo singing "What can we do with a drunken sailor." Don't ask why.

A video of the song features Terry Gilliam–like animation with Ringo singing to Carrie Fisher, who was 17 at the time (pre–*Star Wars*). Let's not dwell on the fact that a 32-year-old man was singing about a girl half his age. Things were different then.

23. "Goodnight Tonight"
Wings
1215 points
Chart appearance: 3/31/1979
Highest position: 5
Weeks on the chart: 16

Paul's first single with his new record company Columbia was recorded during the *Back to the Egg* sessions, but Paul kept it off the album. A disco-flavored beat complemented a song that was pretty much just a really catchy bass line repeated over and over again. Sometimes the chorus would kick in, sometimes a lead guitar, sometimes some echoey vocals, and then it faded out. There aren't too many pop songs that start with a verse and then stuff happens and the second verse doesn't even appear until the song is almost over.

Anyway, it was a big hit, reaching #5. It stayed there for three weeks and spent sixteen on the chart in total. The original track was over seven minutes long but was edited to 4:18 for the single. And that's a good thing; the long version tends to be overkill. Still, this was at a time when disco was king and bands often released "extended dance versions" of their singles.

Paul's insistence on keeping singles off albums may have hurt *Back to the Egg*'s success, as including this song certainly would have increased sales.

22. "Junior's Farm / Sally G"

Paul McCartney and Wings
1241 points
Chart appearance: 1/9/1974
Highest position: 3
Weeks on the chart: 17

Paul's first single after *Band on the Run* was this excellent rocker, which reached #3. This may be the only Top 40 single to mention Oliver Hardy.

Promotional ads for the single show the band in a casino, dressed as a card dealer, a farmer, and an Eskimo (referencing characters in the song), and there's even a sea lion. There wasn't a picture sleeve in the United States, but other countries used that promo picture for theirs. Paul has admitted in interviews that the lyrics don't mean a thing; he's just having fun with the words and images.

As "Junior's Farm" fell off the Top 40, Apple flipped it over and started promoting its B-side, the country-flavored "Sally G." It started rising again, got up to #39, and then fell off completely. However, since by this time *Billboard* was not listing B-sides separately, both songs are listed here together as one.

21. "My Sweet Lord"

George Harrison
1269 points
Chart appearance: 11/28/1970
Highest position: 1 (4 weeks)
Weeks on the chart: 15

George's first single took everyone by surprise, becoming the first #1 by a solo Beatle. From *All Things Must Pass*, it stayed at the top of the chart for an entire month over the Christmas holidays. An acoustic guitar ballad, the song was catchy and religious, perfect for the holiday. In fact, at the time there were a lot of religious rock songs on the radio, from "Spirit in the Sky" to the entire double album *Jesus Christ Superstar*. The fact that George's song included chants to Krishna didn't seem to matter to anyone who picked this up.

The song also grabbed the attention of Bright Tunes Music, the company owning the rights to The Chiffons' earlier hit "He's So Fine." After years of litigation, George lost, with the judge ruling that he had "subconsciously" stolen the music. George later responded with "This Song" (which has "nothing Bright about it").

The B-side "Isn't It a Pity" also received some airplay, and so *Billboard* listed it as if this was a double A-side record—but by this time, they were not listing B-sides separately on the chart. On the other hand, unlike most Apple records where the B-side featured an apple cut in half, this B-side had the full, green apple just like the A-side. "Isn't It a Pity" was not edited for the single, and comes in at 7:10—exactly one second less than "Hey Jude" (which is heard in the background as "Pity" fades out).

20. "No More Lonely Nights"

Paul McCartney
1273 points
Chart appearance: 10/13/1984
Highest position: 6
Weeks on the chart: 18

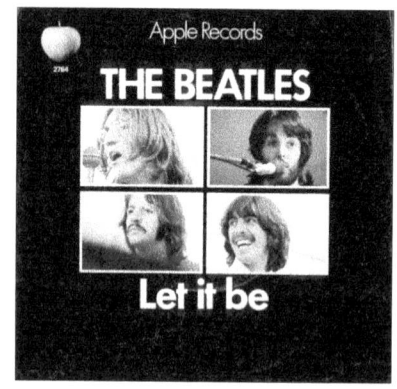

Paul's film *Give My Regards to Broad Street* was a failure, but the signature tune from the film reached #6 and stayed on the charts for an impressive eighteen weeks.

The B-side was the same song, but done with a techno beat, used for the closing titles, and was called the "playout version." There was also a long extended dance version that was available on a 12-inch release.

David Gilmour plays the lead guitar solo and Paul actually let someone else play bass for this one: Herbie Flowers. Eric Stewart and Linda provided backup vocals.

19. "Let It Be"

The Beatles
1287 points
Chart appearance: 3/21/1970
Highest position: 1 (2 weeks)
Weeks on the chart: 14

Like "Get Back," there are two versions of this song. The single was produced by George Martin and was released early in 1970, and a few months later, the album came out with Phil Spector's version. Spector used a different, heavier guitar solo, but if you listen closely, you can hear the old one in the background as well as a third one deep in the mix! And there's even *another* one on *Let It Be.... Naked*!

"Mother Mary" in this song is not a religious reference; Paul is specifically talking about his own mother who had appeared to him in a dream, telling him that to deal with his stress, he should "let it be." John didn't like the song much, and on the *Let It Be* album, Phil Spector has him introduce it in a high falsetto, proclaiming it to be "Hark, the Angels Come."

John once claimed that this was Paul's attempt to write a "Bridge Over Troubled Water" (the song that was #1 just before this one), but that ignores the fact that "Let It Be" was recorded a year earlier, long before Simon and Garfunkel recorded their song.

The B-side is the hilarious "You Know My Name (Look Up the Number)," which Paul once called his "favorite Beatles track, just because it's so insane." Sometimes people complain that this song is too silly, ignoring completely the history of The Beatles' senses of humor and the fact that their name is a literal pun.

18. "With a Little Luck"

Wings
1300 points
Chart appearance: 3/25/1978
Highest position: 1 (2 weeks)
Weeks on the chart: 18

Recorded during the *London Town* sessions, "With a Little Luck" turned out to give a lot of luck to Paul, by staying at the top position for two weeks and remaining on the chart for eighteen weeks, eight of those in the Top 10. Although the single lasted almost six minutes, radio stations often played a shorter version.

On the other hand, some of the luck was bad. Wings split apart again during the sessions, so the album was completed with just Paul, Linda, and Denny Laine.

The song itself is rather simple, keyboard-driven, and light. Paul was apparently not that impressed with his own work, as he has never played this live despite it being one of his biggest hits.

17. "She Loves You"

The Beatles
1336 points
Chart appearance: 1/25/1964
Highest position: 1 (2 weeks)
Weeks on the chart: 15

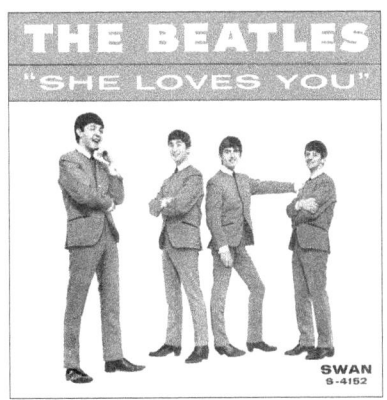

Swan had gained the American rights to this song in 1963, but it had not sold well, despite it being one of the great rock songs of all time. In fact, in the United Kingdom, it is still The Beatles' best-selling single and is their biggest selling single of the entire '60s.

Less than a year later, Beatlemania hit America, and Swan re-released it, to have it hit #1 and stay for two weeks.

It's a clever song full of hooks, and George Martin's suggestion to start the song with the chorus was genius. Unlike many love songs of the day, this one isn't about the singer, which made it a bit unique.

"Yeah yeah yeah" became a Beatles catchphrase (which they repeated in the fade-out of "All You Need Is Love," and Paul brought back again for "What's That You're Doing?" from his *Tug of War* album).

Also noteworthy is the closing chord (George's idea) with a major sixth. The perfect rock song, deserving of all its accolades.

16. "The Girl Is Mine"
Michael Jackson/Paul McCartney
1360 points
Chart appearance: 11/6/1982
Highest position: 2
Weeks on the chart: 18

Half of the songs left in our countdown are from Paul, and half of those are ones he did with other Big Name Stars whose fans also bought these records, thus increasing their popularity. A smart move on Paul's part.

This one is a Michael Jackson song, appearing on his album *Thriller*. It's probably the weakest song on that album. In fact, as it was the first single issued prior to that album's release, critics were worried that *Thriller* would be a major disappointment.

Paul is merely a singer on this one, not having contributed to the writing of the song or any of the instrumentation.

15. "I Want to Hold Your Hand"
The Beatles
1402 points
Chart appearance: 1/18/1964
Highest position: 1 (7 weeks)
Weeks on the chart: 15

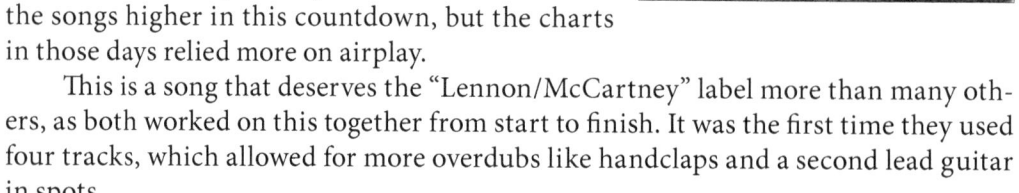

This was the song that broke them here in America, dominating the top spot for seven weeks, only to lose it to "She Loves You" which then lost it to "Can't Buy Me Love."

Sales-wise, it probably did better than some of the songs higher in this countdown, but the charts in those days relied more on airplay.

This is a song that deserves the "Lennon/McCartney" label more than many others, as both worked on this together from start to finish. It was the first time they used four tracks, which allowed for more overdubs like handclaps and a second lead guitar in spots.

Capitol went to work promoting their new artists before the record was released, but import singles had gotten into the hands of DJs in America who were playing them despite Capitol's legal threats. Of course, all this did was raise expectations, and when the single was finally released here, the stores could hardly keep it in stock.

And why not? It's a great song. It's not just hype that has us still listening to Beatles albums and buying Beatles books all these years later.

14. "Band on the Run"
Paul McCartney and Wings
1412 points
Chart appearance: 4/20/1974
Highest position: 1
Weeks on the chart: 18

The third single from *Band on the Run* did even better than the previous two, landing at #1 and staying on the chart for an amazing eighteen weeks. It was also Paul's third #1 hit in America.

Like "Venus and Mars Rock Show" or "Uncle Albert / Admiral Halsey," it contains different parts that all mix together, although not as smoothly as, for example, "You Never Give Me Your Money."

For once, the long song wasn't edited down for the single. A slightly shorter version was provided to radio stations, but most DJs ended up playing the entire version, which runs five minutes. It's become a Paul staple during live shows, and always appears on his greatest hits collections.

The B-side was "Nineteen Hundred and Eighty Five," which also contained the "Band on the Run" reprise at the very end. This was also not edited down from its five-and-a-half minute length.

13. "My Love"
Paul McCartney & Wings
1431 points
Chart appearance: 4/14/1973
Highest position: 1 (4 weeks)
Weeks on the chart: 18

After the mediocre sales for previous Wings projects, this new single prominently proclaimed that it was by "Paul McCartney & Wings," as Capitol was worried the previous poor sales were due to people not knowing Wings was Paul's band. To further emphasize this, the album *Red Rose Speedway* featured only Paul on the cover.

This approach apparently worked, as this single hit number one and stayed there for a month—tying the record George had set for post–Beatles hits with "My Sweet Lord."

Although it was roundly criticized for its simple lyrics, record buyers didn't care. It brought Paul back to the success he had previously known with The Beatles, sitting on the top of the chart like he belonged there. In fact, it only lost that spot in the fifth week to George's "Give Me Love (Give Me Peace on Earth)."

Paul wanted emotion in the song and had it recorded live with an orchestra instead of overdubbing them later. They spent three hours doing take after take, with a different guitar solo each time so Paul could choose his favorite. It's an interesting but expensive way to record (those orchestra studio musicians aren't cheap), but Paul could afford it.

12. "Come Together"
The Beatles
1438 points
Chart appearance: 10/18/1969
Highest position: 1
Weeks on the chart: 16

Here we have an unusual situation, as mentioned in the "About the Charts" chapter earlier. "Something" was backed with "Come Together" on a single at a time where *Billboard* counted each song separately. They both zoomed up the chart. One week, "Something" would be ahead, and the next week, "Come Together" would take the lead. By their fifth week on the chart, "Come Together" was #2 and "Something" was #3. Then *Billboard* said, "That's enough of that," and decided that they would no longer count B-sides separately, so by week seven, "Something/Come Together" was #1.

For purposes of this book, they were counted separately and the time they spent together was given to each. And, interestingly enough, only one point separates them on our chart here.

Although Paul desperately wanted "Maxwell's Silver Hammer" to be released as a single from *Abbey Road*, he was on the outs with their new manager Allen Klein, who instead chose a song from John and a song from George for the next Beatles single.

John's "Come Together" started off with a similar feel to Chuck Berry's "You Can't Catch Me" and John even rewrote a few lines as a tribute—which led to a later lawsuit resulting in the *Rock 'n' Roll* album. (The lines from Berry were "Here come a flat top / He was movin' up with me.") Paul suggested slowing it down, adding that distinctive bass riff and electric piano, and the swampy tune distanced itself from its origins.

The song was originally written for Timothy Leary's campaign for governor of California, as "Come Together" was his slogan. John later came up with something that didn't really fit a political campaign.

During an interview recently on Stephen Colbert's show, Ringo called this his favorite Beatles song of all time.

11. "Something"

The Beatles
1439 points
Chart appearance: 10/18/1969
Highest position: 1
Weeks on the chart: 16

George finally gets an A-side to a single (unless you count VeeJay's release of "Do You Want to Know a Secret?"), and what an A-side! It's one of The Beatles' biggest hits, and is the second most covered Beatles song after "Yesterday." Frank Sinatra did a cover and reportedly called it "One of Lennon/McCartney's greatest songs." Ahem.

You have to admit, though, that when you think of *Abbey Road*, the two songs that tend to get the most downloads are this one and George's other composition "Here Comes the Sun." Imagine if Paul and John had allowed him a few more tunes—he certainly had enough ready to go, as evidenced by the following year's *All Things Must Pass*.

George apparently copied the opening line from Apple recording star James Taylor's album, which included the song "Something in the Way She Moves." The songs bear no other resemblance to each other. George had been working on the song for a year or so before it was recorded, and in the *Get Back* film, he's talking to John about it, saying he was having some trouble with the lyrics. "Something in the way she moves attracts me like ... *what?*" he asked John, who replied that it didn't matter at this point and to just use any word as a filler. He suggested "attracts me like a cauliflower."

This is a great song to showcase George's ability as a lead guitarist. Its lead is simple yet memorable and perfect for the song's mood. George had come a long way from the early, amateurish leads on the first few albums.

A promotional film was made which featured each Beatle with their wives but not together. And, of course, it was soon after that John announced he was leaving the group.

10. "Silly Love Songs"

Wings
1513 points
Chart appearance: 4/10/1976
Highest position: 1 (5 weeks)
Weeks on the chart: 19

And now we're in our Top 10, which contains a few surprises.

In response to criticism over his simple "I love you" lyrics (see "My Love" at #13), Paul gets the last laugh. "What's wrong with that?" he asks, and the public agrees, keeping him at the top of the charts for five weeks and giving him one of the biggest hits of his career. In fact, *Billboard* proclaimed it as the number one hit of 1976, making Paul the only person to have written two year-end number one hits (the other being "Hey Jude").

Propelled by a catchy prominent bassline, and inspired by the then-current disco trend, this proved quite popular. It's Paul's longest single as a solo artist, running almost six minutes, even beating "With a Little Luck." It has different vocal parts over the same backing which eventually all run at the same time to produce some very nice counter melodies. Paul has featured this song in many of his live shows, and it appears on every greatest hits collection (where it belongs).

9. "Ebony and Ivory"
Paul McCartney and Stevie Wonder
1519 points
Chart appearance: 4/10/1982
Highest position: 1 (7 weeks)
Weeks on the chart: 19

Paul's ode to racial harmony, using the keyboard as a metaphor, was the first time he had worked with another recording artist and shared credit. The success of this certainly encouraged him to later partnerships with Michael Jackson, Elvis Costello, Kanye West, and others.

Taken from the *Tug of War* album, this single stayed at the top of the charts for an amazing seven weeks. Paul was reunited with Beatles producer George Martin (although they had also worked on "Live and Let Die" a half a dozen years earlier) and the result is a great recording of what is, ultimately, a rather weak song. Paul and Stevie play all the instruments on the song except for the addition of some Scottish bagpipes in the background.

While this song is completely written by Paul, he and Stevie co-wrote "What's That You're Doing" for *Tug of War* during the same sessions.

The song stayed at #1 for seven amazing weeks, making this both Paul and Stevie's longest run at #1 (not counting "Hey Jude").

8. "Got My Mind Set on You"
George Harrison
1540 points
Chart appearance: 10/24/1987
Highest position: 1
Weeks on the chart: 22

"Got My Mind Set on You" is an old obscure B-side from 1962 that George always liked. He recorded it for his *Cloud 9* album and released it as the first single. It slowly moved up the chart, reaching #1 in its thirteenth week! It then slowly moved back down, staying an impressive twenty-two weeks in total on the chart. That length helped place it in our own Top 10.

This is the last song done by any Beatle to hit #1, and only the second #1 single not written by any of them (the first being Ringo's "You're Sixteen"). It hit #1 just as The Beatles were being inducted into the Rock and Roll Hall of Fame, showing clearly that they were not has-beens.

The single was helped along by two very creative videos, but one received the majority of airplay. It featured George sitting in a chair performing the song as the decorations in the house came to life around him. "Weird Al" Yankovic later did his own parody version, called "This Song's Just Six Words Long."

7. "FourFiveSeconds"
Rihanna, Kanye West, and Paul McCartney
1585 points
Chart appearance: 2/7/2015
Highest position: 4
Weeks on the chart: 20

The most recent addition to our singles countdown never reached #1 but it stayed on the chart a very long time, as is more common these days.

It allows Paul to rightly claim the longest career of any artist to hit the Top 10, from 1964 to 2015 (fifty-one years!).

Like many singles these days, it was written by a committee using scientific ways to determine what will be a hit—commerce over art. On the other hand, one of the ten (10!) writers listed was Paul, so there's that.

It's basically a Rihanna single with extra vocals from Kanye West. Paul plays acoustic guitar and looks a bit out of place in the video, as he only sings backup. It's only on our list because he is credited on the record. Ignore its placement here if you wish.

6. "Woman"
John Lennon
1629 points
Chart appearance: 1/17/1981
Highest position: 2
Weeks on the chart: 20

John's senseless assassination reminded everyone of his talent, and his records (as well as many Beatles albums) reappeared on the charts. This second single from his *Double Fantasy* album benefited from this sad situation, and remained on the chart for an amazing twenty weeks. It stayed at #2

for three weeks, but was unable to defeat REO Speedwagon's "Keep on Loving You" and Blondie's "Rapture" from the top spot.

John said he considered this his "grown-up" adult version of his song "Girl." Although the song is inspired by Yoko, he meant it to be addressed to all women and how we should appreciate them. It's a much more accessible song on the topic than the one he did in 1972 that didn't make the Top 40 due to its title.

If you listen closely, you can hear John whisper "For the other half of the sky" at the start of the song.

Paul, of course, had previously written a song called "Woman" that had been recorded by Peter and Gordon, but it has nothing in common with John's song. Still, it's the only song title shared by both Paul and John in their solo careers.

5. "Coming Up"
Paul McCartney
1631 points
Chart appearance: 4/6/1980
Highest position: 1 (3 weeks)
Weeks on the chart: 21

Paul had recorded this song for his *McCartney II* album, playing all the instruments himself (like he did for *McCartney*) and having fun with strange things he could do with his voice recording. He then produced a wonderful video with him leading a band composed entirely of other Pauls, dressed as Buddy Holly, Ron Mael, himself as a 1964-era Beatle, and various stereotypical rock stars. (Linda also appears as two characters.)

The song had previously been part of Wings' live show, and a recording was made of a performance at the Apollo in Glasgow on December 17, 1979. Paul placed the live version on the B-side … only to find that in America, the B-side was preferred. Radio stations ignored the studio version, and the live version hit #1 and stayed on the chart for twenty-one weeks, becoming Paul's most successful solo single on the charts!

Because of this, if you get certain greatest hits albums in the rest of the world, you get the Paul solo version, but here in America, you get the live version.

Some people theorize that the song was a message to John, with lyrics like "You want some peace and understanding, so everybody can be free. I know that we can get together, we can make it, stick with me!" John and Paul had put aside their problems by this time and they had even hung out together, and it's also said that John was so impressed by this song that it encouraged him to once more get into the studio to record his *Double Fantasy* album. In fact, John said this about it: "I thought that 'Coming Up' was great and I like the freak version that he made in his barn better than that live Glasgow one…. And I thought that the record company had a nerve changing it round on him, and I know what they mean, they want to hear the real guy singing, but I like the freaky one."

4. "Twist and Shout"

The Beatles
1707 points
Chart appearance: 3/21/1964
Highest position: 2
Weeks on the chart: 26

Vee-Jay (through its subsidiary Tollie) released this single at the height of Beatlemania, where it reached #2, staying on the chart for eleven weeks. It would have made #1 but for this song called "Can't Buy Me Love."

It's the only Beatles song not written by The Beatles to reach the Top 10.

You wouldn't expect this to be so high in our countdown, but there's a good reason: In 1986, Matthew Broderick lip-synced to the song in the film *Ferris Bueller's Day Off* and Rodney Dangerfield "sang" his own version in his film *Back to School*, coincidentally released at the same time. Capitol took advantage of that and re-released the song as a single, where it reached #23 and stayed on the chart for an additional fifteen weeks! Combine those two and this song has the longest Beatles chart life.

Despite this song being such a hit and so closely associated with The Beatles, you never find this on any greatest hits collections because it's a cover version, recorded in one basic take. The Beatles never considered the covers as being a part of their catalog, as they were always just used as filler songs for their albums.

It's an Isley Brothers tune that The Beatles learned in 1962 to perform in their live shows. It was already a cover at that time—the Isley Brothers version may have been what The Beatles took and made their own, but it was originally performed by The Top Notes (Remember them? Didn't think so).

When one more song was needed to fill the *Please Please Me* album, The Beatles decided to record this crowd pleaser. Their first album had to be recorded in just one day, so they didn't have time to write, learn, or practice something new. John sang his heart out and knew he could never do that again, as it really ripped his throat.

This popular song was often used to close their live shows, including their Royal Command performance for the Queen, where John introduced it by saying, "For our last number, I'd like to ask your help. The people in the cheaper seats clap your hands. And the rest of you, if you'd just rattle your jewelry."

3. "Hey Jude"

The Beatles
1770 points
Chart appearance: 9/14/1968
Highest position: 1 (9 weeks)
Weeks on the chart: 19

"Hey Jude" holds The Beatles record for the longest time at #1: Nine weeks! From September to late November 1968, no other song could unseat it from the top. However, it only stayed on the chart for nineteen weeks total, so doesn't make our top slot.

Remember that in those days, this was not unusual. Had they paid more attention to sales as opposed to radio play (as they started doing a few years later), this probably would have remained on the charts a few more weeks at least and thus made our #1 spot. Instead, it lost out to songs that were released over twenty years later. Keep in mind that the fact that this scored so high despite having to compete against so many songs that were released later under different qualifications is *very* impressive. (If I were better at math, I'd come up with a formula to take the different standards into consideration when making this list.)

It was recorded during the *White Album* sessions, but was so well received by the band that it was decided to release it as a single before the album was done. George Martin protested, saying no radio station would play a song lasting that long (more than seven minutes!), but John replied, "They will if it's us." He was right!

But it might have also had something to do with how great a song it is. Years later, during an interview, John complained that Paul was always getting the A-sides of singles, and "Revolution" should have been an A-side. When he was reminded that "Hey Jude" was the A-side, John backed down, acknowledging that "Hey Jude" deserved that position.

Paul plays piano and rather than overdubbing his bass later, John played bass (as he would later do for "Let It Be" and "Long and Winding Road"). Sadly, though John was an excellent rhythm guitarist who doesn't always get the credit he deserves, his bass playing was merely adequate.

Paul very much enjoyed it when a song would have something different playing during the fade-out, such as with "Ticket to Ride" and "Hello Goodbye," and took it to an extreme here, with a four-minute fade-out (longer than the basic song itself) that has implanted itself into our collective consciousness. Everyone knows this song, and it is constantly a crowd-pleasing closer at Paul's live shows.

Keep in mind what the previous year or so had been for the band. After Brian Epstein's death, they had struggled a bit. The *Magical Mystery Tour* film was a bust, "Lady Madonna" didn't make it to #1, and almost four months had gone by without any singles on the chart and (in England at least) it had been more than a year since their last album. So when this amazing song blasted through the radio with its inspiring lyrics and happy sing-along fade-out, it was clear that The Beatles were far from finished.

This was the first Beatles song to be released on their new Apple label, which also generated some publicity and attention. But hey, this could have been released on Tollie and it still would have been a hit.

2. "Say Say Say"

Paul McCartney and Michael Jackson
1826 points
Chart appearance: 10/15/1983
Highest position: 1 (6 weeks)
Weeks on the chart: 22

This duet with Michael Jackson was recorded during the *Tug of War* sessions and produced by George Martin using the amazing Beatles engineer Geoff Emerick (who deserves a lot more credit than he often receives). It was done around the same time that Michael was releasing "The Girl Is Mine."

However, rather than releasing it at that time, Paul saved the song for his follow-up album *Pipes of Peace* a year later.

It was the perfect time for Paul to release the song. Michael's album *Thriller* had spent most of 1983 at or near #1, and he was proclaimed the King of Pop—with an unprecedented seven singles from that album reaching the Top 10. Anything he touched turned to gold.

So for a song with Michael *and* Paul to hit #1 and stay there for six weeks? Not too surprising. It became Michael's seventh Top 10 hit for the year, breaking a record previously jointly held by The Beatles and Elvis Presley.

Both Paul and Michael are credited as writers, but apparently Michael's contribution was mostly lyrics. Paul plays most of the instruments in the recording but not, strangely enough, bass.

The song didn't impress a lot of critics, but the public didn't care. It didn't stay at #1 as long as "Hey Jude," but it remained on the chart a few weeks longer, enabling it to bypass The Beatles' most successful chart single.

However, it didn't help *Pipes of Peace* much. Even with this huge hit single, *Pipes* never got any higher than #15 on the chart—which seems to indicate that this single was more popular with Michael Jackson fans than Paul McCartney fans.

Paul and Michael worked well together but the friendship didn't last. Paul had advised Michael that investing in music publishing was a wise choice. Michael then outbid Paul for the publishing rights to The Beatles' catalog. Paul never forgave him after that, and it wasn't until 2017, after Michael's death, that Paul (at age 74) was able to finally gain control over his own publishing rights.

1. "(Just Like) Starting Over"

John Lennon
1838 points
Chart appearance: 11/1/1980
Highest position: 1 (5 weeks)
Weeks on the chart: 22

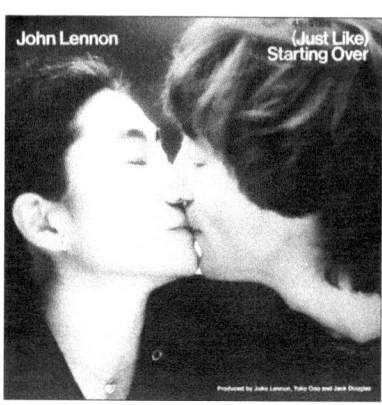

After five years with no new music, John was finally back with a new album (*Double Fantasy*) and a brand new single. It inched its way up the charts, hitting the Top 10. Things looked good for John. He was contentedly back with Yoko, his son Sean was healthy and happy, and his latest album looked successful.

Then the unimaginable happened.

People around the world mourned, gathered around the apartment building where he lived, and sang his songs.

But let's not dwell on the sadness and relive our pain.

John's assassination reminded everyone of what he had brought all of us, and most of his albums as well as many Beatles albums reappeared on the charts. "(Just Like) Starting Over" hit #1 (where it might have found itself anyway) and stayed there for five weeks. It then took its time moving back down the charts, staying for a total of twenty-two weeks and placing it at #1 on our countdown (just slightly ahead of "Say Say Say").

The song itself leads off the album and fits the theme of John returning to recording after five years away. It has a 1950s style to it, although with modern production and musical performances. John admitted he was trying to channel Elvis Presley and Roy Orbison in his approach to both the writing of the song and the singing.

John was indeed starting over. A tour was being planned, and even before December 8, it appeared that *Double Fantasy* was set to become one of his biggest hits ever.

So there's our singles countdown, which is unlikely to change unless Paul or Ringo surprise us.

Albums

164. *Gimme Some Truth*
John Lennon
5 points
Chart appearance: 10/23/2010
Highest position: 196
Weeks on the chart: 1

At the very bottom of our Albums chart is a four-disc box set from John. While it's a complete collection, it didn't sell that well, mostly because by this time, everyone had one of the many other John Lennon greatest hits sets out there. You get your money's worth though, with eighteen songs per CD, so that's at least something. Or, if you really wanted everything plus the kitchen sink, you could get the eleven CD set *Signature Box* which was released on the same day!

This box set really didn't add anything new from older collections other than the sequencing, which organized each disc by subject matter (protest songs, love songs, life, rock and roll roots).

163. *Long Tall Sally (EP)*
The Beatles
5 points
Chart appearance: 12/13/2014
Highest position: 196
Weeks on the chart: 1

In order to keep people from downloading everything these days, record stores have created "Record Store Day" with specials that can only be obtained by getting off your computer and actually going somewhere to buy music just like your crazy grandparents used to do in the Dark Ages. This is one of those specials, and is actually just a re-release of a British EP from 1964.

It sold well enough on that day to make the next chart, after which it fell right off.

Just don't ask why *Billboard* placed this on the album chart instead of the singles chart like they did with EPs that made the singles chart in 1964.

162. *Standing Stone*
Paul McCartney
7 points
Chart appearance: 11/1/1997
Highest position: 194
Weeks on the chart: 1

Paul has been determined to show that he can write any type of music ever since *The Beatles* (White Album) where he proved he could write rock and roll, country, ska, folk, heavy metal, and so on.

Standing Stone is his second classical selection, performed by the London Symphony Orchestra. It fills two CDs and has a very large booklet. The cover photo is from Linda.

Paul said it was about a Celtic man wondering about his place in the cosmos. Reviewers said it falls somewhere between classical and soundtrack music, but come on, for someone who is not classically trained, it's not bad.

It appeared on the chart for one week only in 1997.

161. *Electronic Sound*
George Harrison
19 points
Chart appearance: 7/5/1969
Highest position: 191
Weeks on the chart: 2

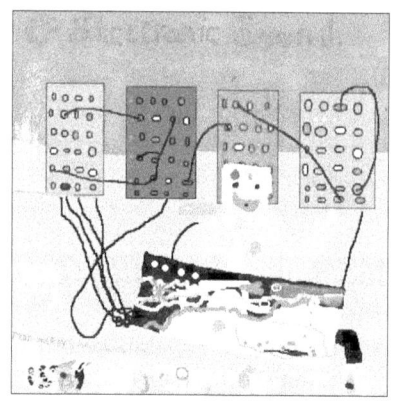

Once The Beatles created Apple, it gave them a way to put out whatever they felt like, without some label bigwig stopping them by saying, "That'll never sell!" So George and John took that opportunity to release a few experimental albums on the Zapple label which, just like the bigwigs predicted, didn't sell.

Okay, admittedly, they sold a few copies to Beatles fans who had to collect everything they ever did, and that allowed this to be on the chart for a few weeks.

Each side of *Electronic Sound* is a separate track and there was some confusion when the album was initially released because the record was mislabeled. It was corrected with the CD version which, not surprisingly, never made the chart.

The album is just George doodling around with one of the few Moog synthesizers available at the time, but if you didn't know it was George, there's no reason you'd be buying this album. It's interesting historically as the first all-electronic album, but that's about it. The Beatles learned how to use the Moog to great effect by *Abbey Road*, where it appears often.

160. *Zoom In*

Ringo Starr
22 points
Chart appearance: 4/3/2021
Highest position: 179
Weeks on the chart: 1

In the midst of the pandemic, Ringo released a five-song EP which spent a week on the chart. It was mostly produced by Ringo and he co-wrote two of the songs.

They were all recorded in his home studio, and with everyone using Zoom to talk to each other during that time, I guess he felt he should comment on it—and thus the EP was named. Much of the album was patched together remotely, but there were some real people playing live with Ringo.

Later in the year, a second EP was released called *Changeced the World*. It did not make the chart. Ringo was asked why he didn't just save up the songs from the two EPs to make one album and he shrugged the question off, saying he just liked to get things out as they were done.

159. *With The Beatles*

The Beatles
22 points
Chart appearance: 12/4/2010
Highest position: 179
Weeks on the chart: 1

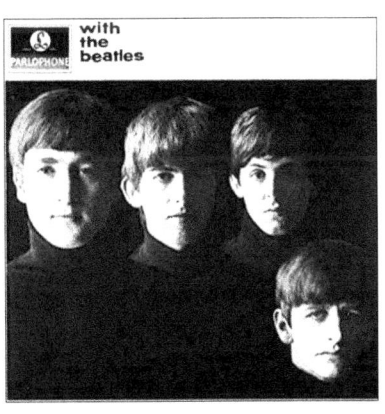

"What in the world?" you ask. "What is their second album doing here near the bottom of the list?" Well, you need to remember that in America, you couldn't get this album at all. Oh sure, the cover was used for *Meet The Beatles!*, but the only way you could get *With The Beatles* was as an import. Once The Beatles albums became available on CD, the British versions were all that were available (for a while).

This appeared on the chart when this album and others were remastered and re-released in 2010. It only spent a week on the chart, but of course, more copies were included in the box sets which Beatles fanatics bought the first week.

158. *The Beatles Bootleg Recordings 1963*

The Beatles
29 points
Chart appearance: 1/4/2014
Highest position: 172
Weeks on the chart: 1

This unusual recording was probably planned by a lawyer for Apple, who noted that under British law, early Beatles recordings would become public domain if not issued.

Thus this download-only album from iTunes, which contains 59 out-takes, rehearsal sessions, and demos, with the largest percentage as live performances at the BBC.

And so the song rights were saved, and everyone lived happily ever after.

157. *The Apple Years 1968–75*

George Harrison
34 points
Chart appearance: 10/4/2014
Highest position: 167
Weeks on the chart: 1

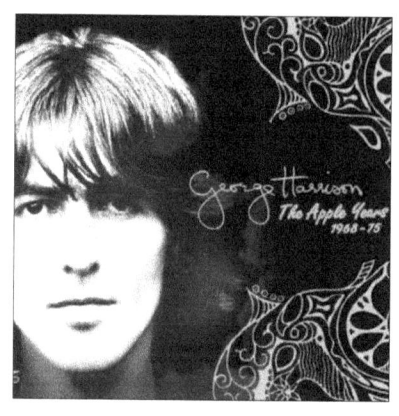

This huge box set includes all of George's Apple albums, including *Electronic Sound* and *Wonderwall Music* but also *All Things Must Pass*, *Living in the Material World*, *Dark Horse*, and *Extra Texture*. It does not include *The Concert for Bangla Desh*.

This eight-disc set includes a few extra bits. For instance, there's an instrumental version of "The Inner Light," a remixed "Bangla Desh," a new version of "This Guitar (Can't Keep from Crying)," and all of the B-sides that had never made the albums.

The eighth disc was a DVD of videos and concert footage.

It sold well enough in its first week to hit #167, but fell off immediately afterward.

The companion album (*The Dark Horse Years*), containing later albums, had been released ten years earlier but legal problems held back this one. *The Dark Horse Years* did not make the chart.

156. *Please Please Me*

The Beatles
46 points
Chart appearance: 12/4/2010
Highest position: 155
Weeks on the chart: 1

Like *With The Beatles*, this re-release of the remastered album appeared the same week and dropped off the chart immediately afterward.

Since this book only looks at the American charts, our British friends flipping through the book are sure to stop here and wonder why this album is so low on our chart!

155. *Signature Box*

John Lennon
53 points
Chart appearance: 10/23/2010
Highest position: 148
Weeks on the chart: 1

This box set was released the same week as *Gimme Some Truth*, so for people who didn't get enough from that four CD box set, this one goes up to eleven. It includes every solo album, non-album single, and demos.

It does not include John and Yoko's experimental albums such as *Two Virgins* or *Life with the Lions*.

154. *Ocean's Kingdom*

Paul McCartney
58 points
Chart appearance: 10/22/2011
Highest position: 143
Weeks on the chart: 1

This was the fifth classical McCartney album.

This was a commission from the New York City Ballet, which performed it to good response. It tells the story of a conflict between the Ocean Kingdom and the evil Land Kingdom.

153. *Wedding Album*
John Lennon and Yoko Ono
63 points
Chart appearance: 12/13/1968
Highest position: 178
Weeks on the chart: 2

Another of John and Yoko's experimental albums, and something that might be interesting to listen to once. There's no real music here (except for bonus tracks later added to the CD version) and one side consists of nothing but John and Yoko saying each other's name over and over again. Side two has John and Yoko talking about peace and otherwise being interviewed. Hey, it's art.

The packaging of the original album was impressive, however. It came in a box, like *All Things Must Pass*, but instead of three albums, it had a copy of the marriage license, lots of photos, drawings by John, and other things to make you feel like maybe you had attended the wedding itself.

This was released in December of 1968, just after *The Beatles* (White Album), when it seemed as if these guys could put anything out and it would sell.

152. *Past Masters*
The Beatles
71 points
Chart appearance: 1/02/2010
Highest position: 177
Weeks on the chart: 2

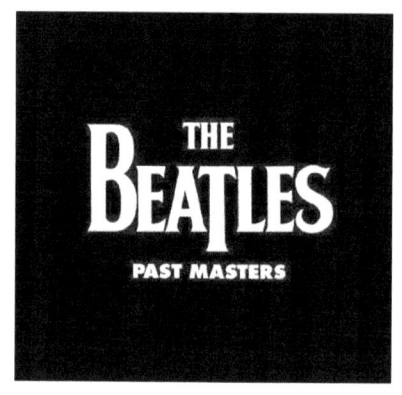

In 1988, all The Beatles' British albums were released on vinyl in a big box set which included two albums of all the non-album singles. The *Past Masters* albums placed these songs in proper chronological order, from the single version of "Love Me Do" all the way through "You Know My Name (Look Up the Number)."

In 2010, when the remastered albums were released on CD, the two *Past Masters* albums were combined into a double CD set, which stayed on the chart for two weeks. It was also the first time that the songs "From Me to You" and "Thank You Girl" were made available in stereo on CD.

Boring cover, though. It's not like there aren't pictures of The Beatles available.

151. *Give More Love*

Ringo Starr
73 points
Chart appearance: 10/7/2017
Highest position: 128
Weeks on the chart: 1

Ringo's most recent albums tend to appear on the chart as all the fans buy them the first week and then the albums disappear immediately afterward, which is kind of sad since some of them are quite good. This one contains his regular crowd these days (Joe Walsh, Edgar Winter, Peter Frampton) and is once again produced by Dave Stewart. Paul plays bass on a few songs and adds some backing vocals as well.

The album also includes a bonus CD featuring new versions of his songs "Back Off Boogaloo," "Photograph," "Don't Pass Me By," and "You Can't Fight Lightning" (an obscure Starkey tune off his album *Stop and Smell the Roses*).

150. *What's My Name*

Ringo Starr
74 points
Chart appearance: 11/9/2019
Highest position: 127
Weeks on the chart: 1

Once more, we have a Ringo album spending one week on the chart, but at least this time, it was one position higher than his previous album!

This was Ringo's 20th studio album, featuring the same gang from *Give More Love*. Ringo's tours with this "All-Starr Band" are almost all available on CD, but none of the live albums ever made the charts.

The title song was written by Colin Hay from Men at Work and is based on a chant Ringo liked to perform in concert. Joe Walsh and Dave Stewart also contributed songs.

Paul plays bass and provides backing vocals again on one of the songs, a cover of John's "Grow Old with Me." Ringo decided to record it when he learned that the original demo John had recorded on a cassette tape included John's comment that this would be a great song for Ringo. Ringo also added his own version of "Money (That's What I Want)."

149. *Live in Japan*

George Harrison
75 points
Chart appearance: 8/1/1992
Highest position: 126
Weeks on the chart: 1

George's tour of Japan in 1991 with Eric Clapton was recorded and turned into this double album set.

Almost half are Beatles songs, including a few obscure ones that had never been performed live before, such as "Piggies," "Old Brown Shoe," and "Taxman." It ends with an exciting version of "Roll Over Beethoven."

148. *Liverpool Oratorio*

Paul McCartney
83 points
Chart appearance: 11/16/1991
Highest position: 177
Weeks on the chart: 6

Paul's first orchestral album performed best of the ones he's done, probably because it was a bit of a novelty when it was released. Written with composer and conductor Carl Davis, the Oratorio was recorded live at a performance of the Liverpool Philharmonic Orchestra and follows a story similar to Paul's own upbringing.

147. *Photograph*

Ringo Starr
83 points
Chart appearance: 9/15/2007
Highest position: 130
Weeks on the chart: 2

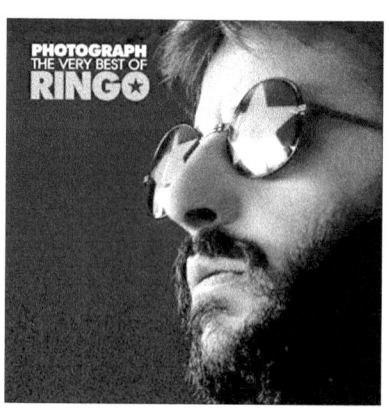

This collection of Ringo's greatest hits is an excellent look at his career, and includes many great songs from later years that have been overlooked, such as "Weight of the World," "Fading in Fading Out," and his tribute to George, "Never Without You" (featuring Eric Clapton).

146. *Postcards from Paradise*

Ringo Starr
102 points
Chart appearance: 4/18/2015
Highest position: 99
Weeks on the chart: 1

Ringo produced this one himself, and there are some nice highlights here. The title track should be heard by all Beatles fans. It was co-written with Todd Rundgren and basically uses Beatles song titles as its lyrics. The album also features Ringo's pre–Beatles memories in the song "Rory and the Hurricanes," which was the band he was in when asked to join The Beatles.

This was released at the same time as a book Ringo had written (with the same title) which shared all the postcards his fellow Beatles had sent him over the years.

145. *Ringo Rama*

Ringo Starr
103 points
Chart appearance: 4/12/2003
Highest position: 113
Weeks on the chart: 2

Ringo's work with Mark Hudson provided his most creative period. Mark was the leader of The Hudson Brothers, who had their own TV show in the '70s (remember them?). Hudson knew how to write and produce clever pop songs that should have been bigger hits. He had produced best-selling albums for many others, including Aerosmith, winning a Grammy for the song he wrote for them called "Livin' On the Edge."

Ringo invited friends Eric Clapton, Dave Gilmour, Willie Nelson, and others to play along, and many Ringo fans consider this one of his best albums. Sadly, the quality of the album was not reflected in its chart performance.

Of note is the song "Missouri Loves Company," which the state now uses as one of its mottos … not sure if Ringo gets any credit. Another highlight is "Elizabeth Reigns" which concludes with Ringo saying, "Well, there goes me knighthood." Turns out Sir Richard Starkey was proven wrong fifteen years later.

144. *Paul Is Live*
Paul McCartney
117 points
Chart appearance: 12/4/1993
Highest position: 78
Weeks on the chart: 4

This live album from Paul's 1993 "Off the Ground" tour did rather poorly on the charts, and the probable reason for that was because the market had enough live albums from Paul: within the previous three years we had *Tripping the Live Fantastic* (two versions), *Unplugged*, and the cover album *Choba B CCCP*, which, although not live, was recorded mostly live. A fourth live album may have been pushing it, but then again, the costs of putting out a live album have to be cheaper than a studio album, so it's not likely the record company lost any money on this.

In his defense, Paul made sure that the songs on *Paul Is Live* were different from *Tripping*, with only "Live and Let Die" appearing on both. It's not like he doesn't have a huge selection of songs to choose from.

The title itself is a play off the "Paul is dead" rumors of the late '60s and so Paul is Photoshopped into the *Abbey Road* cover looking a bit silly, acting like he's being pulled by his dog Martha who is standing completely still. Note the VW Beetle license plate: Instead of "28IF" (as in "Paul would have been 28 if he had lived," as per the rumor), it now says "51IS" (since Paul was 51 at the time).

143. *The McCartney Interview*
Paul McCartney
118 points
Chart appearance: 1/31/1981
Highest position: 158
Weeks on the chart: 3

Here's an interesting one: It's exactly what it looks like. It's an interview with Paul that originally was just sent to radio stations but then got released to the public.

One of the reasons it made the chart at all is probably due to sad timing. John's murder had occurred just a month or so earlier and The Beatles were once more all in the news and the albums were once more on the charts. People couldn't get enough Beatles news, and this album appeared at just the right time to take advantage of that sad circumstance.

142. *Working Class Hero*

John Lennon
124 points
Chart appearance: 10/22/2005
Highest position: 135
Weeks on the chart: 3

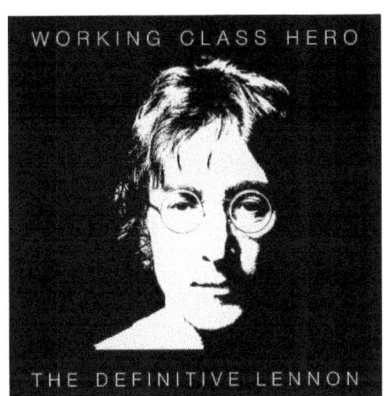

Yet another greatest hits collection from John, remixed and remastered.

It contains thirty-eight songs over two discs, with all the cuts you'd expect, plus his demos of "Real Love" and "Grow Old with Me."

It was released on what would have been his 65th birthday, but only stayed on the chart for three weeks.

141. *Gimme Some Truth: The Ultimate Mixes*

John Lennon
128 points
Chart appearance: 12/19/2020
Highest position: 157
Weeks on the chart: 5

Ten years after the *Gimme Some Truth* box set comes this new album with remastered greatest hits but with the confusing same name. To confuse things even more, you could get the single CD version of this album (or two vinyl albums), containing nineteen songs, or the double CD version (or four vinyl albums) containing thirty-six songs (two less than the *Working Class Hero* collection). So when you say you have the album *Gimme Some Truth*, people will ask, "Which one? The one CD version, the two CD version, or the four CD version?"

Some of these sets included a poster, some stickers, and a nice booklet. The album was released on what would have been John's 80th birthday. It reappeared on the chart the following Christmas season in 2021.

Reviewers held that the remixes improved the sound quality greatly.

140. *Ringo 2012*

Ringo Starr
130 points
Chart appearance: 2/18/2012
Highest position: 80
Weeks on the chart: 2

This unimaginatively named album (which was almost called "Motel California") is Ringo's shortest album, containing only nine songs and lasting less than half an hour. Included are two remakes from Ringo's earlier albums: "Step Lightly" (from *Ringo*) and "Wings" (from *Ringo the 4th*). There's another song about Liverpool, and Ringo once more looks back on his life in some autobiographical songs, which he says is his way of telling his story (as opposed to writing the book everyone keeps asking him to do).

139. *Unfinished Music No. 2: Life with the Lions*

John Lennon and Yoko Ono
137 points
Chart appearance: 6/28/1969
Highest position: 174
Weeks on the chart: 8

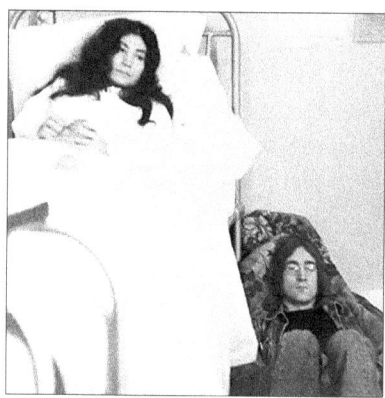

This is the second of three experimental albums from John and Yoko. The first side is a live performance of Yoko making noises while John produces guitar feedback sounds, recorded live on March 2, 1969, at Cambridge University. It lasts almost a half an hour. Side two consists of John and Yoko talking, a baby's heartbeat, two minutes of silence, and then ten minutes of John turning a radio dial to get random snippets, because there's no way you or I could do that.

There's a quote from George Martin on the back cover: "No comment."

138. *The U.S. Albums*

The Beatles
153 points
Chart appearance: 2/8/2014
Highest position: 48
Weeks on the chart: 1

Many Beatles fans are completists. Since the U.S. albums had different sequences—along with more echo and a few other minor differences—they had to have this box set of the remastered U.S. albums.

Once *Sergeant Pepper* was released, the albums in the United States and Britain were the same, so this box set contains only those earlier albums, plus the *Hey Jude* album, which was only available in the United States.

This appeared in the Top 50 from all the fans buying it the first week and then disappeared off the charts immediately after.

137. *The Beatles vs. The Four Seasons*

The Beatles
169 points
Chart appearance: 10/10/1964
Highest position: 142
Weeks on the chart: 3

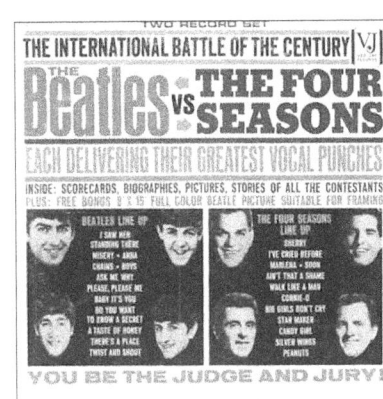

The label Vee-Jay had the rights to The Beatles' first album *Please Please Me* for release in America, but when the singles they released didn't sell, they held back on releasing the album.

Once Capitol had a success with "I Want to Hold Your Hand," Vee-Jay jumped on The Beatles bandwagon and finally released it, renamed *Introducing The Beatles*, even though they did not have the rights to do so by that time since they had not released it earlier as per their contract. They also re-released "Please Please Me" as a single and cheered as both hit the charts.

More singles followed, as well as any other reconfigurations of the album they could come up with to milk as much money out of The Beatles as possible before they were sued into oblivion.

This is one of those rip-off albums: a double album, with the second being songs from The Four Seasons. Since everyone had these songs by this time, it only stayed on the chart for three weeks.

136. *Tomorrow Never Knows*

The Beatles
178 points
Chart appearance: 8/11/2012
Highest position: 24
Weeks on the chart: 2

Here's one most Beatles fans aren't even aware of: An iTunes-only downloadable album of fourteen great heavier songs that may not have gained attention previously, including "Hey Bulldog," "Revolution," "I'm Down," and "She Said She Said." Despite this being a downloadable-only album, the boring cover shows a vinyl album. Go figure.

It debuted at 24 and dropped the next week, then disappeared after that, as the current trend seems to go (especially for downloadable albums).

135. *Menlove Avenue*
John Lennon
182 points
Chart appearance: 11/22/1986
Highest position: 127
Weeks on the chart: 4

Menlove Avenue was the address of John's boyhood home and has absolutely nothing to do with this posthumous album, which consists of only ten songs. The first side has outtakes from his *Rock 'n' Roll* album, and the second has early versions of songs from *Walls and Bridges*. It's kind of an official bootleg album in that regard.

The album was organized by Yoko, and while fans enjoyed hearing some of these songs, it wasn't something the general public wanted, and only stayed on the chart for four weeks.

134. *Past Masters 1*
The Beatles
182 points
Chart appearance: 4/2/1988
Highest position: 149
Weeks on the chart: 6

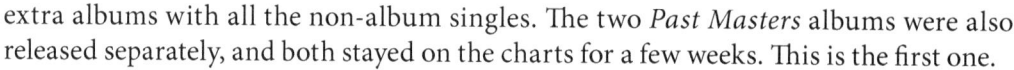

As mentioned previously (at number #152 in our countdown), the release of the British albums on vinyl in America in a box set in 1988 included two extra albums with all the non-album singles. The two *Past Masters* albums were also released separately, and both stayed on the charts for a few weeks. This is the first one.

133. *Choba B CCCP*
Paul McCartney
182 points
Chart appearance: 11/16/1991
Highest position: 109
Weeks on the chart: 3

Over a period of two days in 1987, Paul recorded an album of rock and roll favorites for release in the Soviet Union, which was in its last days. The title is Russian for "Back in the USSR" (although that song is not on this record). It was a popular bootleg and import in the rest of the world for years after that until Paul agreed to release it in 1991, where it was grabbed up by any fans who did not already have it.

Among the songs Paul recorded were "Kansas City," "Twenty Flight Rock," "Lucille," and "Ain't That a Shame."

132. *McCartney III Imagined*
Paul McCartney
182 points
Chart appearance: 8/7/2021
Highest position: 19
Weeks on the chart: 1

Paul's third completely solo album *McCartney III* had fallen off the chart earlier in the year, and this followed soon thereafter, containing "reinterpretations, remixes, and covers" of the original songs. It was grabbed by all the fans, allowing it to debut at an impressive #19 on the top 200, but it disappeared the very next week. Among the people involved were Beck and Dominic Fike.

131. *Ringo the 4th*
Ringo Starr
185 points
Chart appearance: 10/15/1977
Highest position: 162
Weeks on the chart: 6

Apparently, Ringo wanted you to forget his first two albums, *Beaucoups of Blues* and *Sentimental Journey*. Thus the title of his sixth album.

After the hits of *Ringo* and *Goodnight Vienna* and even the middling success of *Ringo's Rotogravure*, his label Atlantic decided to ditch the successful formula of using Ringo's talented friends (which included Beatles) for songwriting and performing and instead put out an album of contemporary music, which meant dance music (as disco was the rage).

Singles were released that went nowhere, never hitting the charts, and the album bombed. Atlantic dropped him after, as if they had nothing to do with the failure of the album.

130. *Liverpool 8*
Ringo Starr
195 points
Chart appearance: 2/02/2008
Highest position: 94
Weeks on the chart: 2

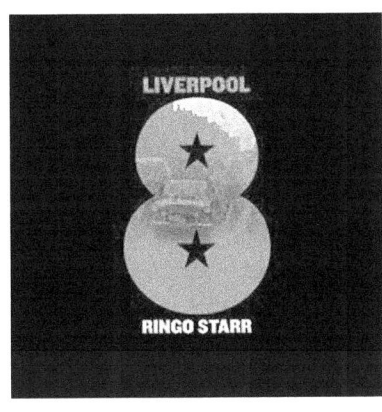

Ringo's fifteenth album found him back with EMI, but came about after a breakup with his previous producer Mark Hudson. Apparently, Mark had an offer to be in a TV show and took it, which angered Ringo, who wanted him to tour with him again.

Most of the songs are co-written by Hudson and feature him playing guitar, singing backup, and otherwise producing the songs, but once he was gone, Dave Stewart (of Eurythmics fame) then took over.

The title track has Ringo once more singing about his life, and was co-written with Stewart. (Lyrics include the line "Went to Hamburg, the red lights were on / With George and Paul and my friend John.")

This album also includes his tribute to his friend Harry Nilsson ("Harry's Song") done in a style reminiscent of Nilsson's music.

Despite being a pretty good album, it only stayed on the chart for two weeks.

129. *Y Not*
Ringo Starr
208 points
Chart appearance: 1/30/2010
Highest position: 58
Weeks on the chart: 2

The follow-up to *Liverpool 8* did only slightly better, despite containing a vocal duo with Paul ("Walk with You") who also plays bass on the song "Peace Dream."

Also on the album are Joe Walsh, Van Dyke Parks, and others who would form the basis of Ringo's new recording group.

And, of course, there's another biographical song in "The Other Side of Liverpool."

Ringo wrote or co-wrote all the songs and produced the album. The loss of Mark Hudson is noticeable.

128. *The Capitol Albums Volume 2*
The Beatles
227 points
Chart appearance: 4/29/2006
Highest position: 46
Weeks on the chart: 2

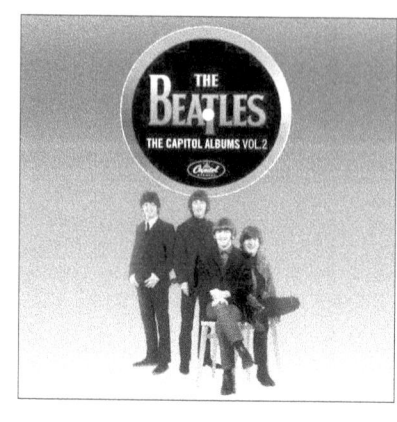

This box set included CDs of the American releases *The Early Years*, *Beatles VI*, *Help!*, and *Rubber Soul* in both mono and stereo.

Beatles fans know that the American versions have added reverb on some songs as well as other noticeable changes (such as the false start on "I'm Looking Through You"), so if you want every version, you'd need to get these.

Many fans did, allowing this to appear at #46 only to fall off after one more week.

127. *The Best of Dark Horse 1976-1989*

George Harrison
242 points
Chart appearance: 11/4/1989
Highest position: 132
Weeks on the chart: 4

This collection of George's greatest hits from the Dark Horse years includes three songs that were never on an album before ("Poor Little Girl," "Cockamamie Business," and the wonderful "Cheer Down") but failed to get much attention.

For some reason, it does not include two singles released during this period—"This Song" and "This is Love"—but does contain three songs from the *Gone Troppo* album, despite that album's poor reception.

The album only reached a high of #132, staying on the charts for a month before falling off.

126. *Bad Boy*

Ringo Starr
309 points
Chart appearance: 5/18/1978
Highest position: 129
Weeks on the chart: 6

After *Ringo the 4th* bombed, Ringo took control and tried a comeback. He once more did away with famous guests writing songs for him, which was probably a mistake. A prime-time TV special was filmed to help promote the album, and featured Ringo playing two parts in a "Prince and the Pauper" type of story. But none of that mattered because, well, the album isn't that good.

His new label dropped him afterward just like his last one had. It stayed on the charts for six weeks but never made the Top 100.

125. *Tripping the Live Fantastic Highlights*

Paul McCartney
352 points
Chart appearance: 12/15/1990
Highest position: 141
Weeks on the chart: 9

Paul released this live album from his '89–'90 tour in two versions: The two CD version and this one for anyone who wanted the "highlights"

without having to spend so much money. Surprisingly, the two CD version did better on the charts but over time, this one ended up outselling the other. Just goes to show, once again, that the charts are not the ultimate resource for determining overall sales.

124. *Vertical Man*

Ringo Starr
365 points
Chart appearance: 7/4/1998
Highest position: 61
Weeks on the chart: 4

Ringo's previous album *Time Takes Time*, released in 1992, was a wonderful return to great pop, full of engaging songs—with guests like Brian Wilson, Jeff Lynne, Harry Nilsson, Andrew Gold, Jeff Baxter, and Mark Hudson. Sadly, it didn't make the charts at all, and it took another six years before Ringo tried again.

This time, he got Mark Hudson to produce, and the resulting album is even better. Hudson is a huge Beatles fan who appears often at Beatles festivals, where he raves about how much he loved working with Ringo. The album has a definite Beatles feel to it from start to finish and is full of great, catchy songs.

Ringo and Hudson grabbed a lot of famous friends to play on the album, including Paul, George, Brian Wilson, Alanis Morissette, Ozzy Osbourne, Tom Petty, Joe Walsh, Steven Tyler, and others.

Sadly, despite having been released soon after the success of the *Anthology* albums, it did not do well on the chart, although admittedly it performed better than many of Ringo's more recent albums.

123. *Past Masters 2*

The Beatles
379 points
Chart appearance: 4/2/1988
Highest position: 121
Weeks on the chart: 7

This CD was released the same week as *Past Masters 1* (#134 on our chart here) but did better, probably due to the more recent hits that did not sound as dated as the earlier material.

You can't miss with an album that includes huge hits such as "Hey Jude," "Paperback Writer," "Get Back," "We Can Work It Out," "Let It Be," "Day Tripper," and "Lady Madonna," among other great songs.

Sadly, "You Know My Name (Look Up the Number)" was only available in mono for this recording.

122. *Live at the Star Club*
The Beatles
387 points
Chart appearance: 7/2/1977
Highest position: 111
Weeks on the chart: 7

This was recorded live from a small portable mono recorder and a cheap microphone, and the quality is not something you'd listen to other than for historical purposes. It's just after Ringo joined, when Beatlemania was just beginning in Britain.

The album absolutely shows the excitement in their performance and it's interesting to hear some of the differences between these performances and later recordings of the same songs.

Not surprisingly, it didn't sell that well and was soon available in cut-out overstock bins in record stores everywhere.

121. *Pure McCartney*
Paul McCartney
388 points
Chart appearance: 7/2/2016
Highest position: 15
Weeks on the chart: 4

This greatest hits collection was available in both a two CD set or a four CD box set. The four CD set isn't just the first two with two more added, but a completely different track listing. For some reason, there are no songs from *Flowers in the Dirt* or *Driving Rain*.

120. *Early Takes Volume 1*
George Harrison
390 points
Chart appearance: 5/19/2012
Highest position: 20
Weeks on the chart: 3

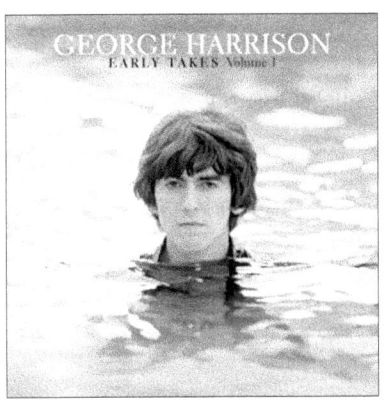

This posthumous album contains early versions of songs that later appeared on albums such as *All Things Must Pass*, *Living in the Material World*, and even *Thirty Three and ⅓*. They were produced by Giles Martin specifically for use in Martin Scorcese's biographical film of George.

Even though all the songs are from 1970 and later, the album cover features a 1965-era George.

119. *Gone Troppo*
George Harrison
412 points
Chart appearance: 11/27/1982
Highest position: 108
Weeks on the chart: 7

This is George's lowest ranking original album (not counting *Electronic Sound*). He didn't seem very interested in promoting it and was apparently in a poor mood at the time, because it took another five years before he released another.

This didn't even make the Top 100.

"Wake Up My Love" was released as a single and did poorly. It's a mystery why the catchy "Dream Away" wasn't released instead, given its placement in the *Time Bandits* film in which George was executive producer.

118. *The Beatles in Mono*
The Beatles
442 points
Chart appearance: 9/26/2009
Highest position: 40
Weeks on the chart: 5

It's difficult to remember sometimes that The Beatles would release two separate versions of each album in the '60s up through *The Beatles* (White Album), and that the emphasis was on the mono version which they considered the "official" versions. Recording studios even had a very small speaker set up on the control board so you could hear what the song would sound like coming out of a small, mono car radio.

Stereo was a gimmick, people thought. But over the years, as stereo became common, the stereo versions of the albums have become the "official" versions simply because that's what everyone's gotten used to.

It's quite interesting to compare the two versions because there are some major differences (which we are not getting into here). Some of the new remixes have been done with the mono mixes in mind to meet somewhere in the middle.

If you want to make sure you have their original mixes as The Beatles initially intended them, this box set is the way to go.

117. *Acoustic*
John Lennon
446 points
Chart appearance: 11/20/2004
Highest position: 31
Weeks on the chart: 5

This album of John's acoustic songs, demos, live solo performances, and practice sessions performed fairly well on the chart for this sort of collection, but many fans were upset because the vast majority had already been previously released, either in one of the box sets or collections.

Interestingly, the booklet contained the chords for each of the songs, so guitarists could play along.

116. *McCartney III*
Paul McCartney
475 points
Chart appearance: 1/2/2021
Highest position: 2
Weeks on the chart: 4

Paul's third completely solo album (with Paul playing all the instruments from his home studio) was recorded during the COVID-19 pandemic. It shot up to #2 in its very first week and was gone within a month.

Although it hit that high point, its lack of staying power has made this the weakest original Paul album that isn't a greatest hits collection, live album, album of cover songs, or classical piece.

It was nominated for two Grammy Awards, Best Rock Album and Best Rock Song ("Find My Way"), but did not win either.

115. *In the Beginning (Circa 1960)*
The Beatles
488 points
Chart appearance: 5/16/1970
Highest position: 117
Weeks on the chart: 7

In 1961, The Beatles (with Pete Best) went into the studio in Hamburg to provide backing for singer Tony Sheridan. John was allowed to sing one song, "Ain't She Sweet," and the album also contains the Harrison/Lennon instrumental "Cry for a Shadow." Polydor released this in 1970, where it did well for what it's worth.

114. *Two Virgins*

John Lennon and Yoko Ono
506 points
Chart appearance: 2/8/1969
Highest position: 124
Weeks on the chart: 8

John and Yoko's first experimental album was released in a brown paper package because John and Yoko decided to pose nude for the cover. This, of course, increased sales in some ways and decreased them in others, in that most record stores refused to carry it.

This album is closer to "Revolution 9," with its tape loops and effects, than it is to the later experimental albums the two produced. Each side is only about 15 minutes long, and at the end, John says, "I've had enough now, thank you." Many listeners agreed.

The other Beatles tried their best to encourage John not to release this, but finally he was able to do so, although he had to go to a different record label for distribution. Still, this was at a time where anything Beatles would sell, so it did spend a few weeks on the chart.

113. *Jolly What! The Beatles & Frank Ifield*

The Beatles
518 points
Chart appearance: 4/4/1964
Highest position: 104
Weeks on the chart: 6

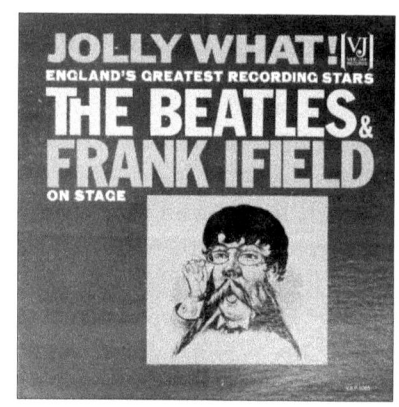

In another blatant attempt to milk as much as possible from The Beatles songs it had in its possession, Vee-Jay rushed out another album, this time including British singer Frank Ifield, who they claimed deserved to share an album with The Beatles (who only get four songs!). On the other hand, for years, this was the only place you could get "From Me to You" in stereo, so there's that.

This album doesn't deserve the attention we're giving it here, but it's such a blatant rip-off, it deserves further comment. For one thing, it promises that the performances are "on stage" on the cover, yet these are all studio recordings. Then there's the fact that Frank Ifield's country music (which included a generous amount of yodeling) has nothing that Beatles fans would want. But the best part is the liner note which states, "It is with a good deal of pride and pleasure that this copulation has been presented." Yes, you read that right. This isn't a compilation, it's a copulation, because if you buy this, you're getting screwed.

112. *Run Devil Run*

Paul McCartney
586 points
Chart appearance: 10/23/1999
Highest position: 26
Weeks on the chart: 6

After Linda died, Paul understandably had trouble getting enthused about making music. Finally, after a year or so, he gathered some pals including Pink Floyd's David Gilmour, and just had fun recording some of his favorite rock and roll songs, similar to his *Choba B CCCP* album. He also wrote three new ones of his own, done in the same style: "Run Devil Run," "Try Not to Cry," and "What It Is."

The result is a tremendously fun album that deserved to do much better than it did.

The cover photo is of a drug store in Atlanta which impressed Paul enough to use it, inspiring him to write the title song.

111. *The Capitol Albums Volume 1*

The Beatles
622 points
Chart appearance: 12/04/2004
Highest position: 35
Weeks on the chart: 6

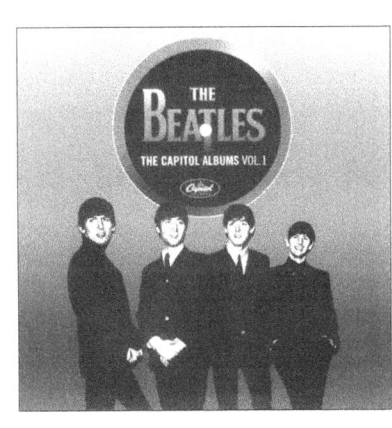

This box set contained the albums *Meet The Beatles!*, *The Beatles' Second Album*, *Something New*, and *Beatles '65*. Since the American mixes were different from the British, fans who wanted every version rushed out to get this.

It took another two years before *Volume 2* was released (see #128).

110. *Remember*

John Lennon
681 points
Chart appearance: 10/02/2010
Highest position: 44
Weeks on the chart: 5

Another Lennon compilation album. This one contained eighteen songs, and was part of Starbucks' "Hear Music" series (as opposed to "See Music" or "Smell Music," one supposes). It did well enough to stay on the chart for five weeks, peaking at #44.

It contained most of John's best known songs, but omitted the singles "Cold Turkey," "Give Peace a Chance," "Happy Xmas (War Is Over)," and "Woman Is the Nigger of the World."

The packaging contained a very basic bio of John and a few pictures, but any fan already had all these songs.

109. *Heartplay: Unfinished Dialogue*
John Lennon and Yoko Ono
751 points
Chart appearance: 1/14/1984
Highest position: 94
Weeks on the chart: 12

This is a spoken word album consisting of discussions between John and Yoko in 1980, and also contains some of the interviews John did with *Playboy* magazine.

It was released right before *Milk and Honey* (the follow-up to *Double Fantasy*) at the same time Paul was riding high with Michael Jackson and "Say Say Say," and so the time was just right for another wave of Beatles interest. A few weeks later, other Beatles albums appeared on the chart as well.

108. *Lennon Legend*
John Lennon
778 points
Chart appearance: 3/14/1998
Highest position: 65
Weeks on the chart: 9

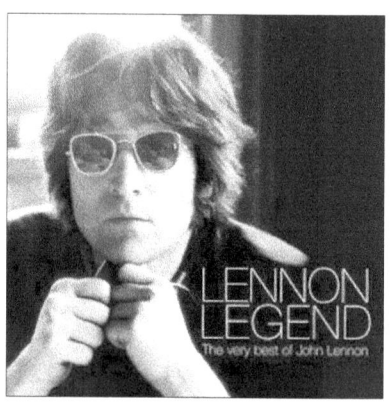

One more compilation of John's greatest hits, but this was the first to come after *Milk and Honey* to contain the singles from that album. It's the best compilation on one CD, containing twenty songs.

107. *Driving Rain*
Paul McCartney
835 points
Chart appearance: 12/01/2001
Highest position: 26
Weeks on the chart: 9

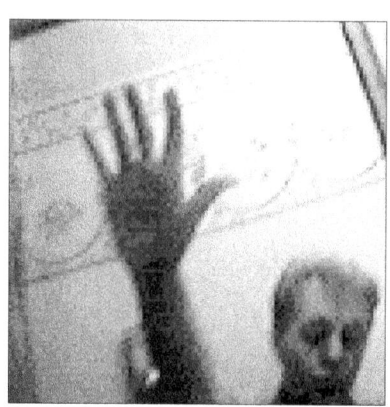

This album was released to good reviews but failed to generate many sales. Perhaps the cover had something to do with it. Paul was impressed with the technology that allowed him to take low resolution pictures with his watch, and used one of them for the cover. This also made the album cover kind of dated quickly. When the album failed to sell, a new wrap-around cover with a color picture of Paul replaced this one.

The album was completed when the 9/11 attack on the World Trade Center happened. Paul was a witness, sitting in a plane waiting to take off. He wrote the song "Freedom" about the incident and had it added as a bonus song on the CD, as it was too late to list it on the cover.

Paul later organized the Concert for New York City in the next year as a fundraiser.

106. *Brainwashed*

George Harrison
899 points
Chart appearance: 12/07/2002
Highest position: 18
Weeks on the chart: 9

George's final album didn't sell well, and that's a shame, as it's quite good. Perhaps the unappealing cover had something to do with it in the same way Paul's *Driving Rain* failed to impress.

It had been more than a decade since his last album *Cloud 9*, but George had some basic tracks done in the meantime. These were completed by his son Dhani along with long-time producer (and Traveling Wilbury) Jeff Lynne.

George was aware that the cancer that was eating away at him would be terminal, and worked on finishing as much as he could with the assistance of Dhani, who knew exactly what George wanted for the songs.

The song "Marwa Blues" won a Grammy award for Best Instrumental, George's first (and last) for his solo work.

105. *Stop and Smell the Roses*

Ringo Starr
930 points
Chart appearance: 11/14/1981
Highest position: 98
Weeks on the chart: 12

After the failures of *Ringo the 4th* and *Bad Boy*, Ringo went back to what gave him success in the past: Good friends. He got Paul and George to write songs for him, as well as Harry Nilsson, Ronnie Wood, and Stephen Stills. Despite the cast, the album failed to generate much attention, although the George-penned song "Wrack My Brain" got Ringo back into the Top 40 (for the last time).

There's also a new version of "Back Off Boogaloo" that opens with the rift from "It Don't Come Easy" and then in the background, you can hear all sorts of Beatles songs. Ringo has never forgotten why he is where he is, and his love for his past is shared by his fans.

104. *Power to the People*
John Lennon
1016 points
Chart appearance: 10/23/2010
Highest position: 24
Weeks on the chart: 14

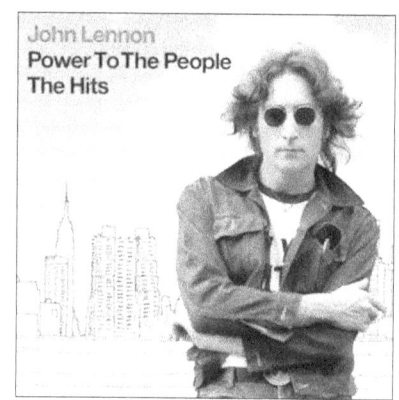

Yet another Lennon compilation album. Now, admittedly, four of these were released at the same time, so you could pick and choose which one you wanted: *Gimme Some Truth*, *Signature Box*, *Remember*, or *Power to the People*. This one performed the best on the charts, though, being a single album collection that you didn't have to go to Starbucks to get.

103. *Unplugged*
Paul McCartney
1023 points
Chart appearance: 16/22/1991
Highest position: 14
Weeks on the chart: 8

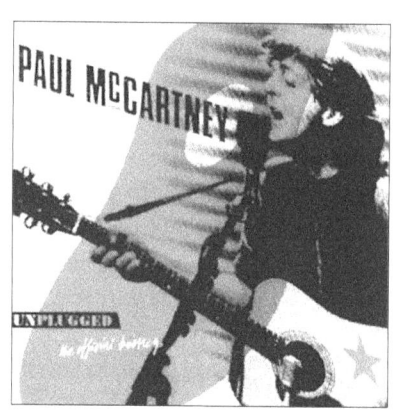

Back when MTV had music, many musicians would appear on a show called *Unplugged* where they'd perform their songs acoustically. Paul was the first to release an album of his show. The album features old rock and roll classics and a few Beatles favorites. Interestingly enough, the only songs performed from his solo career were all from his first album *McCartney*: "Junk," "Every Night," and "That Would Be Something."

This could have been a two album set, given that there were many other songs on the show that were not included here.

102. *Songs, Pictures and Stories of The Fabulous Beatles*
The Beatles
1026 points
Chart appearance: 10/31/1964
Highest position: 63
Weeks on the chart: 11

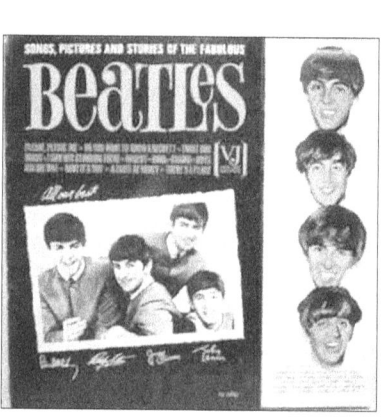

Upon the horrible realization that they had run out of Beatles songs to release, Vee-Jay put together this further rip-off, with the same songs in a new package. And just like the last Vee-Jay rip-off (*Jolly What!*), the mistakes on the cover are part of its, um, "charm." For instance, notice how Ringo's last name is listed as "Star" or its claim that George met President Kennedy, and how it got John's age wrong at the time of his mother's death. "Stories?" More like fables.

101. *Ringo's Rotogravure*

Ringo Starr
1062 points
Chart appearance: 10/16/1976
Highest position: 28
Weeks on the chart: 9

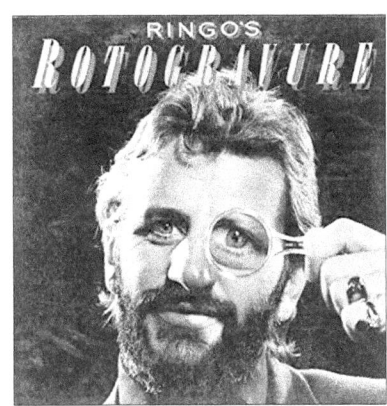

Just outside of our countdown's top 100, we find Ringo's fifth album. He got rid of producer Richard Perry, who had managed his past success, but stuck to using friends to contribute songs, with John, Paul, and George all rising to the task. You'll also find Eric Clapton, Peter Frampton, Melissa Manchester, Harry Nilsson, Dr. John, and more.

However, all this talent didn't lead to the successes of the previous albums *Ringo* and *Goodnight Vienna*. The album never even hit the Top 20, and disappeared after about two months.

The single "A Dose of Rock 'n' Roll" made the charts but not impressively so. The follow-up single was a remake of an old rock and roll classic "Hey Baby" which did even worse. Why they didn't release either the song John wrote for him ("Cookin' in the Kitchen of Love") or the one George wrote ("I'll Still Love You") is a mystery, as is the album's title itself. (A rotogravure is a printing process that has absolutely nothing to do with music, records, drums, or this album.)

100. *Let It Roll*

George Harrison
1138 points
Chart appearance: 7/04/2009
Highest position: 24
Weeks on the chart: 14

Arranged by George's widow Olivia, this collection has all his major hits along with a few live versions of some Beatles songs, but is missing some lesser hit singles such as "Crackerbox Palace," "This Song," "Bangla Desh," and "You." It does have three songs from the *Brainwashed* album, so maybe people buying this collection might check that one out.

This was released right around the time of the remastering releases of all The Beatles albums, so you'd think interest would have been a bit higher and it would have done better on the charts. Instead, it peaked at #24 and only stayed on the charts for fourteen weeks.

99. *Egypt Station*

Paul McCartney
1149 points
Chart appearance: 9/22/2018
Highest position: 1
Weeks on the chart: 8

Paul's album debuted at #1, and the media took note: He's still hitting #1 after all these years! It was indeed his first #1 album since *Tug of War* thirty-six years earlier, but it dropped tremendously immediately after and was gone in two months.

This is the lowest rated #1 on our list, which is sad because it's not a bad album. Paul did extensive publicity for it, with "surprise" concerts in places like Grand Central Terminal and the Cavern in Liverpool (both televised, of course).

It's a full album of an hour's worth of music (more if you buy a special edition with two extra songs), and the reviews were almost all positive.

A couple of singles were released, but neither made the charts. One highlight is the six-minute song "Despite Repeated Warnings," which Paul admitted is about climate change deniers and specifically Donald Trump, who is referenced as the "mad captain." Another is "Fuh You" which is kind of a strange way for a man in his late seventies to wink like a kid who thinks he got away with saying something naughty.

By the way, people have noted how much the cover art of *Egypt Station* (painted by Paul) can be placed next to George's *Gone Troppo* as if they were planned that way. (It looks better in color than what you see here.)

98. *On Air: Live at the BBC Volume 2*

The Beatles
1214 points
Chart appearance: 11/30/2013
Highest position: 7
Weeks on the chart: 11

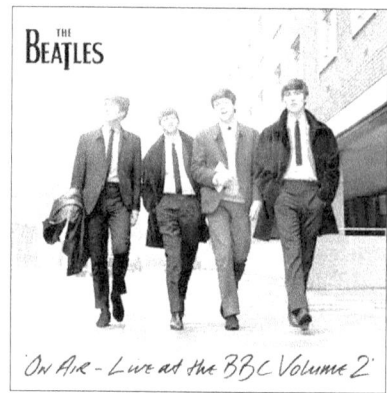

Live at the BBC Volume 1 was released in 1994 and here, almost twenty years later, is *Volume 2*. It was released alongside a remastering of *Volume 1*, which also appeared back on the charts for a few weeks.

This collects forty songs The Beatles performed on BBC radio in 1963 and 1964. These are mostly covers that they had been performing for years in Liverpool and Hamburg. The rest are from their albums of the time, including performances of hits like "She Loves You," "I Want to Hold Your Hand," and "Please Please Me."

The sound quality is not up to modern standards but it's still much more listenable than, say, the *Live at the Star Club* album.

There's also some interesting and humorous chatter with the DJs that displays The Beatles' charm.

97. *Live in New York City*

John Lennon
1224 points
Chart appearance: 3/22/1986
Highest position: 41
Weeks on the chart: 11

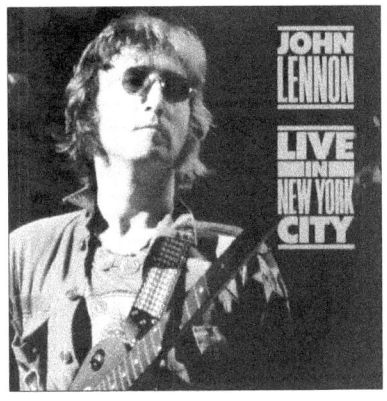

In 1972, John performed at a fundraising event for the Willowbrook State School for Retarded Children in New York, along with Stevie Wonder, Roberta Flack, Melanie, and Sha-Na-Na. John is backed by the band Elephant's Memory, fresh from recording the album *Sometime in New York City*.

John performs only one Beatles song ("Come Together") and the rest are from his solo career with the exception of a cover of the Elvis Presley hit "Hound Dog."

Although Yoko had also performed some of her songs at the show, these were edited out to make a John-only album.

96. *Beaucoups of Blues*

Ringo Starr
1309 points
Chart appearance: 10/17/1970
Highest position: 65
Weeks on the chart: 15

Ringo followed his first album *Sentimental Journey* five months later with this country-and-western album. (Strange how no one ever uses the "and western" part of that phrase these days.) Ringo obviously enjoyed some country music, as seen in his cover of "Act Naturally," and his own "Don't Pass Me By" from his Beatles days. In fact, he admitted that he chose the name "Ringo" partially because it was a "cowboy name."

When he met pedal steel guitarist Pete Drake, he was encouraged to go to Nashville to do his own album, especially after he was told he could do it in days instead of the months he was used to with recording an album.

Ringo and Pete gathered some country stars to write all new songs for him, and they came through. Who wouldn't? The picture on the back cover includes most of them. Ringo's voice works well with these songs.

Recorded in Nashville (of course), it stayed on the chart for quite a while, reaching #65. It also appeared on the Country chart.

95. *The Beatles with Tony Sheridan and Guests*

The Beatles with Tony Sheridan and Guests
1321 points
Chart appearance: 2/15/1964
Highest position: 68
Weeks on the chart: 14

So it's February of 1964 and any record company with anything even slightly Beatles related is releasing it to make a quick buck.

This album collects four songs The Beatles played on, with only one with vocals by any Beatle ("My Bonnie," a single of which even charted for a short time).

The rest of the album is basically Tony Sheridan, who lucked out at having the boys play backing for him when they were in Hamburg. Notice how small his name is next to The Beatles, despite the fact that most of the songs on this album are his.

94. *Good Evening New York City*

Paul McCartney
1380 points
Chart appearance: 12/05/2009
Highest position: 16
Weeks on the chart: 10

This double CD set is from Paul's concerts at Citi Field in July of 2009, which is the successor to Shea Stadium ... at least this time, the sound system was better than it was when The Beatles used the baseball announcer's loudspeakers!

And then, to promote it, Paul revisited the Ed Sullivan Theater and did a live free concert for Times Square from atop the marquee for the David Letterman show. So now he has performed both inside the theater and on top of it!

Paul runs through his typical set of Beatles hits and solo hits, but also included songs from his recent more experimental album as "The Fireman," which never made the charts.

The set also includes a DVD with highlights from the concert.

93. *Blast from Your Past*

Ringo Starr
1474 points
Chart appearance: 12/6/1975
Highest position: 30
Weeks on the chart: 11

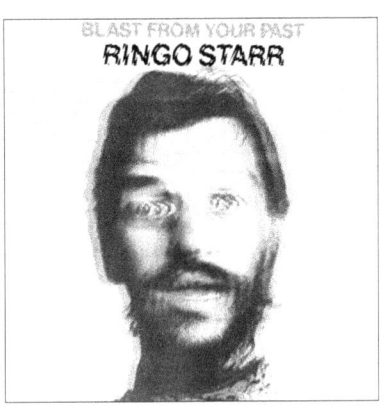

This greatest hits collection included all of Ringo's very successful hits from the albums *Ringo* and *Goodnight Vienna* along with his non-album singles "It Don't Come Easy," "Back Off Boogaloo," and one non-album B-side ("Early 1970"). It only has ten songs and the entire album is less than half an hour long in total. They could have easily included "Goodnight Vienna," which charted much higher than "Beaucoups of Blues," found on side two. Similarly, there was plenty of room for "Snookeroo," a B-side here but a single in Britain—especially since they included the B-side "Early 1970."

While the phrase "blast from your past" seems like it would be looking back at years gone by, the album came out shortly after "No No Song" fell off the charts, so apparently the "past" in this case means "five months ago." It reached the Top 30 at a time when these songs were still fresh in everyone's minds, but only stayed there for eleven weeks.

92. *Yellow Submarine Songtrack*

The Beatles
1478 points
Chart appearance: 10/2/1999
Highest position: 15
Weeks on the chart: 16

What a great improvement over the original *Yellow Submarine* album! This includes every song from the film, remixed and remastered to beauty. Finally, we get a true stereo version of "Only a Northern Song," and "Nowhere Man," with its vocals surrounding you, really makes one drool for a remixing of *Rubber Soul* we all hope is coming.

Also included on the album are complete songs that are only heard in snippets in the film, such as "Baby You're a Rich Man," "Love You To," and "Think for Yourself."

This album was released to coincide with the DVD release of the film, with the "Hey Bulldog" scene returned after being edited out from the original film for time considerations.

91. *The Traveling Wilburys Collection*
The Traveling Wilburys
1522 points
Chart appearance: 6/30/2007
Highest position: 9
Weeks on the chart: 13

This is a box set of the two Traveling Wilburys albums, along with four bonus songs. A couple of the bonus songs were actually just unfinished Wilburys songs that were completed for this release by George's son Dhani with Jeff Lynne.

To make it even sweeter, it also includes a DVD with all the promotional videos, as well as a documentary about the group.

The two albums had actually been out of print for some time, so when this was released by George's estate, it was grabbed up by many fans. It did quite well on the charts for a reissue, hitting the Top 10.

90. *All the Best*
Paul McCartney
1523 points
Chart appearance: 1/2/1988
Highest position: 62
Weeks on the chart: 15

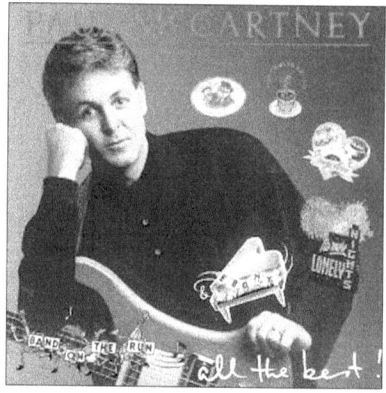

This collection of Paul's greatest hits should have performed much better, given all the hits contained within. However, it only reached #62.

The albums and covers are different depending on your country, because some songs were hits in the UK but not here, and vice versa. For instance, the British version contains the brand new song "Once Upon a Long Ago" as well as the *McCartney II* version of "Coming Up" which was a hit in England (as opposed to the live version that hit #1 in America). The track arrangements are different as well.

89. *New*
Paul McCartney
1588 points
Chart appearance: 11/2/2013
Highest position: 3
Weeks on the chart: 14

Paul used four different producers for this album, which gives it some variety. Giles Martin (George Martin's son) oversaw the entire production.

It contained a secret track at the end of the CD, and later special edition versions had a few more songs as well as live versions of some of them. Some of the songs are clearly based on Paul's early life pre–Beatles. "Queenie Eye" refers to a game he played as a child, "On My Way to Work" was about a job he had, and "Early Days" is about how he would hang out with John.

It debuted high, stayed on the charts for a while, but none of the singles from the album made the Top 100.

88. *The Beatles in Stereo*
The Beatles
1603 points
Chart appearance: 9/26/2009
Highest position: 15
Weeks on the chart: 18

The box set of all the remastered stereo versions of the albums performed much better than the mono version. No other musical act could put out a fifteen disc set of forty-year-old music and have it hit the Top 20.

87. *Reel Music*
The Beatles
1692 points
Chart appearance: 4/10/1982
Highest position: 19
Weeks on the chart: 9

In the late '70s and early '80s, Capitol Records once more had control of The Beatles' catalog and started repackaging the songs into various specialty albums. This had the effect of not only reintroducing The Beatles' music to a younger crowd, but also helped generate enough enthusiasm that often, the original albums would reappear on the chart as well.

The Beatles, however, were not impressed, and have not allowed any of these to be released anymore. As such, they're all collector's items.

This album featured songs from the four films and *Magical Mystery Tour*. A medley single was also released to promote the album, and The Beatles were once more heard on Top 40 radio because of it.

86. *The Best of George Harrison*

George Harrison
1702 points
Chart appearance: 11/27/1976
Highest position: 31
Weeks on the chart: 15

This is just another example of Capitol once again taking music it now owned and doing their best to capitalize on it, with another compilation album being released without the artist's approval or knowledge. To make it worse, this was released within weeks of George's album *Thirty Three and ⅓* for his new label Warner Brothers, creating competition for the two albums on the chart. It almost seemed that Capitol was angry at George and wanted to sabotage his success at the new label.

This is a unique album in that side one contains George's most popular Beatles songs and side two is his own solo career hits. Apparently, George was insulted that the record company didn't think he had enough hits of his own to fill the album and had to rely on Beatles songs.

Once The Beatles regained control of their music, this album also disappeared.

85. *Kisses on the Bottom*

Paul McCartney
1709 points
Chart appearance: 2/25/2012
Highest position: 5
Weeks on the chart: 15

Kisses features Paul crooning traditional pop songs like "Bye Bye Blackbird" that he would sing with his musician father when he was a child. Paul also throws a couple of his own new songs into the mix (and for a special edition, also included a cover of his own "Baby's Request" from *Back to the Egg*, which fits in perfectly).

The album features guest musicians Eric Clapton and Stevie Wonder on some tracks, but not singing.

"My Valentine," written by Paul, was released as a single from the album but it didn't chart.

84. *Wonderwall Music*

George Harrison
1729 points
Chart appearance: 1/11/1969
Highest position: 49
Weeks on the chart: 16

George's first album is an instrumental-only soundtrack to a movie remembered primarily for having George's music. Being the first solo musical album from a Beatle at the time, it gathered tremendous attention and did quite well for what it was.

Unlike *Electronic Sound*, this album actually contains music. It's primarily Indian sitar-based music, but there are snippets of all sorts of influences. George's soundtrack also includes musical guests Eric Clapton, Ringo Starr, and Peter Tork.

Supposedly The Beatles B-side "The Inner Light" was recorded during this period.

The original album does not have all of the music from the film, but a later extended CD version is complete. A remastered version was included in the Apple box set in 2014.

And yes, Beatles fans: Oasis definitely named their hit song "Wonderwall" from this.

83. *Sentimental Journey*

Ringo Starr
1789 points
Chart appearance: 5/16/1970
Highest position: 22
Weeks on the chart: 14

Ringo's first album was, like Paul's *Kisses on the Bottom*, a collection of old pop standards he had grown up hearing (and even includes "Bye Bye Blackbird"). He gave George Martin a list of songs he wanted to do and asked him to produce the album, which was almost named "Ringo Stardust."

It sold quite well, coming out at a time when anything from a Beatle would sell. Then again, it was the spring of 1970 and everyone was talking Beatles. Paul had just announced that he was quitting the group, and had released *McCartney*. John was there with *Live Peace in Toronto* and his single "Instant Karma." "Let It Be" was still in the Top 40, soon to be joined with "The Long and Winding Road." And The Beatles were about to release the *Let It Be* album, which would join *Abbey Road*, still on the charts from its release in the fall of 1969, along with the collection *Hey Jude*. So all that certainly helped Ringo's sales and chart activity.

82. *Extra Texture (Read All About It)*
George Harrison
1796 points
Chart appearance: 10/11/1975
Highest position: 8
Weeks on the chart: 11

After the disappointing reception to *Dark Horse* and the subsequent tour, George came back with an album he thought would recapture his audience. Devoid of any spirituality, George hoped *Extra Texture* would get back fans who had been alienated by his preaching. He resurrected the old tune "You" originally written for Ronnie Spector (and co-produced by Phil Spector), which did well on the singles chart, but that didn't translate well to album sales. The album generated poor reviews and only rose to #8, where it stayed for three weeks until falling off the charts.

"This Guitar (Can't Keep from Crying)" is a song that seems to give George's feelings about his reception at the time and is not, as it seems, an actual sequel to "While My Guitar Gently Weeps." Still, it made it seem like George was running out of ideas, and when it was released as a single, the song didn't even make the Top 100.

The album contains a few fine offerings but an awful lot of filler. George was going through a tremendously depressing time of his life, complicated by alcohol and drugs, and that may have played a part.

81. *Wingspan: Hits and History*
Paul McCartney
1815 points
Chart appearance: 5/26/2001
Highest position: 2
Weeks on the chart: 14

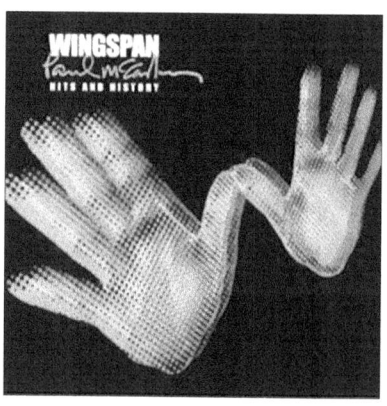

This is another greatest hits collection from Paul, and features songs from his solo career as well as those from Wings. The first disc is called "hits" and the second, featuring mostly album cuts, is the "history." The British version is slightly different (just like *All the Best* was), because of the different hits and singles between the two countries.

This contains many great album tracks but is missing some of Paul's singles that made the charts, such as "Give Ireland Back to the Irish," "I've Had Enough," "Getting Closer," and "Letting Go." Its sales were helped by a TV documentary on Paul's music that was released at the same time, helping it to debut on the chart at #2.

80. *Somewhere in England*
George Harrison
1855 points
Chart appearance: 6/20/1981
Highest position: 11
Weeks on the chart: 13

Apple was still in litigation, so none of The Beatles were releasing anything on their own label. Therefore, The Beatles didn't have as much control over their own music as they were used to, which George sadly learned with this album. He presented it to Warner Brothers in the fall of 1980 and they refused to release it, saying it was too "laid back."

George had to add some new songs in order to get the label excited, so he recorded a few, including "Blood from a Clone" (clearly about the Warner Brothers executives) and the basics for what would become "All Those Years Ago." After John's death, George rewrote the lyrics to pay tribute to his friend and bandmate, and had Ringo play drums and Paul provide backing vocals to it.

The album was finally released almost a year later, but didn't quite make it into the Top 10, despite the #2 hit of "All Those Years Ago."

79. *Back in the U.S.*
Paul McCartney
1910 points
Chart appearance: 12/14/2002
Highest position: 8
Weeks on the chart: 15

Paul loves to tour and his fans love to come to his concerts, so it makes absolute sense that he would release a live album after each major tour. Why not? They may not be huge, gigantic sellers, but there's no way the record label would lose money on them. This one was from the tour for his album *Driving Rain*, and it did better on the chart than the album the tour was meant to promote. It was his first tour in almost ten years, so that grabbed some of the attention. A DVD was also available of highlights from the concert tour. The double CD set includes many Beatles hits but only one song from the *Driving Rain* album.

78. *Sometime in New York City*

John Lennon and Yoko Ono
1941 points
Chart appearance: 7/1/1972
Highest position: 48
Weeks on the chart: 17

In 1972, John and Yoko and their backup band Elephant's Memory rushed out an album of timely protest songs, using a cover designed like a newspaper to emphasize their immediacy. While the song topics are important and the issues real, dedicating an entire album to them may have been overkill, and it certainly dated the material. With the exception of the poorly named single "Woman Is the Nigger of the World," none of the other songs ever seem to show up on any Lennon greatest hits collections or be mentioned by fans.

The album includes a second disc, containing live performances and jam sessions with Frank Zappa and the Mothers (and others), some of which is only slightly more interesting than the jam album George included in *All Things Must Pass*. In fact, much of it is unlistenable. This extra record did not increase the price of the album, but getting two discs for the price of one didn't seem to help sales at all.

The album bombed and received poor reviews, which was especially depressing after John's previous well-received album *Imagine*. John didn't record again for over a year, and then he put all his effort into making as commercial an album as possible with *Mind Games*.

77. *Rarities*

The Beatles
1984 points
Chart appearance: 4/12/1980
Highest position: 21
Weeks on the chart: 15

A British import called *Rarities* had been released in 1978 as part of a collection of all the British albums, in the same way *Past Masters* later came to be. The British version featured songs that had not appeared on any album.

A few years later, Capitol issued its own *Rarities*, which had nothing in common with the British version. The idea was to provide much better quality for songs that had previously only appeared on bootlegs.

Beatles fans ate it up for things like a remixed "I Am the Walrus" with a few extra bars of music, "Penny Lane" with the extra piccolo trumpet solo at the very end, and a few extra bars at the end of "And I Love Her." There was the original version of "Across the Universe" which had only appeared on a charity fundraising album previously. It even included the run-out groove from *Sergeant Pepper's Lonely Hearts Club Band* that had been removed from the American version.

The rest of the album included stereo and/or mono versions of songs that were noticeably different from the official releases and which were unavailable elsewhere at the time.

76. *Tripping the Live Fantastic*
Paul McCartney
2005 points
Chart appearance: 11/24/1990
Highest position: 17
Weeks on the chart: 20

This is the two CD version (or three vinyl album version) of Paul's "Flowers in the Dirt" tour (as we discussed with the single CD version at #125).

This was Paul's first live album since *Wings Over America*, so it did quite well, and features many of the classic hits Paul fans expect when they attend one of his concerts. The album is not a straight-forward recording of a specific concert, but instead contains songs from various performances during the tour. It also includes a few soundcheck jams.

75. *Off the Ground*
Paul McCartney
2031 points
Chart appearance: 11/24/1990
Highest position: 31
Weeks on the chart: 16

After the success of *Flowers in the Dirt* four years earlier, Paul went into the studio for a follow-up that performed poorly chart-wise. "Hope of Deliverance" failed to ignite the singles chart, and the highlights were the two songs co-written with Elvis Costello. Other than those songs, the rest were written in the studio with his touring band, and while the songs are more politically oriented than usual for Paul, the lyrics were still rather uninspiring.

It ended up being Paul's first album not to produce a hit single. For young record buyers in the '90s, The Beatles were now "oldies" music.

A two CD set was made available in some parts of the world, including the B-sides and some songs that were left off the *Unplugged* album. That version was never made available in the United States and is now quite the collector's item.

74. *Memory Almost Full*
Paul McCartney
2033 points
Chart appearance: 6/23/2007
Highest position: 3
Weeks on the chart: 15

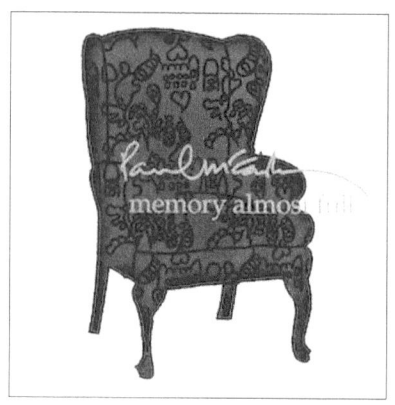

By the 2000s, The Beatles were still popular but Paul and Ringo's solo albums didn't perform the way they did years earlier. That can be a sad situation, as some of these are excellent albums. *Memory Almost Full* deserves far better than its chart activity may demonstrate (and in fact, was even nominated for a Grammy).

"Dance Tonight" from the album became Paul's first charting single in six years (after "Freedom"), and also his last. The album also has an *Abbey Road*–like medley on side two, with the songs merging and fading into each other. The final song is "The End of the End" with lines like "On the day that I die I'd like bells to be rung and songs that were sung to be hung out like blankets that lovers have played on and laid on while listening to songs that were sung...."

The album's title came when Paul noticed the phrase on his cell phone, and thought it applied to his life in general. People later pointed out that the title is an anagram of "for my soulmate LLM" (Linda Louise McCartney) but Paul has denied this, while being amazed at the creativity of the fans to find secret messages that were never intended.

73. *The John Lennon Collection*
John Lennon
2050 points
Chart appearance: 12/4/1982
Highest position: 33
Weeks on the chart: 16

And yet another John Lennon greatest hits collection.

This was the first to be released after his death, and includes most of his hit singles, with the addition of "Jealous Guy" (from *Imagine*) and "Love" (from the *Plastic Ono Band* album). "Love" was released as a single to promote this collection but did not chart.

Added to this were all of his songs off of *Double Fantasy*, so if you liked that album but skipped over Yoko's songs, you can get this one instead.

It sold very well, and even though it didn't make the Top 20, it remained on the chart long enough to place it here in our countdown.

72. *Chaos and Creation in the Backyard*
Paul McCartney
2107 points
Chart appearance: 10/1/2005
Highest position: 6
Weeks on the chart: 16

Another very good album from Paul that deserves more attention than it had received. This was the first time in a while that Paul did not produce his own music, and that's a good thing. While some of Paul's self-produced albums are masterpieces, sometimes it's a good idea to have an editor (as my publishers always tell me). Nigel Godrich took the helm after producing acts like Radiohead and Beck, and Paul plays almost all of the instruments. Paul was apparently not used to having someone tell him a song wasn't good enough to record, but he wisely listened and the result is an excellent album that did quite well, considering.

The excellent song "Fine Line" was released as a single but failed to chart. The album contains fourteen songs (one a "hidden" track), but other songs from the sessions have appeared on CD singles.

The cover picture is of Paul as a young lad, literally in his family's backyard.

71. *Let It Be.... Naked*
The Beatles
2121 points
Chart appearance: 12/06/2003
Highest position: 5
Weeks on the chart: 16

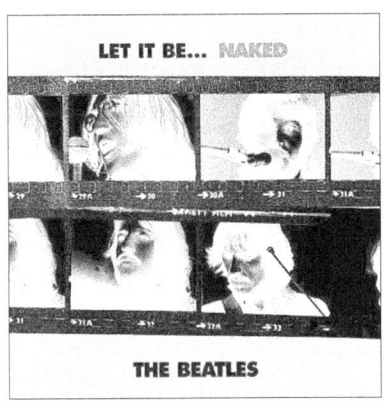

Paul never liked Phil Spector's production of the *Let It Be* album, so when all the legal rights were wrapped up, he put out his own version, stripping away all the strings and choral voices on songs like "The Long and Winding Road" to make the album he always imagined.

Gone is the studio chatter, as well as bits like "Maggie Mae" and "Dig It." In their place is "Don't Let Me Down," which should have been on the original album in the first place.

Fans are split on whether this remix was an improvement. While George approved this project before his death, John and Ringo had never disapproved of the Spector mix.

Let It Be, by the way, is the only Beatles album that does not contain a song sung by Ringo.

70. *Imagine: John Lennon*

John Lennon
2135 points
Chart appearance: 10/22/1988
Highest position: 31
Weeks on the chart: 18

Don't get confused: This is not the *Imagine* album, but instead the soundtrack album for the documentary film of the same name. It contains music from John's entire career, starting with "Twist and Shout" and including John's Beatles hits like "A Day in the Life," "Strawberry Fields Forever," and "Revolution." The other half consists of his solo career, up through "(Just Like) Starting Over."

Also included is the original demo of "Real Love" that was later taken by the remaining Beatles and completed for the *Anthology* albums.

It only reached #31 on the chart but remained long enough to place it higher than many of the other Lennon greatest hits albums.

69. *Wings Greatest*

Wings
2135 points
Chart appearance: 12/9/1978
Highest position: 29
Weeks on the chart: 18

This was the first greatest hits collection for Paul, and while it never reached the Top 10, it stayed on the chart a while and sold well. Even though it is labeled as a Wings album, it contains two pre-Wings songs: "Another Day" and "Uncle Albert / Admiral Halsey."

Four of the songs had never appeared on an album before, as well as "Live and Let Die," which had never appeared on a Paul album. For some reason, the number one hit "Listen to What the Man Said" is not here at all. "Mull of Kintyre" is included as it was a gigantic hit in England but did not make the chart at all here in the United States.

The Art Deco statuette on the cover reappears on the cover of the next album *Back to the Egg*. Check the mantelpiece!

68. *Flaming Pie*

Paul McCartney
2167 points
Chart appearance: 6/14/1997
Highest position: 2
Weeks on the chart: 18

The title of this wonderful Paul album refers to John's response to a reporter who asked where The Beatles name came from: "A man appeared on a flaming pie and said unto them 'From this day on you are Beatles with an A.' Thank You, Mister Man, they said, thanking him."

After completing the *Anthology* project, Paul was inspired to work harder on this release to meet the standards The Beatles had always set for themselves. The result gave him a hit and almost a #1 album. (It was kept out of the top spot by The Spice Girls!) The single "The World Tonight" appeared on the charts but didn't make the Top 40.

Paul produced some of the songs on the album, but others were produced by George Martin and Jeff Lynne. Guests included Ringo (who shares writing credit with Paul on the song "Really Love You") and Steve Miller (who co-wrote "Used to Be Bad" with Paul). In 2020, the album was re-issued in various versions, including a collector's edition containing four vinyl LPs, five CDs, and two DVDs!

67. *Anthology 3*

The Beatles
2270 points
Chart appearance: 11/16/1996
Highest position: 1
Weeks on the chart: 16

In 1996, Apple finally released all the outtakes and unreleased songs that had been appearing on various bootlegs and organized them into the *Anthology* albums, much to the delight of the hardcore Beatles fanatics. To add to the fun, Paul, George, and Ringo went back to the studio to take some of John's demo tapes of unreleased songs to finish them, using producer Jeff Lynne.

The third *Anthology* collection hit #1 like the previous two, but it fell off the charts much quicker. The original plan was for "Real Love" and "Free as a Bird" to be on the previous ones, and this one would have John's "Now and Then"—but that plan was abandoned when George vetoed it, saying he didn't like the song. (Or perhaps it was because the previous two had not sold as well as expected for "new" Beatles songs.) If a new song had been included, maybe this would have sold better. Then again, this was the first appearance of George's "Not Guilty," which was left off the *White Album*. Maybe that should have been the single.

It also includes the often bootlegged song "What's the New Mary Jane," featuring

John's fun lyrics that were just too weird for the other Beatles to release as a single (as John wanted).

66. *Give My Regards to Broad Street*

Paul McCartney
2408 points
Chart appearance: 11/10/1984
Highest position: 20
Weeks on the chart: 16

Paul decided to get back into the movies and hired Isaac Asimov to write a script for him, which Paul immediately threw out, thinking, "I can write as well as one of the best-selling authors of my time." So we get a ridiculous story about a rich musician who is in deep trouble because someone has stolen the master tapes for his next album—you know, something we can all relate to. Then, at the end, we find out it was all a dream!

Anyway, the movie does contain some excellent music, including remakes of some of Paul's best songs with The Beatles. The new song "No More Lonely Nights" was a big hit, but that didn't seem to translate to album sales. Ringo is in the film and plays on some of the songs but refused to play on The Beatles remakes.

65. *Rock 'n' Roll*

John Lennon
2414 points
Chart appearance: 3/8/1975
Highest position: 6
Weeks on the chart: 15

John had been sued by Morris Levy, the publisher of Chuck Berry's music, because of his use of a few lines from Berry's "You Can't Catch Me" in "Come Together." As part of the settlement, John agreed to record an album of rock classics and include some Berry songs so the publisher could get his royalties.

John got Phil Spector to produce and gave him a list of songs he wanted to do. John told Spector to do all the backing tracks so all John would have to do is come in one day and add the vocals. However, Spector was notoriously hard to work with (once shooting a gun into the air in front of John) and at one point, it was announced that Spector could not continue because he had been in a car accident—although there doesn't seem to be any evidence of that happening.

John ended up taking the project over to complete it. He hated Spector's production on many of the songs and had to redo them completely. As such, the album took more than a year to complete.

The album is quite good, although clearly still Spectorish in parts. At one point during the fade-out of "Just Because," John says, "There's two basses in this. I hope you appreciate it."

Meanwhile, Morris Levy, the corrupt publisher known for his ties to organized crime, got ahold of the tapes before the album was completed and released his own version of the album, which he sold through TV ads offering mail-order delivery. Lawsuits ensued, Levy was forced to pay John damages, and the actual album was finally released. The cover features John in a doorway in Germany, with blurred images of Paul, George, and possibly Stu Sutcliffe walking by.

64. *20 Greatest Hits*
The Beatles
2430 points
Chart appearance: 11/13/1992
Highest position: 50
Weeks on the chart: 27

Fitting twenty songs onto one vinyl album certainly hurt the sound quality (especially considering they included the lengthy "Hey Jude," albeit slightly edited) but having so many great Beatles songs together on an affordable album helped sales tremendously.

The British version of this album differs because of different singles being released in each country. The American version, for instance, contains "Eight Days a Week" and "Yesterday," neither of which were singles in Britain, and is missing "Yellow Submarine." Strangely, it contains "Come Together" but not "Something" even though the *Billboard* charts listed "Something" as the #1 hit.

Previously, the only official greatest hits collection were the two disc sets of *1962–1966* and *1967–1970*.

This was released at a time when Capitol had the rights to The Beatles' catalog and were doing their best to make as much money as possible from it, even against the band's desires or knowledge.

63. *George Harrison*
George Harrison
2445 points
Chart appearance: 3/17/1979
Highest position: 14
Weeks on the chart: 18

Spurred by the success of the single "Blow Away," this album performed strongly despite never making the Top 10. It was critically well received in addition.

George was at a happy period in his life, having

just married Olivia and with the birth of his son Dhani. The album has a lighter, happier feel to it than his previous albums.

Among the songs on this album are George's version of "Not Guilty," which was originally planned for the *White Album* and never saw the official light of day until *Anthology 3*, and a sequel of sorts in a song called "Here Comes the Moon." The song "Love Comes to Everyone" can still sometimes be heard on oldies stations despite not being released as a single, and George's sense of humor comes through in the song "Soft-Hearted Hana," where, as it is fading, the speed on the song varies, making listeners think their vinyl has warped.

62. *Love Songs*
The Beatles
2542 points
Chart appearance: 11/12/1977
Highest position: 24
Weeks on the chart: 30

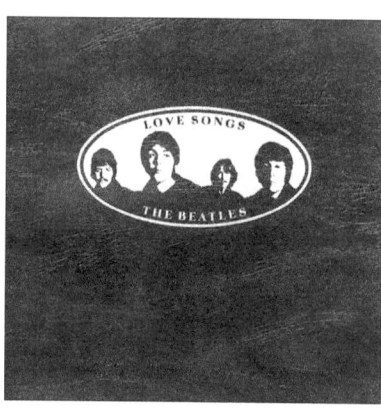

It's 1977, the Apple lawsuit is still progressing, and Capitol keeps coming up with ways to reissue Beatles songs despite The Beatles' objections.

This is a two-record set of their love songs, although one might question whether "She's Leaving Home" and "Norwegian Wood" actually qualify. And there's no "Oh! Darling" or "Do You Want to Know a Secret?" or even "I Want You (She's So Heavy)"—okay, maybe not the last one.

It never reached the Top 20, but stayed on the chart for 30 weeks, placing it here at #62 on our list.

The original cover was simulated leather with a gold embossed picture of The Beatles, and the whole thing came with a booklet with all the lyrics.

Like all '70s Capitol collections, this is no longer available.

61. *Dark Horse*
George Harrison
2563 points
Chart appearance: 12/28/1974
Highest position: 4
Weeks on the chart: 17

George's third studio album was rushed to promote his upcoming tour, the first from any Beatle. Unfortunately, George was suffering from laryngitis for much of the recording and the tour, and it shows. He mixed his voice down in many of the songs to hide it, but that just resulted in a Spectorish muddiness.

It was also a stressful time in George's life, having just been divorced, trying to create a new record label (Dark Horse), and dealing with former Beatles manager Allen Klein and their lawsuit. George was doing drugs again, having affairs with married women (including Ringo's wife at the time), and otherwise seemed to be in a bit of a self-destructive period (as he admitted in his book *I Me Mine*). This turmoil comes through in the songs, many of which are about lost loves and broken idealism. A few are more direct, such as his version of "Bye Bye Love" which specifically mentions his ex-wife and her new lover Eric Clapton. It makes for a bit of cringe-worthy listening.

Two singles from the album charted ("Dark Horse" and "Ding Dong; Ding Dong") but neither made the Top 10. The latter makes a good holiday song to ring in the New Year, but the single was released too late to capitalize on that.

60. *The Beatles' Story*

The Beatles
2619 points
Chart appearance: 12/12/1964
Highest position: 7
Weeks on the chart: 17

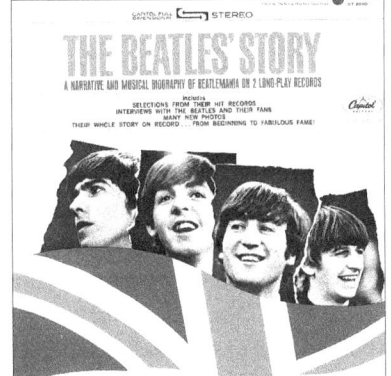

This two-disc documentary about The Beatles was released at a time when anything with their name on it would sell. And sell it did, reaching #7, and staying on the chart for an impressive 17 weeks.

This American-only album is composed mainly of interviews and commentaries, with just snippets of Beatles songs. The whole thing could have fit on one album, as one of the sides doesn't even last ten minutes—but with a double album, you can charge more.

59. *Milk and Honey*

John Lennon and Yoko Ono
2688 points
Chart appearance: 2/11/1984
Highest position: 11
Weeks on the chart: 19

Yoko arranged this album, released three years after John's death. It includes brand new songs from her but John's practice sessions and outtakes of songs left off the *Double Fantasy* album. While this was always planned as the follow-up, it's not clear that these particular songs would have been on that planned album.

These songs were completed at her direction, but still have the feel of unfinished work, especially when a demo of "Grow Old with Me" was needed to fill the album.

Yoko had a falling out with Geffen Records as well as Jack Douglas, the original producer of *Double Fantasy*, and as such the work Douglas did with the original recordings was uncredited on the album, which was released through Polydor. It sold well, though, and produced a Top 10 hit with "Nobody Told Me," which was originally written for Ringo's *Stop and Smell the Roses* album.

58. *Live at the BBC*

The Beatles
2766 points
Chart appearance: 12/24/1994
Highest position: 3
Weeks on the chart: 25

This first collection of BBC recordings made it to #3. These were recorded during various appearances on BBC radio, including a period where they had their own show called "Pop Go The Beatles."

The songs are almost all cover versions never before released, but there are some originals, including a Lennon/McCartney song that they never recorded in the studio but had been given to Billy J. Kramer and The Dakotas in 1963: "I'll Be on My Way." Among The Beatles originals, you'll find most of their hits of the time, including "A Hard Day's Night," "Can't Buy Me Love," "Ticket to Ride," and "Love Me Do."

57. *The Beatles at the Hollywood Bowl*

The Beatles
2825 points
Chart appearance: 5/21/1977
Highest position: 2
Weeks on the chart: 21

The Beatles' performances at the Hollywood Bowl were recorded by George Martin with the idea of releasing highlights as an album. However, the sound quality wasn't up to Martin's standards, and it was difficult to avoid the constant screaming of the fans. As such, the recordings remained unreleased until the '70s, when Capitol was doing everything they could to milk as much out of The Beatles as possible.

In 2016, the album was remastered and re-released with a new cover and a new title: *Live at the Hollywood Bowl*. It was released to coincide with the Ron Howard documentary on their touring years called *Eight Days a Week*. At this second release, it once more entered the chart, reaching a high of #7.

56. *Wild Life*
Wings
2838 points
Chart appearance: 12/25/1971
Highest position: 10
Weeks on the chart: 19

After the success of *Ram*, Paul decided he wanted to start touring again and thus needed a band. He first called Denny Laine (is in my ears and in my eyes), who Paul had known from 1965 when The Moody Blues had opened for The Beatles. Deciding that Denny was a great name, he then got Denny Seiwell for drums, who had played on *Ram*. The only thing left was to teach Linda to play keyboards, and Wings was born.

This album was rushed out, recorded in just more than a week, as Paul thought it would show the enthusiasm and excitement of the band. And while it did that, it was not the success one would expect from an ex-Beatle.

It contains only eight songs, one of which was a complete jam that was made up on the spot and has Paul singing nonsense words as lyrics ("Mumbo"). One was a cover version of an old song by Mickey & Sylvia ("Love Is Strange"). "Wild Life" meanders on for more than six minutes, and "Dear Friend" is just as long, with only a few lyrics repeated over and over. There were little jams thrown in at odd places (such as after the last song when you think the album's over). While there are some high points, the album feels unfinished, like it's a collection of obscure B-side fillers.

There was no single from the album to help promote it, although some radio stations played a few. Of note is "Tomorrow," a fine song which uses the same chord structure as "Yesterday" (get it?).

55. *Press to Play*
Paul McCartney
2869 points
Chart appearance: 9/13/1986
Highest position: 30
Weeks on the chart: 28

After the failure of the *Give My Regards to Broad Street* movie, Paul hired producer Hugh Padgham (XTC, The Police, Genesis) to give him a more contemporary sound. The result is a well-produced album, but there's only so much you can do with weak songs. This is surprising, as Paul often works best when collaborating with another. In this case, it was 10cc founder Eric Stewart. Ironically, some of the B-sides released from these sessions are better and more commercial than the songs chosen for the album.

The single "Press" performed well enough, but a follow-up single of "Stranglehold" only reached #81 on the chart, and the album barely made it into the Top 30.

54. *Back to the Egg*

Paul McCartney and Wings
3115 points
Chart appearance: 6/30/1979
Highest position: 8
Weeks on the chart: 24

Riding high on the success of the single "Goodnight Tonight," Paul released the very last Wings album, which didn't do as well as expected. Perhaps he should have included the single on the album to help sales. Instead, the follow-up single "Getting Closer" failed to get any higher than #20, even though it is one of Paul's catchier works.

Of note is the "Rockestra Theme" which features way too many musicians, including David Gilmour, John Bonham, John Paul Jones, Pete Townshend, Brian Thomas, and Ronnie Lane. To top John's "two basses" on his *Rock 'n' Roll* album, Paul has *four* on this song, which won a Grammy for Best Rock Instrumental.

A tour to support the album got off to a bad start when Paul was arrested in Japan for marijuana possession and spent nine days in jail. That was the end of Wings.

53. *Thirty Three & ⅓*

George Harrison
3178 points
Chart appearance: 11/27/1976
Highest position: 11
Weeks on the chart: 21

Most critics felt that *Thirty Three & ⅓* was George's best album since *All Things Must Pass*. This was especially welcome after the disappointing performances of *Dark Horse* and *Extra Texture*, and is reflected in its placement on the chart, where it almost made the Top 10 and stayed on the charts for almost half a year.

George went out of his way to promote the album, including appearing on "Saturday Night Live" and doing many radio and TV interviews.

It contained two hit singles, "Crackerbox Palace" and "This Song," the latter being a humorous look at the lawsuit George had lost over the similarities between "My Sweet Lord" and "He's So Fine." Funny promotional clips by Eric Idle were made of these two songs as well as a cover of "True Love" (the old Cole Porter song).

Thirty three and ⅓, of course, refers not only to the speed at which albums are played, but also George's age at the time of the recording.

52. *McCartney II*

Paul McCartney
3279 points
Chart appearance: 6/14/1980
Highest position: 3
Weeks on the chart: 29

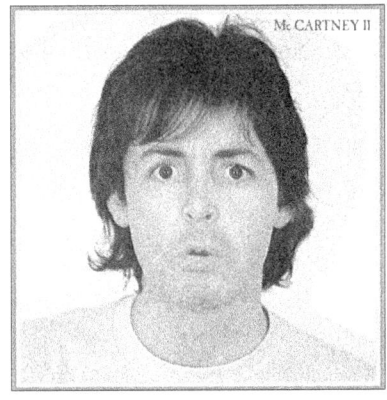

Wings was no more, so Paul decided to do another at-home recording while playing all the instruments. While this allowed him to be more experimental and creative, it also made the album less accessible and hit-worthy.

And then he released the single "Coming Up," with its clever video. The B-side was a superior live version performed by Wings, and American radio stations chose that one to play instead. It went to number one, stayed there for weeks, and became Paul's biggest hit since "My Love."

Despite this huge hit, two follow-up singles ("Waterfalls" and "Temporary Secretary") failed to chart.

A lot of the album involves Paul's enchantment with new technology, such as synthesizer keyboard sequencers that allowed him to create interesting musical patterns. This is especially obvious in "Temporary Secretary" and the B-sides "Check My Machine" and "Secret Friend" (which lasts over ten minutes!). Although it did not receive great reviews when it was released, in retrospect, many critics feel this was an influential album for '80s synthpop bands and as such deserves more recognition.

Also recorded during this time but not on the album is Paul's holiday song "Wonderful Christmastime."

A remastered version of the album was released in 2011 with a dozen more tracks, including the B-sides previously issued.

51. *Volume 3*

The Traveling Wilburys
3344 points
Chart appearance: 11/17/1990
Highest position: 11
Weeks on the chart: 22

The first Traveling Wilburys album was a huge success, which one might expect with a supergroup consisting of George, Tom Petty, Bob Dylan, Roy Orbison, and Jeff Lynne. Despite the sad loss of Orbison soon after the first album, the remaining Wilburys pressed on with a second album they called "Volume 3" just to drive record store employees mad when people demanded Volume 2.

Volume 3 did not do as well as the first album, even though the songs themselves are of the same high quality. One might complain that the majority of vocals on this seemed to be from Dylan, whose voice, while distinctive and expressive, is the weakest of the four.

50. *Rock 'n' Roll Music*
The Beatles
3359 points
Chart appearance: 6/26/1976
Highest position: 2
Weeks on the chart: 30

Yet another collection by Capitol, *Rock 'n' Roll Music* has terrible artwork that makes The Beatles look like they were from the '50s, with images of Marilyn Monroe and cars with huge tailfins. The cover upset Ringo, who publicly told journalists, "It made us look cheap!" John complained as well, saying it made them look like a "Monkees reject" (although the Monkees also were not from the '50s…).

It's a two-disc set with mostly the cover songs from the early albums, but is arranged in a semi-chronological order so that by the time you get to side four, it's all Beatles originals.

Sales were good though, as Paul was touring at the time and interest in The Beatles was renewed.

Capitol issued "Got to Get You Into My Life" as a single to promote the album and surprised everyone by having it get into the Top 10.

49. *The Early Beatles*
The Beatles
3363 points
Chart appearance: 4/24/1965
Highest position: 43
Weeks on the chart: 34

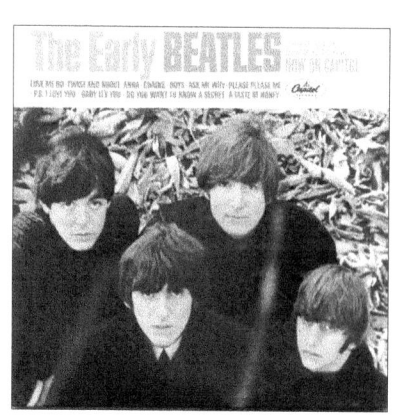

When the lawsuit with Vee-Jay was finally resolved, Capitol jumped in and immediately released this, containing the songs from Vee-Jay's *Introducing The Beatles*. Because everyone pretty much had all these songs by that time, the album only reached #43, but it stayed on the chart for an impressive thirty-four weeks. It continued to sell after that but, in all honesty, finding discounted old copies of *Introducing* wasn't difficult.

48. *Anthology 2*
The Beatles
3389 points
Chart appearance: 4/6/1996
Highest position: 1
Weeks on the chart: 34

This second collection was released only a few months after the first, and it easily hit #1 as well. Buoyed by the single "Real Love," it almost met the chart success of the first.

Consisting of outtakes and rehearsals from their "middle period," the album is also noticeable for two songs which were recorded but never released: "If You've Got Trouble" is a Ringo-sung rocker that was originally planned for *Help!* and has the wonderful Ringo comment at the lead, "Rock on, anybody!" Then there's Paul's echo-laden "That Means a Lot" which was given to P.J. Proby.

Unlike *Anthology 1*, however, most of the cuts are rehearsals and early versions as opposed to complete songs that had just never been released (other than on bootlegs).

This is also where you can get the complete version of "You Know My Name (Look Up the Number)" in stereo for the first time, although for some reason it fades out instead of letting John do his hilarious upper class twit impersonation long after the song has ended.

47. *Anthology 1*
The Beatles
3532 points
Chart appearance: 12/9/1995
Highest position: 1 (3 weeks)
Weeks on the chart: 29

The *Anthology* albums were a great boon to Beatles fans who could finally get good, clean copies of songs that previously had only been available on poorly mastered bootlegs. The additions of the Decca audition tapes and the hit single "Free as a Bird" were enough to justify the cost. But wait, there's more! You could also get the Tony Sheridan songs, the original recording of "One After 909," and the previously unreleased cover "Leave My Kitten Alone." There are poor recordings of the Quarrymen, and the unreleased "How Do You Do It?" that almost became their second single until John and Paul brought forth "Please Please Me."

Sales were huge, and were assisted by a TV documentary airing in prime time. (The massive coffee-table book of their career came a few years later.)

46. *John Lennon/Plastic Ono Band*
John Lennon
3608 points
Chart appearance: 12/26/1970
Highest position: 6
Weeks on the chart: 28

For John's first real solo album, he enlisted Phil Spector to produce and then wisely held him back from turning the album into another "Wall of Sound." John wanted it simple, and he got it. After the lush George Martin productions of The Beatles, this sounds raw and emotional, just like the lyrics. John used his music to deal with unresolved issues from his past, such as feeling abandoned by his parents. "Mother" was one of the stronger pieces in this regard. It was released as a single but never even made it into the Top 40.

John's songs by this time had become almost completely autobiographical, which pretty much discourages anyone from doing cover versions of them. Almost every song on this album mentions himself or Yoko by name. It was an album of introspection and truth, exemplified by the song "God," where he proclaimed he didn't believe in many things, including "Beatles."

Critics loved the album. However, as this was not a traditional Beatles-sounding record, radio stations didn't really know how to deal with it, and so it didn't get much airplay and as such, not as many sales as one would expect from a John Lennon release.

Let's take a moment to point out how each of The Beatles, though still tied together with Apple, did their best to differentiate themselves from each other. John's apple on the label was white, George had an orange one for *All Things Must Pass*, Ringo had a bluish-tinted one, and Paul stopped using the apple logo altogether for a time.

45. *Pipes of Peace*
Paul McCartney
3611 points
Chart appearance: 11/19/1983
Highest position: 15
Weeks on the chart: 26

The single "Say Say Say" from this album was a gigantic hit, staying at number #1 for an amazing six weeks. So why couldn't the album get any higher than #15? One has to assume it's because Michael Jackson, who was at the top of his popularity at the time, had more to do with the song's success than Paul did.

A follow-up single "So Bad" did poorly and didn't help rescue the album.

In any event, this follow-up to *Tug of War* contains songs that were originally recorded for that album. Once more we have George Martin producing, Ringo on drums, and Eric Stewart from 10cc assisting.

44. *Goodnight Vienna*

Ringo Starr
3642 points
Chart appearance: 11/30/1974
Highest position: 8
Weeks on the chart: 25

This follow-up to the hugely successful *Ringo* album reunites Ringo with his producer Richard Perry and friends Harry Nilsson, Billy Preston, and Klaus Voormann. John once again contributes the opening song: "Goodnight Vienna." He plays keyboards and you can hear him do the count at the start. Paul and George aren't to be found this time.

Singles from this album were the old classic "Only You," Hoyt Axton's "No No Song," and John's "Goodnight Vienna." Elton John was at the peak of his popularity at the time and provided the song "Snookeroo," but it was relegated to the B-side of "No No Song."

The album hit #8, not as high as *Ringo*, but quite impressive nonetheless. However, other than those four songs mentioned here, the rest of the album is rather forgettable.

As all science fiction fans know, the cover is from the film "The Day the Earth Stood Still" with Ringo's head superimposed, ready to say "Klaatu Barada Nikto" (where the band Klaatu got its name).

43. *Yellow Submarine*

The Beatles
3745 points
Chart appearance: 2/8/1969
Highest position: 2
Weeks on the chart: 25

This is the first album we see on our list that was an original Beatles album of (mostly) new music released during The Beatles years (not counting the reissues). Although it hit #2, it didn't stay on the chart for long, mostly because it only has four new songs on side one and side two is filled with George Martin's background music for the film. Two of the new songs are George's that were rejected for *Sergeant Pepper*, one was a "throwaway" kid's singalong ("All Together Now"), and the last is the excellent "Hey Bulldog," created and recorded during a promo shoot for "Lady Madonna" (and which probably should have been the single instead).

42. *Living in the Material World*

George Harrison
3815 points
Chart appearance: 6/6/1973
Highest position: 1 (5 weeks)
Weeks on the chart: 26

George's second studio album hit the top of the chart, pushing Paul's *Red Rose Speedway* out of the #1 position, while the single "Give Me Love (Give Me Peace on Earth)" replaced Paul's "My Love." It was an interesting time for Beatles fans.

George's spiritual side is prominent on this album, but there are a few Beatles references as well. In the title song, he sings "John and Paul here in the material world / though we started off quite poor, we got Richie on a tour," which is followed by a short Ringo drum solo. And it's not hard to guess what "Sue Me, Sue You Blues" is about.

While he had originally planned to use Spector as a producer again, George was rightfully worried about the future murderer's stability, and decided to produce it himself.

It didn't garnish the great reviews that *All Things Must Pass* got, with critics complaining about too many slow songs and the constant preaching. That didn't seem to hurt sales too much, though. The album was a big success, hitting #1 and staying there for five weeks.

41. *London Town*

Wings
3862 points
Chart appearance: 4/15/1978
Highest position: 2
Weeks on the chart: 28

After the success of *Wings Over America*, Wings was down to three people again, but this time the three did not produce a masterpiece like *Band on The Run*. You certainly got your money's worth with *London Town*, however, as it clocked in at more than fifty minutes. Of course, that much time on vinyl reduced the sound quality quite a bit.

The album contained "With a Little Luck" which hit #1, but follow-up singles from the album barely cracked the Top 40. Recorded around the same time was Paul's biggest hit in Britain "Mull of Kintyre" but the song does not appear on the album.

The album reached #2 on the Top 200, staying there for six weeks, but held back by the soundtrack to *Saturday Night Fever*. Disco beat The Beatles, but only temporarily.

40. *Mind Games*

John Lennon
3923 points
Chart appearance: 11/24/1973
Highest position: 9
Weeks on the chart: 31

Fans who were disappointed with *Sometime in New York City* might have been too cautious about trying John's next album, as it never reached higher than #9. This is disappointing, because it's a much more accessible collection of great pop songs.

John had waited more than a year to record this. He was saddened by the reaction to *New York City* and had separated from Yoko. However, once he decided to go for it, this led to his most creative period, music-wise (although it's clear that most of the lyrics are still about Yoko).

This time, John stayed away from Phil Spector and produced the album himself.

The single "Mind Games" didn't do that well on the charts, though, and there wasn't a follow-up single from the album despite there being some fine contenders. Perhaps the prominent profile of Yoko on the cover may have scared away listeners who thought it was another joint album of the two.

39. *Walls and Bridges*

John Lennon
3933 points
Chart appearance: 10/12/1974
Highest position: 1
Weeks on the chart: 35

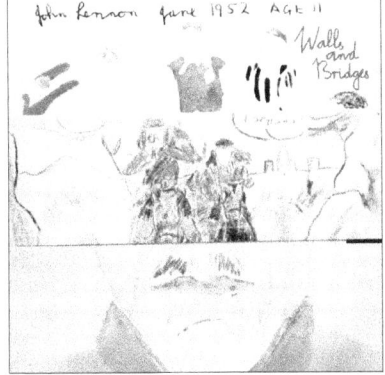

During John's eighteen-month separation from Yoko, he recorded three albums, helped David Bowie write and produce the hit single "Fame," played on Elton John's #1 version of "Lucy in the Sky with Diamonds," performed live with Elton at Madison Square Garden, produced an album for his pal Harry Nilsson, and wrote and played on *Goodnight Vienna* for Ringo.

And then, he finally had a #1 single, the only one during his lifetime. "Whatever Gets You Thru the Night," sung with Elton John, zoomed to the top of the charts, helping this album reach the top itself. The follow-up single "#9 Dream" reached #9 (of course).

Many Beatles fans consider this John's best album. It's certainly the most pop-oriented and accessible.

The album features artwork from John's school years, and the cover was done in such a way that you could fold it back and around to make new collages. It certainly appeared from this album that John was in a happy mood.

38. *Shaved Fish*

John Lennon
3957 points
Chart appearance: 11/8/1975
Highest position: 12
Weeks on the chart: 32

After returning to Yoko, John decided to take a few years off to raise his son Sean. To fill the gap, he arranged this "greatest hits" album, the only one released during his lifetime. It contains all of his singles except "Stand by Me" from the *Rock 'n' Roll* album, which wasn't written by John anyway.

Beatles fans were happy to get five songs that had previously only appeared on singles: "Give Peace a Chance," "Instant Karma," "Cold Turkey," "Happy Xmas," and "Power to the People." Unfortunately, many of the songs are edited versions for some reason. "Give Peace a Chance" and "Happy Xmas" are mixed together to make a medley where one never existed; "Mother" and "Woman Is the Nigger of the World" are significantly trimmed, and even "Instant Karma" and "Power to the People" fade early.

37. *Live Peace in Toronto*

John Lennon
3975 points
Chart appearance: 1/10/1970
Highest position: 10
Weeks on the chart: 32

The 1969 Toronto Rock and Roll Festival asked John if he would like to be the Master of Ceremonies for the festival, never thinking he'd agree. Instead, John asked if he could perform. You can imagine how quickly they said, "Yes!" John then got Eric Clapton, Klaus Voormann, and Alan White and they rushed to the festival, practicing on the plane on the way there.

The result was the first live album from The Beatles or any solo Beatle. They played some uncomplicated classic rock songs that they all knew (plus "Cold Turkey"). Side two features long jam-like songs from Yoko with John providing guitar feedback, and is probably the least played side two of any best-selling album.

Capitol originally didn't want to release this, but John pointed out the bootlegs that were already available, and they eventually gave in. The original album also came with a 1970 John and Yoko calendar which helped sales. It didn't hit the top of the charts, but it had staying power.

36. *Red Rose Speedway*
Paul McCartney and Wings
4427 points
Chart appearance: 5/12/1973
Highest position: 1 (3 weeks)
Weeks on the chart: 32

After *Wild Life*'s lackluster performance, Paul took some time and came back more than a year later with *Red Rose Speedway*. He had originally planned on releasing a two album set but EMI convinced him not to, afraid that it would do poorly. A few of the songs left off were later released on B-sides ("I Lie Around," "The Mess," "Country Dreamer"). Other songs were cut that would have made the album more of a group effort. Instead, Paul wrote and sings lead on every song. One wonders how the band members felt when they discovered their contributions were left off but there was still enough room for an instrumental.

But EMI insisted they needed a Paul McCartney album, not a Wings album. To doubly ensure the album would sell, it was prominently credited to "Paul McCartney and Wings" and the cover only featured him. It included a gatefold sleeve, a full-color booklet, and a sticker on the plastic wrap to make sure you knew "Hey, look, it's Paul McCartney!"

The album was given mediocre reviews by the critics, but the inclusion of the hit single "My Love" increased sales, and the album stayed at #1 for three weeks, until it was replaced by George's *Living in the Material World*.

The album starts with Paul singing "Who's that coming around that corner?" which had originally been sung as "Ram On" was fading from the *Ram* album a few years before. This turns into the opener "Big Barn Bed," which was featured on Paul's TV special at the time called "James Paul McCartney," used to promote the album.

Three Wings singles came before the album, including the hit "Hi Hi Hi" and the rocker "Give Ireland Back to the Irish," and one wonders if their inclusion on the album would have helped both sales and reviews.

35. *Tug of War*
Paul McCartney
4673 points
Chart appearance: 5/15/1982
Highest position: 1 (3 weeks)
Weeks on the chart: 30

Paul's first album since *McCartney II* was postponed a while after John's death, and you can't blame him for going through a period of depression over the loss of his childhood friend and songwriting partner. For *Tug of War*, Paul decided to reunite with George Martin, and the result was one of his best reviewed and best-selling albums.

Teaming up with Ringo, Carl Perkins, Stanley Clarke, and Stevie Wonder produced some excellent music as well as a very sappy but tremendously successful single "Ebony and Ivory." It was even nominated for a Grammy.

Tug of War spent three weeks at #1 and stayed on the chart for an impressive thirty weeks. It would be thirty-six years before Paul would hit #1 on the album chart again, with *Egypt Station* (#99 on our chart).

34. *Yesterday and Today*

The Beatles
4732 points
Chart appearance: 7/9/1966
Highest position: 1 (5 weeks)
Weeks on the chart: 32

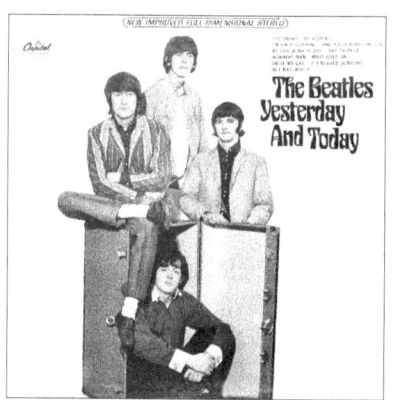

Capitol was still stiffing American record buyers by cutting songs from the albums and throwing together brand new albums that did not exist in The Beatles' original catalog. The Beatles were apparently so frustrated with this that they posed for the cover of this album as butchers, with decapitated baby dolls surrounding them (a collector's item now). That was quickly squelched, replaced by this boring cover.

"Yesterday" was pulled from the *Help!* album and released as a single, which leads to this oh-so-clever album title. In order to have enough songs for this release, they grabbed three finished John songs that were planned for The Beatles' next release *Revolver*, making the American release of *Revolver* Paul-heavy and ruining the sequencing The Beatles planned.

33. *Hey Jude*

The Beatles
4906 points
Chart appearance: 3/21/1970
Highest position: 2
Weeks on the chart: 36

Finally, The Beatles were free from Capitol destroying their albums and making new unplanned ones to cash in. Right? Not so fast. Seeking to grab some quick cash, Allen Klein (the new Beatles manager) threw together another compilation album in America comprised mostly of non-album singles. *Hey Jude* became a big seller because it was the first time most of the songs had appeared on an album, and the first time you could get them in stereo. For some reason, "Can't Buy Me Love" and "I Should Have Known Better" were included even though they had been released on an album before, but that was on the soundtrack for *A Hard Day's Night*, which was from United Artists instead of Capitol. This is still a strange decision to make, especially when you consider they could have included "The Inner Light" and "I'm Down" instead, neither of which had appeared on an album by that point.

It also includes "Don't Let Me Down," which was the B-side to "Get Back," and that may be why it wasn't later included on the *Let It Be* album where it clearly belonged.

It was originally going to be called "The Beatles Again" and some of the albums had that on the label. The album got to number 2 on the chart and stayed there for three weeks, held back by Simon and Garfunkel's classic *Bridge Over Troubled Water* LP.

32. *Cloud Nine*
George Harrison
4977 points
Chart appearance: 12/19/1987
Highest position: 8
Weeks on the chart: 27

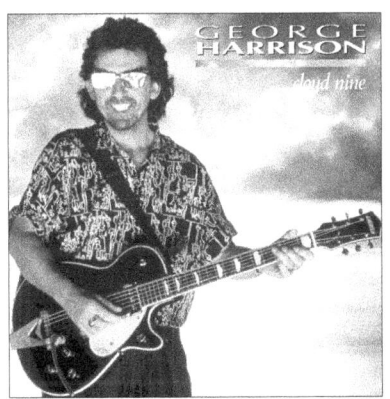

George's last album released during his lifetime was a major success. Coming five years after the disappointing *Gone Troppo*, *Cloud Nine* proved that George still had it. Although it never reached any higher than #8, it stayed in the Top 10 for an impressive nine weeks. The first single from the album ("Got My Mind Set on You") reached #1 and was the last song by any Beatle to hit the #1 spot. Ironically, it was a cover of an old obscure song from 1961 that George always loved. The follow-up single "When We Was Fab" was a George original which should have performed much better.

It was produced by Jeff Lynne, who also co-wrote a few of the songs.

31. *Wings Over America*
Paul McCartney and Wings
5435 points
Chart appearance: 12/25/1976
Highest position: 1
Weeks on the chart: 88

Wings' only live album hit #1, dropped quickly, but continued to sell, bubbling at the bottom of the chart for an amazing eighty-eight weeks. This is even more impressive when you consider it was a three-album set, which knocked the price up a bit.

Beatles fans were thrilled when Paul finally played some of his Beatles hits in concert, something he had previously avoided. So by getting this album, you could hear him sing "The Long and Winding Road," "Blackbird," "I've Just Seen a Face," "Lady Madonna," and "Yesterday."

A live version of "Maybe I'm Amazed" (originally from the album *McCartney*) was released from this and hit the Top 10.

30. *Flowers in the Dirt*

Paul McCartney
5452 points
Chart appearance: 6/24/1989
Highest position: 21
Weeks on the chart: 50

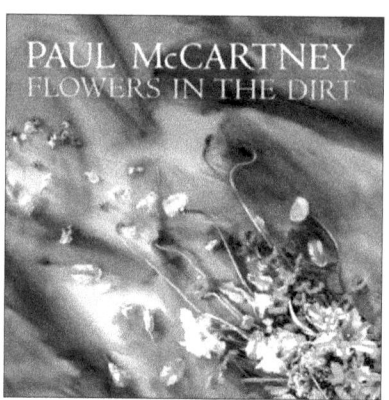

We're down to the top thirty albums in our countdown and every single album in our top thirty hit the Top 5 in the *Billboard* chart—except this one, which didn't even reach the Top 20!

However, Paul spent 1989 on a world tour, promoting it everywhere, thus keeping this album on the chart for almost an entire year.

Disappointed with the reception for *Press to Play*, Paul enlisted Elvis Costello, known not only for catchy music but clever lyrics, and the two got to work writing songs. Their collaboration produced the single "My Brave Face" and other excellent songs, including "You Want Her Too" and "Back on My Feet" (which only appeared as a B-side to the British single "Once Upon a Long Ago"). However, despite the excellent songs the two produced, they did not get along well (two very strong personalities), and so we shouldn't expect any more from them.

"My Brave Face" couldn't make it out of the Top 20, and "This One" (the follow-up single) never made it higher than #94—and then "Figure of Eight" did only slightly better, hitting #92. It would be four years before Paul attempted another studio album.

29. *Ringo*

Ringo Starr
5663 points
Chart appearance: 11/17/1973
Highest position: 2
Weeks on the chart: 38

So it had been a few years since The Beatles split. Paul and George each had two #1 hits under their belt, John was still waiting for his, and Ringo decided instead of doing the kinds of songs Beatles fans didn't care much about (with *Beaucoups of*

Blues and *Sentimental Journey*), he'd make a proper album. He recruited producer Richard Perry who had helmed Nilsson's greatest albums, which had Ringo playing on a few songs. He then began his trend of asking his famous friends to chip in.

John, Paul, and George all contributed songs and performed, making this the first album where all four Beatles appeared on the same disc since their break-up, although not all four of them together on the same song. John, George, and Ringo recorded John's song "I'm The Greatest" together, George appears on a few others, and Paul performed on his song "Six O'Clock" and "You're Sixteen." Add other guests like Harry Nilsson, Billy Preston, Mark Bolan, Levon Helm, Tom Scott, Nicky Hopkins, and Jim Keltner, and you have an all-star band (pun intended). And to make sure that was known to the record-buying public, they can all be seen in the cover painting, cheering Ringo on.

Packaging was extensive and certainly helped sales, with a huge booklet featuring all the lyrics and illustrations by Klaus Voormann—you know, that artist/bassist The Beatles met in Germany who ended up designing the *Revolver* album cover.

With three singles in the Top 5, this album holds the record of "Most Hit Singles from a Solo Beatles Album." (The closest competitor is *Band on the Run*, which had three singles hitting the Top 10, and then only if you count the American version of that album.)

The album never made it to #1, however, as it couldn't push Elton John's *Goodbye Yellow Brick Road* out of the top spot.

28. *All Things Must Pass*

George Harrison
5854 points
Chart appearance: 12/29/1970
Highest position: 1 (7 weeks)
Weeks on the chart: 40

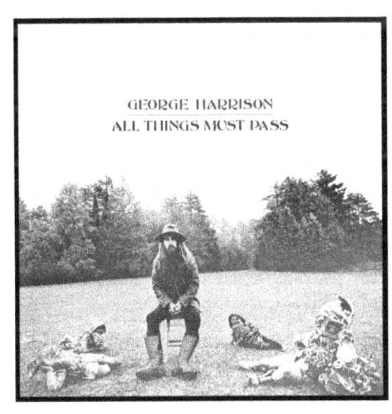

Since John and Paul usually only gave George two or maybe three songs per album, he had a lot saved up. George realized the others would never give him equal time on a Beatles album, and during the "Get Back" sessions, talked to John about it, saying he wanted to do a solo album but still be able to have songs on Beatles albums—and John agreed. However, when The Beatles split, George figured it was time. He brought out the songs he'd been saving up and hired Phil Spector to produce his debut album.

We ended up with a three-disc set, containing two of George's music and a third (called "Apple Jam") containing improvised instrumentals which, honestly, went nowhere. On the other hand, it was meant as a bonus disc, not really part of the album, and didn't add to the price.

The result was a huge hit, staying at number 1 for an impressive seven weeks. It produced two hit singles: "My Sweet Lord" and "What Is Life." The B-side to "My Sweet Lord" was "Isn't It a Pity," which also got major airplay.

Many critics still consider this the best Beatles solo album.

The musicians who participated in the creation of the album read like a who's who of the time: Ringo, Billy Preston, Eric Clapton, Gary Wright, Peter Frampton, Dave Mason, Bobby Keys, Klaus Voormann, Alan White, and the members of Badfinger, just to name a few.

Sometimes when musicians want to sound like The Beatles, they'll add slide guitar work like the type that George became famous for and which first appeared on this record. Yes, it's true: George never played slide on a Beatles song during their original run (we're not counting the *Anthology* reunion songs). John does, though, in George's "For You Blue"!

In 2021, for its 50th anniversary, the album was remastered and re-released, where it hit #7 on the charts. Some critics were hoping the remastering would un–Spectorize it and get rid of the "Wall of Sound" but that didn't happen. However, there were versions available with all sorts of outtakes, rehearsals, and background information for the true fan.

27. The Concert for Bangla Desh

George Harrison
6216 points
Chart appearance: 1/8/1972
Highest position: 2
Weeks on the chart: 41

After the success of *All Things Must Pass*, George turned his attention to the plight of those in Bangla Desh, and organized this fundraising concert. Recorded in Madison Square Garden in August of 1971, the album took months to be issued because of legal problems between record labels as to who had the rights, with most of the dispute coming from Bob Dylan's label. Then when that was settled, George ended up fighting with Capitol, who would be releasing the album, because they refused to waive their profits to help the cause, unlike all the musicians involved.

The album features George with a huge backing band consisting of Ringo, Jim Keltner, Eric Clapton, Jesse Ed Davis, Billy Preston, Leon Russell, Klaus Voormann, the members of Badfinger on acoustic guitars, six horns, and seven back-up singers. Can you tell Phil Spector was involved? On the other hand, this line-up helped fill Madison Square Garden and raise lots of money, which was the whole point.

George had invited his fellow Beatles, but Paul wasn't ready to appear with them yet and John apparently didn't want to participate if Yoko wasn't invited.

Ravi Shankar takes up one side of this three-disc package, and Bob Dylan takes another. Ringo gets to sing "It Don't Come Easy" and Billy Preston sings "That's the Way God Planned It" but the rest belongs to George.

One of the sides is only eight minutes long and another is only eleven minutes long, so you have to wonder why this couldn't all fit on two vinyl discs instead.

The album stayed at #2 for five weeks, unable to dislodge Don McLean's *American Pie* from the #1 spot. It had the last laugh, though, by winning the Grammy for Album of the Year.

26. *Imagine*

John Lennon
6428 points
Chart appearance: 9/18/1971
Highest position: 1
Weeks on the chart: 47

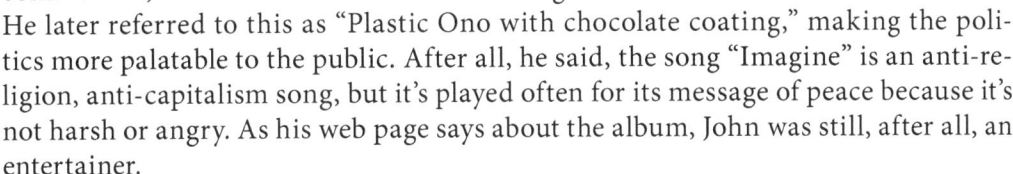

John's second musical album was his first #1 hit, although the iconic song somehow never made it that high. It received good reviews, although some thought the previous album (*Plastic Ono Band*) was superior.

It appears that John was trying to be more commercial, and he was successful in that regard. He later referred to this as "Plastic Ono with chocolate coating," making the politics more palatable to the public. After all, he said, the song "Imagine" is an anti-religion, anti-capitalism song, but it's played often for its message of peace because it's not harsh or angry. As his web page says about the album, John was still, after all, an entertainer.

The song "How Do You Sleep?" grabbed attention for its blatant attack on Paul at a time when their lawsuit was destroying their friendship ("Those freaks was right when they said you was dead…. The only thing you done was Yesterday and since you've gone you're just Another Day" [referencing two of Paul's hits in one line]). The fact that the album contained a postcard of John posing with a pig in the same way Paul had posed with a ram erased any doubt.

Also notable was the beautiful ballad "Jealous Guy," which probably should have been released as a second single from the album. The song eventually did get released as a single in 1988 to promote the *Imagine* biographical film, and it stayed on the chart for a month.

Musicians on the album include George and Nicky Hopkins.

The album spent forty-seven weeks on the chart, but not all at the same time. It reappeared along with many of his other albums after John's death.

25. *Wings at the Speed of Sound*

Wings
6567 points
Chart appearance: 4/10/1976
Highest position: 1 (7 weeks)
Weeks on the chart: 53

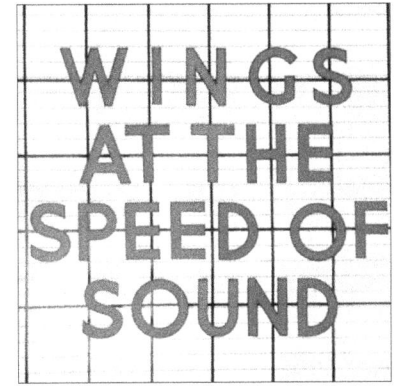

Paul was at the peak of his career when *Speed of Sound* was released. His previous two albums (*Band on the Run* and *Venus and Mars*) had been huge best-sellers, and eight out of the nine singles he had released in the three years previous had hit the Top 10, with three of them reaching #1. So anticipation for this album was huge.

It spent seven weeks at #1, but not in a row, falling back to #2 a few times. In all, it spent sixteen weeks in the Top 3!

The first single from the album ("Silly Love Songs") became Paul's fifth #1 hit, and the follow-up ("Let 'Em In") spent a month at #3. Disco was all the rage at the time, and many felt that the feel and production of "Silly Love Songs" was Paul's attempt to grab some of that attention. It worked.

The album is more of a group effort than previous Wings albums, with vocal turns for all the other members of the group. For many Paul fans, this is not an advantage.

Despite its commercial success at the time, reviewers were not too kind. While the album is enjoyable in its own way, this doesn't usually end up on anyone's list as "Best Paul McCartney album."

24. *Ram*

Paul and Linda McCartney
6844 points
Chart appearance: 6/5/1971
Highest position: 2
Weeks on the chart: 42

Although Paul's first solo album *McCartney* had been a great success, he was hurt by some of the reviews which commented on the amateurish album (even though that was the point). They apparently expected Paul to have a lushly-produced Beatles album without the other Beatles.

To combat this, Paul put great effort into his second album, and the result is wonderful. Many consider this his best album even after all this time; there's not a bad song on it.

The album produced his first #1 single, "Uncle Albert / Admiral Halsey." In Britain, "The Back Seat of My Car" was released as a single instead.

The album itself never made it to the top. It debuted at #6 and then hovered in the Top 10 for an amazing twenty-four weeks, hitting #2 in its third month, blocked from the top by Carole King's *Tapestry*.

The album is the only one credited to Paul and Linda, but this time Paul did not try to play all the instruments himself. Linda's contribution was mainly inspiration and backup singing.

Paul's first single "Another Day" was recorded during these sessions and released months before the album was available, but was not included on the album until special edition CDs were released years later. "Too Many People" opened the album with thinly disguised digs at John and Yoko, which did not go unnoticed by the two. "Dear Boy," however, is not about John, despite what some may think—it's actually about Linda's ex-husband ("I guess you never knew what you had missed").

23. *McCartney*

Paul McCartney
6923 points
Chart appearance: 5/9/1970
Highest position: 1 (3 weeks)
Weeks on the chart: 49

Life is a bowl of cherries!

Paul's first album was recorded on his home system, with Paul playing all the instruments. He included some songs that had been previewed with The Beatles ("Junk" and "Teddy Boy") and a few instrumentals to produce what sounds like an album of home demos, because that's kind of what it is.

He then got into a big argument with the other Beatles about its release, which would place it in competition with *Let It Be*. Paul refused to give in, *McCartney* was released, and it zoomed up to #1 until *Let It Be* pushed *McCartney* to the #2 position.

The Beatles had definitely been apart for a while when this happened. John had already told the other three he had quit, and started releasing his own singles. He did not participate when the other three recorded "I Me Mine" for *Let It Be*, but was outraged when Paul included a hand-out with *McCartney* where he announced he had quit The Beatles. This led to some harsh reviews from people who blamed Paul for breaking up the band, unaware that it had already broken up, but also from those expecting Paul to do a slick *Abbey Road* type of album.

The negative publicity didn't seem to hurt sales at all, as it spent thirteen weeks in the Top 10. Being the first album from an ex-Beatle that wasn't experimental certainly helped.

There are some great songs on this album between the fillers, and over time, the critical view has improved. In retrospect, Paul probably should have done an album like *Ram* first, but this was during a period of severe depression for him. After all, he had been a Beatle for a dozen years by that point, for his entire teenage years and beyond. Linda encouraged him to record and to get the album out to dig him out of his situation and it apparently worked.

No singles were released from the album, although "Maybe I'm Amazed" got some radio play. A live version of that song was eventually released from the *Wings Over America* album.

22. *Something New*

The Beatles
7016 points
Chart appearance: 8/8/1964
Highest position: 2
Weeks on the chart: 41

United Artists had the right to issue the *A Hard Day's Night* soundtrack in America, but Capitol still had the rights to some of the songs themselves, and thus produced this release, duplicating eight songs. Added to those were "Slow Down," "Matchbox," and "Komm, Gib Mir Deine Hand," giving the album a meager eleven tracks.

Americans were really getting ripped off in those days, with less songs per album and duplicates.

21. *The Traveling Wilburys*
The Traveling Wilburys
7382 points
Chart appearance: 11/12/1988
Highest position: 3
Weeks on the chart: 47

George's supergroup was tremendously successful, and sales outperformed recent releases from every one of these talented musicians. (Indeed, this is the highest George contribution on our list.) It never got any higher than #3, but it stayed in the Top 10 for an amazing twenty-two weeks!

The name comes from George's comments during the mixing of *Cloud Nine* concerning unwanted mechanical sounds: "*We'll bury* them in the mix." And thus the Traveling Wilburys idea was born.

Sadly, Roy Orbison died within a year of the album's release while it was still on the charts, but at least he left while on top of the world.

20. *Introducing The Beatles*
The Beatles
7515 points
Chart appearance: 2/8/1964
Highest position: 2
Weeks on the chart: 49

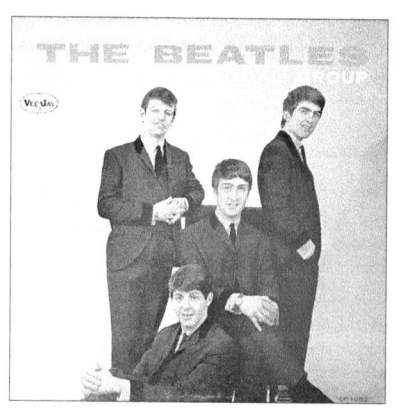

Lucky Vee-Jay. In 1963, they got the rights to some of the early Beatles songs, and had planned on releasing the U.S. version of *Please Please Me*. However, the singles they released didn't do very well and the album was scrapped ... until "I Want to Hold Your Hand" came out in late 1963 and Capitol started pushing their upcoming *Meet The Beatles!* It was clear something big was happening. Vee-Jay rushed out this album, beating *Meet* by a few weeks, and was thrilled to see it reach #2 behind Capitol's official release.

Legally they were not supposed to do that, because they didn't exercise the right to release the album when they had originally promised. Lawsuits ensued, and by the end of 1964, they were forced to stop selling the album, allowing Capitol to basically release it as *The Early Beatles*. Vee-Jay wasn't too unhappy, having sold more than a million copies.

19. *Help!*

The Beatles
7648 points
Chart appearance: 8/28/1965
Highest position: 1 (9 weeks)
Weeks on the chart: 46

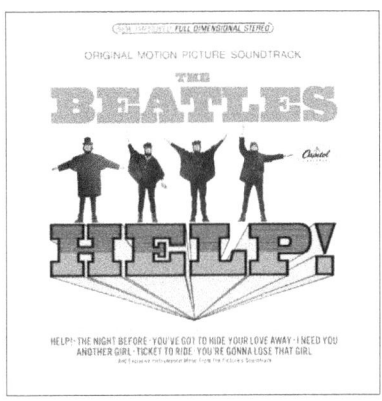

The American version of *Help!* varies from the British version, in accordance with Capitol's goal of milking them for all they can. It contains only the seven Beatles songs heard in the film and ignores the seven new songs on side two of the British LP. Instead, we get instrumental incidental music from the film.

On the other hand, three of the omitted songs had been released two months earlier in the slapped-together *Beatles VI*. Two more would be stuck on the truncated *Rubber Soul* album, and two more would appear on *Yesterday and Today*.

None of this hurt sales and the album quickly rose to #1 and stayed on the chart for almost an entire year. It also was nominated for Best Album of the Year at the Grammy Awards, the first for a rock band's album.

18. *Love*

The Beatles
7861 points
Chart appearance: 12/09/2006
Highest position: 4
Weeks on the chart: 84

Cirque du Soleil wanted to do a show based on The Beatles' music, so George Martin and his son Giles decided to try something new. They mashed up "Tomorrow Never Knows" and "Within You Without You" and nervously played it for Paul and Ringo, who loved it.

By mixing elements from different songs, they created something brand new for Beatles fans, and sales were great. It may have only reached #4 but it stayed on the charts for eighty-four weeks.

A lot of the fun is in listening for parts and, like a Beatles trivia game, trying to identify what song a guitar solo originally was on or where that new bass line came from. George Martin called it "The DaVinci Code for Beatles fans."

And for some Beatles fans, it was wonderful to just hear "I Am the Walrus" in complete stereo for the first time.

17. *Double Fantasy*

John Lennon and Yoko Ono
8026 points
Chart appearance: 12/6/1980
Highest position: 1 (8 weeks)
Weeks on the chart: 77

John had been inspired to record after hearing and loving the B-52s' "Rock Lobster" with its Yoko sounds. A trip to Bermuda rekindled his enthusiasm for life, he was impressed with Paul's "Coming Up," and as his son Sean was now getting old enough to not need constant attention, the time was right.

The album itself had been recorded in secret, and once completed, a search for a label ensued. Not surprisingly, everyone wanted the new John Lennon album. John and Yoko eventually signed with brand new Geffen Records.

After five years without a John Lennon album, fans lined up to buy *Double Fantasy* even if half of the songs were from Yoko. Sales were doing well but not amazingly so (but still better than John and Yoko's last collaboration *Sometime in New York City*, which never even reached the Top 40).

Critics were unimpressed, largely because the album was so personal (as John tended to be in his solo years). They pointed out how John used to criticize Paul for writing songs about simple family life, and here was an entire album from John with the same theme. They also complained that instead of using the musicians John usually employed, the producer chose session musicians that gave the album a slick sound unlike John's previous albums. The album looked like it might not make it into the Top 10.

And then the unimaginable happened.

The album hit #1, not surprisingly, right after December 8, 1980, and stayed there for two months before slowly moving down the chart. All of John's other albums as well as many Beatles albums also reappeared at the time, as everyone was reminded of how great the music was while mourning over the loss of John.

It later won the Grammy for Album of the Year.

16. *Venus and Mars*

Paul McCartney and Wings
8069 points
Chart appearance: 6/14/1975
Highest position: 1
Weeks on the chart: 79

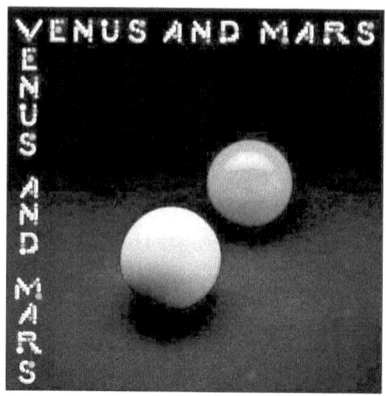

After the success of *Band on the Run*, Paul spent some time with his brother Michael to produce the excellent *McGear* album, which features many contributions by Paul. It's practically a Wings album with someone else handling the lead vocals and writing the lyrics. Despite that, it did not make the chart.

Paul then gathered up his new version of Wings—and then another one when the drummer quit—and came back with *Venus and Mars* and its hit single "Listen to What the Man Said." Since it had been more than a year and a half since *Band on the Run*, anticipation was high.

A follow-up single of "Letting Go" never even made the Top 20 but a third single, a mix of the first "Venus and Mars" with a shortened "Rock Show," rose to #12, helping album sales.

Paul's decision to try and create an album as opposed to a collection of songs is evident. Many songs fade into each other, and each side starts with "Venus and Mars" (with side two's version having extra verses). The first version of "Venus and Mars" even includes a snippet of "You Gave Me the Answer."

The Beatles' contracts with EMI/Capitol had ended by this point, and lawsuits kept Apple from releasing anything for many years. John stopped recording for five years, Ringo went through a number of different record labels, George started Dark Horse which was released through A&M, but Paul signed back up with Capitol. And so the green apple never appeared again on a Beatles solo album.

Venus and Mars was only at #1 for one week, but it stayed in the Top 10 for two months and on the chart for more than a year.

15. *Let It Be*

The Beatles
8531 points
Chart appearance: 5/30/1970
Highest position: 1 (4 weeks)
Weeks on the chart: 72

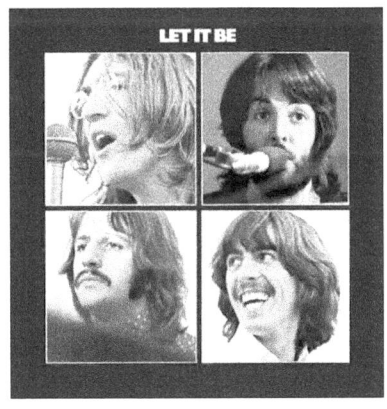

The idea was to "get back" to their roots and do an album without any overdubs live. It turned out to be not as easy as they thought, and perhaps not the best idea after all. It limited what they could play and do and, until Billy Preston showed up, really demonstrated how their music had gotten to the point where they couldn't just play it live easily. They hadn't even done that for *Please Please Me*, where the vocals were recorded afterwards.

The sessions ended and engineer Glyn Johns did his best to give The Beatles what they had asked for, but the end result didn't satisfy them. The tapes were then given to Phil Spector to see if he could do anything with them. He asked the band to record "I Me Mine," which was only done in practice and never finished, so Paul, George, and Ringo went to the studio and finished that number. John had announced that he was leaving the band at that point, but it's not clear the other three thought that would be permanent. After all, Ringo and George had also announced the same thing before and they came back, right?

Spector emerged with the *Let It Be* album, full of strings and female choirs that angered Paul. Apple announced a release date, and Paul objected, wanting his

McCartney album released instead. Between that and his dispute with the other three hiring Allen Klein as their manager, Paul announced that he was leaving. (He later oversaw his own version of the album with *Let It Be.... Naked*.)

When finally released, the album sold very well, with many not realizing that it had been recorded a year earlier, prior to *Abbey Road*.

It's the only original Beatles album with three #1 singles ("Get Back," "Let It Be," and "The Long and Winding Road").

The entire session was filmed and edited in such a way that when the *Let It Be* film was released, everyone saw The Beatles fighting and ending their relationship. As the film came out just as Paul announced he was leaving, everyone viewed the film in that light.

Fifty years later, Peter Jackson was asked by Apple to take all the film from the sessions and make a new version that would show what really happened, as Paul and Ringo especially never liked the film *Let It Be*. So in 2021, an eight-hour version debuted on Disney+ called *Get Back*. It showed that there was plenty of love as well as arguments during the sessions. (Those of us who have been in bands know this is absolutely normal.) *Get Back* also put the album back into the charts, where it remains as of this writing (at the end of 2021).

14. *The Beatles' Second Album*

The Beatles
8544 points
Chart appearance: 4/25/1974
Highest position: 1 (5 weeks)
Weeks on the chart: 55

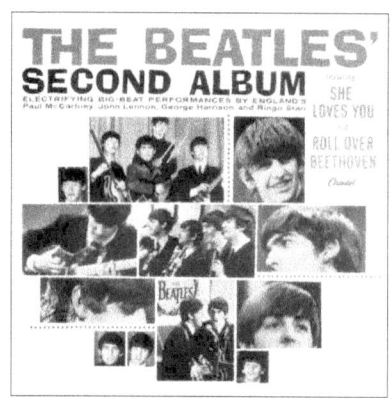

Those folks at Capitol with their clever album titles, hm? Technically, this was their third album in America, but Capitol was not about to acknowledge the existence of Vee-Jay Records.

This patched-together album contained mostly cover versions. Five songs were from *With The Beatles* that had not made the previous *Meet The Beatles!* The rest were various B-sides, along with "She Loves You." There's not a ballad among them—just a half hour of rock and roll.

Whereas in England, Beatles albums had fourteen songs, here Capitol tries and gets away with only eleven songs, which they kept up on many following albums.

It spent five weeks at #1, replacing *Meet The Beatles!*, and fell from #1 in June of 1964 to be replaced by the soundtrack to *Hello Dolly!* "Aha," critics said. "The Beatlemania fad is over." Then, a month later, *A Hard Day's Night* came out, proving them wrong.

13. *Revolver*

The Beatles
9065 points
Chart appearance: 9/3/1966
Highest position: 1 (6 weeks)
Weeks on the chart: 84

Revolver usually ends up near or at the top of "best Beatles album" lists and it's easy to see why. It's a masterpiece, with no bad songs. The quality and variety of the music is an improvement over *Rubber Soul*, which in itself was a huge leap past *Help!* They really started experimenting in the studio with this one, using backward tapes, tape loops, sound effects, and unusual instruments.

One wonders how people would have reacted to this album if The Beatles had treated the packaging with as much reverence as they did for *Sergeant Pepper*.

One of the reasons it didn't get the same respect may be because the album they produced was stripped of three of John's songs for the American release (having been previously issued on *Yesterday and Today*), relegating John to only "She Said She Said" and "Tomorrow Never Knows" ending each side. Even George got more songs. This was fortunately the last time the American version was different from the British version, unless you count *Magical Mystery Tour*, which was only an EP in England.

This also marked the point where The Beatles realized their songs were getting too complex to perform live. They embarked on their last tour after this album was released, but played none of the songs from it.

The album itself was an instant hit, staying at #1 for six weeks. Critics were overwhelmingly supportive and amazed at the progression of the music. Some fans, however, were upset that the four moptops were now playing "adult music."

12. *A Hard Day's Night*

The Beatles
9464 points
Chart appearance: 7/18/1964
Highest position: 1 (14 weeks)
Weeks on the chart: 56

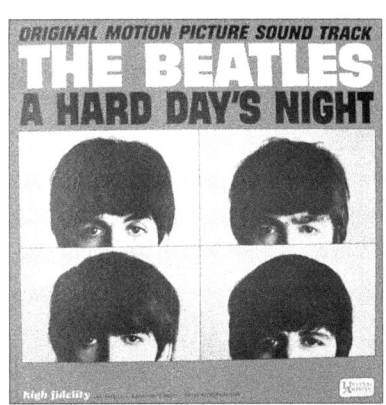

United Artists had the right to distribute the songs from their movie in America, and put out this album featuring eight Beatles songs in the film with instrumentals from the film. For the cover, United Artists apparently thought the most interesting thing about The Beatles was their hair. They rushed the album out about a month before the film's release to properly promote it (as if they needed to do that). In fact, The Beatles were once more at #1 on the album chart and the singles chart when the film opened.

The album stayed at #1 for fourteen weeks, keeping Capitol's *Something New* at #2 despite, or maybe because of, some of the songs appearing on both albums.

This is the first album to contain no cover songs, which is even more amazing when you consider the British version has thirteen original songs, written at a time when The Beatles hardly had a break between touring, recording, and making a movie!

The British version of this album often appears on "greatest rock albums of all time" lists alongside *Abbey Road*, *Rubber Soul*, and *Revolver*.

11. *Rubber Soul*

The Beatles
9817 points
Chart appearance: 12/25/1965
Highest position: 1 (6 weeks)
Weeks on the chart: 70

After almost three years of non-stop touring, recording, and filmmaking, The Beatles finally had some time to spend on their next record. They had recently met with Bob Dylan, who had a great influence on them lyrically (and chemically). Thanks to him, they realized they didn't have to just write teenager love songs. They were growing up, and so was their music.

They also began thinking of albums as more than just a collection of random songs but as a cohesive whole, and put effort into making sure the songs worked well with and against each other.

That meant nothing to Capitol, of course. They cut four songs from the album and added two that had been extracted from *Help!*

The album is considered one of The Beatles' best, and its position on this countdown only emphasizes that point. It was highly successful.

And unlike many pop stars who find their niche and stay with it, The Beatles were never satisfied to stay in one place. They were always experimenting and working to make their music better, and that's one of the reasons we're still listening to them and writing books about them today.

10. *Beatles '65*

The Beatles
10,221 points
Chart appearance: 1/2/1965
Highest position: 1 (9 weeks)
Weeks on the chart: 71

Oh Capitol, with their oh so clever album titles. ("We'll call it *Beatles '65*! It's not like people will still be listening to this sixty years from now, right?")

This is another spliced-together album, grabbing half of the songs off of *Beatles for Sale* and adding a non-album single ("I Feel Fine"), a B-side ("She's a Woman"), and a leftover from *A Hard Day's Night* ("I'll Be Back") to create another Frankenstein album to gather as much Beatles money as possible, with only eleven songs.

However, Beatlemania was still in full swing, and the album held the top spot for nine weeks, staying on the chart for an impressive 71 weeks. It jumped from #98 to #1 in one week, setting a new record for the time.

9. *Magical Mystery Tour*

The Beatles
10,384 points
Chart appearance: 12/23/1967
Highest position: 1 (8 weeks)
Weeks on the chart: 93

After the death of manager Brian Epstein, The Beatles were lost without a father figure (as Paul said in the *Get Back* film). Seeing no one else willing to do it, Paul tried to lead. "Let's make a TV show!" The idea was fine, but what we ended up with was basically an amateurish home movie. To make matters worse, this psychedelic showcase was shown in black-and-white in Britain. It did not go over well.

The good news is that for once, the American version of the album was better than what the British got. There, the songs from the show were placed on a double EP along with a cartoon booklet with photos which attempted to create a plot from the thing. In America, it became an album, with the booklet enlarged to album size, and with recent singles on side two.

And boy, was it successful. It appeared on the charts while *Sergeant Pepper* was still at #3, and it quickly rose to #1, where it stayed for two months while *Pepper* was still in the Top 20.

It also contained some of The Beatles' most experimental and exciting music—mostly from John—including "I Am the Walrus" and "Strawberry Fields Forever" (which was originally recorded for *Sergeant Pepper* but instead released as a single with "Penny Lane"). However, it appears that once they got this out of their system, their interest in psychedelic music disappeared. (The new songs from *Yellow Submarine* appeared later but had been recorded prior.)

The album also includes the first song credited to all four Beatles: the instrumental "Flying." Other instrumentals were recorded during this time for use as background music for the filmed sequences, but they were either unfinished or discarded and have never been officially released.

The cover was taken from the "Walrus" sequence and was the first time The Beatles' faces were not seen on the cover of one of their albums.

8. *Band on the Run*

Paul McCartney and Wings
10,833 points
Chart appearance: 12/22/1974
Highest position: 1 (4 weeks)
Weeks on the chart: 120

Not surprisingly, *Band on the Run* is the most successful on our countdown of any of The Beatles' solo offerings. But it didn't always look that way. Wings was down to just Paul, Linda, and Denny Laine, and the sessions had been disastrous in many ways, including having Paul and Linda robbed at gunpoint of some of the recording tapes, having Paul fainting dead away with what was thought to be a heart attack (but was actually caused by too much smoking), and open hostility from the Nigerian locals where the album was being recorded. (The original idea was to use local musicians but instead of being thrilled at having a Beatle want their contributions, they instead accused Paul of trying to steal their music.)

The initial release didn't give Paul too much encouragement. The previous album *Red Rose Speedway* had gotten to #1 in only three weeks, but *Band on the Run* took five weeks just to get into the Top 10.

And then it just stayed there, moving up slowly, then back down, then getting to #1, then falling back, then moving back up to #1, and so on for an amazing thirty-two weeks in the Top 10, four of which were at #1 (but not consecutively). That's more than half a year in the Top 10!

This is an album that grew by word of mouth, assisted by three hit singles that were released slowly over this period, each one doing better than the previous ("Helen Wheels," "Jet," and "Band on the Run"). Paul had apparently paid attention to how well *Ringo* had sold, with three singles being released from the album, and changed his mind about not having singles come from albums. Or maybe he just saw that *Band on The Run* was not selling as well as it should and he realized singles would help promote it. He even allowed Apple to edit "Jet" down to a shorter size for the radio.

It was critically well received and has gone on to reappear on the charts from time to time, while showing up on many "Best Albums Ever" lists. Even John said it was a great album, which had to mean a lot to Paul.

Some have speculated that Paul's creativity may have been buoyed by the fact that the other three Beatles finally realized what a con artist Allen Klein was and had joined with Paul in suing him. They were talking to each other again. Could a Beatles reunion be in their future?

Paul still loved to create a cohesive album instead of just a collection of songs, and he worked themes from "Jet" and "Mrs. Vandebilt" into the song "Picasso's Last Words" as well as a reprise of "Band on the Run" at the very end of the album as "Nineteen Hundred and Eighty Five" was fading.

Paul thought of the idea of a jailbreak scene for the cover, and gathered up Linda, Denny, and (of all people) Christopher Lee, James Coburn, talk show host Michael Parkinson, singer Kenny Lynch, boxer John Conteh, and Clement Freud (grandson of Sigmund!).

7. *Meet The Beatles!*

The Beatles
10,840 points
Chart appearance: 2/1/1964
Highest position: 1 (11 weeks)
Weeks on the chart: 74

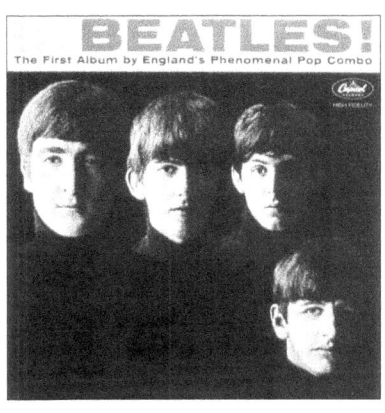

This time, Capitol got it right, but there's a reason. This was the first Capitol Beatles album released in America, and they knew it had to be great to live up to the hype they had been promoting. So Capitol took *With The Beatles* and removed all the cover versions except one ("Till There Was You"). They then added the non-album tracks "I Want to Hold Your Hand" and its British B-side "This Boy" as well as the American B-side "I Saw Her Standing There" (which also was available on Vee-Jay's *Introducing The Beatles*, issued a few weeks prior). Apparently, Capitol was worried that having cover versions of songs already familiar to Americans would turn off record buyers, but since "Till There Was You" was from the musical *The Music Man* and hadn't been performed by any rock and roll star at the time, that one was okay to keep.

The result was impressive by any standard. In the days when most songwriters did not perform their own music, to have these four moptops from England fill almost an entire album with their own creations made even the harshest critics take notice.

It zoomed up the chart, aided by their appearance on "The Ed Sullivan Show" (garnishing the highest ratings ever for a TV show at the time) and stayed at #1 for eleven weeks until it was pushed off the top by *The Beatles' Second Album*.

The back cover consisted of extensive liner notes with the attempt to convince everyone that this was the real thing, and not some flash in the pan. It's all dated now, of course, but you have to remember that rock and roll was just for the kids and "they'll grow out of it." The first rock and roll songs had only really appeared less than ten years previously!

But the kids proved them wrong. The album broke all sorts of records (no pun intended), spending over a year on the chart.

It wasn't until years later when the British albums started becoming easily available in America that we realized how much reverb and echo Capitol had placed on the songs, as if they weren't good enough on their own. Later reissues on CD included both the stereo and mono versions of the album, which differed from the original British release even more.

6. *1962–1966*

The Beatles
15,150 points
Chart appearance: 4/14/1973
Highest position: 3
Weeks on the chart: 183

In the early '70s, a bootleg "Beatles greatest hits" album was actually being promoted in terrible television commercials featuring someone faking a deplorable British accent. The album (called "Alpha Omega") also contained some of the solo Beatles hits, which was a sure-fire way for anyone to realize this wasn't an official release, given the way John and Paul had been arguing in public.

As lawyers pounced and eventually stopped it, Allen Klein realized The Beatles needed to have their own official greatest hits album. Thus came two double albums. Not surprisingly, both sold very well and appeared often on the chart (until the year 2000 when *1* was released).

The cover picture for this is taken from *Please Please Me* which was not released in the United States, so it was new to Americans. This album had a red border and has often been called "the red album" to the later "the blue album."

One problem with this collection is that these early songs are short and more could have fit on each side. In fact, when it was released on two CDs, people pointed out that all of the songs could have fit on one. While the "blue" album had seven songs per side, this one had two sides with only six songs, and the earlier songs are much shorter than the later ones. There was room for much more!

One could also question the selection. *Rubber Soul* was well represented but the only songs from the excellent *Revolver* were "Yellow Submarine" and "Eleanor Rigby." Yes, "Girl" and "In My Life" are great songs, but where was "Got to Get You Into My Life" or "Taxman" or "Tomorrow Never Knows"? For that matter, "Do You Want to Know a Secret?" had hit #2, and "She's a Woman" hit #4, but they're nowhere to be found, either.

5. *1967–1970*

The Beatles
16,978 points
Chart appearance: 4/14/1973
Highest position: 1
Weeks on the chart: 181

The second double album greatest hits collection performed slightly better than the first, perhaps because the later songs tend to not sound as dated as some of the earlier ones.

The cover picture for this was from the aborted *Get Back* album, but what a stroke of luck for having the two covers work perfectly together like this.

The only problem was that, unlike the *1962–1966* album, where more songs could have easily been included, the later songs are much longer. With seven songs per side, the vinyl version of this album was very dense. Each side lasted around twenty-five minutes. Sound quality falters at that level.

4. *The Beatles*

The Beatles
19806 points
Chart appearance: 12/14/1968
Highest position: 1 (9 weeks)
Weeks on the chart: 221

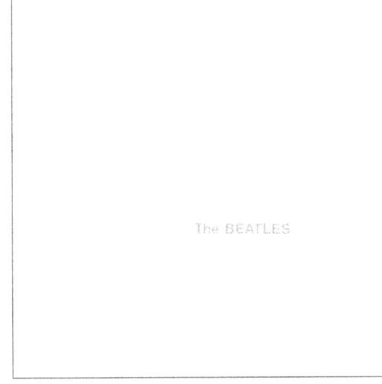

It had been almost an entire year since The Beatles' last album *Magical Mystery Tour* (and even longer in Britain, where *Tour* had only been an EP). "Hey Jude" had dominated the airwaves for months, and everyone was anxiously awaiting the next album only to discover two very full albums' worth of music arriving. Each side was so long that even when this was made available on CD, it needed two discs.

Despite being an expensive two-record set that contained no hit singles, it sold well and continued to sell well for years. Whenever people thought about The Beatles, this album would reappear on the chart. It currently has spent 221 weeks on the chart (that's more than four years total) and who knows? It could reappear again.

The packaging was attention-getting for being as minimal as you could get: an all-white cover with "The Beatles" embossed. No mention of the songs within, no liner notes, nothing. It was like getting a surprise present that you couldn't appreciate until you opened the wrapper. A large poster was included within, backed with all of the lyrics, as well as four glossy portraits of each Beatle.

"The White Album" (as it is more commonly known) contains thirty songs and shows the band's talents for writing in any style. There's rock & roll and country/western and Hollywood musical and lullaby and ska and folk and whatever "Revolution 9" is. Some critics complained that this made the album less cohesive, but others realized *that was the point*.

It's also interesting to note how much of The Beatles' sense of humor is at play here. On side one alone, we get "Back in the USSR" which cheekily sends up both Chuck Berry and The Beach Boys; "Ob-La-Di, Ob-La-Da," with its funny asides and lines like "Desmond stays at home and does his pretty face"; "Wild Honey Pie," which is just silly in and of itself; plus "The Continuing Story of Bungalow Bill" and "Happiness Is a Warm Gun."

The album doesn't show the tension in the band at the time, which even caused engineer Geoff Emerick to leave and not come back. Ringo quit at one point and Paul ended up playing drums on "Back in the USSR" and "Dear Prudence," but fortunately Ringo was persuaded to return. There are also quite a few songs that only feature one or two Beatles, so it is not as much of a group effort as previous albums.

There are huge differences between the stereo and mono versions of this album. For instance, the fade-in at the end of "Helter Skelter" is nonexistent on the mono version. However, this was the last Beatles album to have a mono release with different mixes.

The inclusion of the sound collage "Revolution 9" apparently caused some turmoil in Beatles circles. Paul had been creating sound collages previously just for fun, but had never demanded they be included on an album—but John insisted that his should. While one can once more appreciate The Beatles for always experimenting and pushing music to new things, this probably would have been better saved for one of John and Yoko's experimental albums. Imagine how much greater this album would have been had they included "Hey Jude" at that spot instead.

Still, when people think of great Beatles albums, this is almost always near the top of everyone's list. And rightly so.

3. 1

The Beatles
21,637 points
Chart appearance: 12/3/2000
Highest position: 1 (8 weeks)
Weeks on the chart: 505

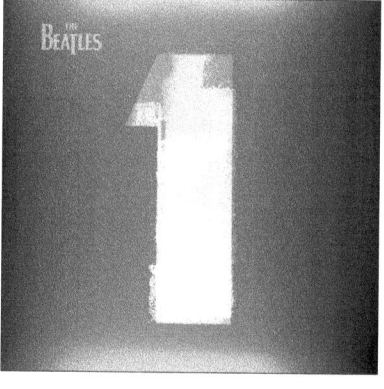

In 2000, Apple decided that with CDs able to hold around eighty minutes of music, a single CD of The Beatles' #1 hits might sell well.

Boy, did it. Look at this: It spent eight non-consecutive weeks at #1 (knocked off for two weeks by The Backstreet Boys, of all things). It ended up being the top selling album of *the entire decade*—pretty good for songs that were all more than thirty years old.

While it has fallen off the charts from time to time, *1* always seems to come back because, you know, *Beatles*. Who doesn't love The Beatles? It's still on the chart as of this writing in December of 2021 and it shows no sign of stopping. It's spent 505 weeks there so far. That's almost ten years if run consecutively.

Besides the CD, this was also released on two vinyl albums in the UK only, with each side lasting at least twenty minutes.

1 contains twenty-seven songs but sharp-eyed readers of this book will realize that some of the songs on the album never actually made #1. While "From Me to You" may have hit #1 in Britain, in America it only got as high as #41 (and if Britain #1s are the standard, then where's "Please Please Me"?). "Day Tripper" only hit #5, "Yellow Submarine" was at #2, "Eleanor Rigby" was #11, "Lady Madonna" got to #4, and "The Ballad of John and Yoko" only hit #8.

But that's okay, because getting all of these songs on one CD is just wonderful.

Of course, this is not the same thing as a "best of" album because let's face it, some of their best songs were never released as singles ("A Day in the Life" and "Here Comes the Sun," for instance), and some great B-sides aren't there ("Strawberry Fields Forever" and "I Am the Walrus," for instance). But then again, if you asked ten Beatles fans to list the twenty greatest Beatles songs, you'd get completely different lists from everyone. And that's okay: It just means there are so many great songs they can't all fit on one CD.

A deluxe edition was later issued which included a DVD of videos and commentary from Paul and Ringo.

2. *Sergeant Pepper's Lonely Hearts Club Band*

The Beatles
25,048 points
Chart appearance: 6/24/1967
Highest position: 1 (15 weeks)
Weeks on the chart: 232

You may have heard of this one.

This album took the world by storm. In the summer of 1967, you couldn't travel anywhere without hearing it playing on the radio, in stores, on the street. It remained at #1 for fifteen weeks and was still in the Top 3 six months later when the follow-up *Magical Mystery Tour* was released.

Critics everywhere took notice. The music was more complex, more adult. The Beatles were no longer the cute moptops, but adults with mustaches even. They had once more topped themselves, dragging the rest of pop music behind them. This was completely by design, as Paul explained years later: "We were fed up with being The Beatles. We really hated that fucking four little mop-top boys approach. We were not boys, we were men." They wanted to be taken seriously. And they were.

The experimentation that had permeated *Revolver* came full force at us, with sound effects whirling around us in stereo, animal sounds, English music hall numbers, Indian sitar music, audience cheers—and then there's "A Day in The Life" with its orchestra crescendo lasting almost a full minute, as we sit there in awe.

The original plan was to do the entire album as if they were another band, introducing Billy Shears and everything. That didn't exactly come to pass, but they did try to make this as complete and whole as possible, by having barely any space between songs and having the songs fade into each other quite often. They weren't the first band to do that for a rock album—Frank Zappa usually gets that credit—but it was used to great effect here.

"Penny Lane" and "Strawberry Fields Forever" were originally planned for the album but when the record company demanded another single after "Yellow Submarine," George Martin gave them those two. He later said that was a terrible mistake, as the inclusion of those two would have made the album even better.

For years, this was The Beatles album that would appear on the charts every time The Beatles were back in the news. When this list was first made for a Beatles fanzine in the 1980s, this was way ahead at the top of the list. That has changed. There's a new #1....

1. *Abbey Road*
The Beatles
36,389 points
Chart appearance: 10/18/1969
Highest position: 1 (11 weeks)
Weeks on the chart: 435

Many bands find that their first album is their best-selling one. As one musician once said, "You spend your entire life writing your first album and you have six months for your second."

The Beatles, on the other hand, only got better with each album. And here we see their last album as being the main one that people are still buying fifty years later.

After the failure of the *Get Back* album, George Martin was lured back to the studio with the promise that he could produce an album like he used to. He brought back engineer Geoff Emerick and assistant engineer Alan Parsons (later known for The Alan Parsons Project). The Beatles deferred to them more than they had previously done, giving us the best-produced and lushest-sounding Beatles record ever. It was their first album to use 8-track recordings, which allowed for more separation of the instruments and overdubs. The drums, for instance, were finally recorded in stereo since they could dedicate two tracks to them.

George brought his new Moog synthesizer to the sessions, which was only one of a few available at the time. (The first, believe it or not, belonged to Micky Dolenz, who had used it on a Monkees album in 1967.) Some feel it was overused on the album, but it certainly had its place.

John wanted to just put out an album with unrelated songs, but Paul and George Martin wanted the songs to be connected. A compromise allowed Paul to arrange the medley on side two, which included a few of John's songs as well.

Some have speculated that The Beatles knew this would be their last album and so put extra effort into it, but recent releases of dialog from the sessions show them discussing what their follow-up album would be.

Still, it was a tense time. Allen Klein was trying to clean up the mess that Apple had become, and Paul was upset that the other three had voted against him to hire Klein when previously, big decisions like that had to be unanimous in the group. John was with Yoko and was getting bored with being a Beatle and indeed would announce his departure soon after the album was finished. And the *Get Back* sessions had left everyone disappointed. But they put all that aside to work.

The first song recorded was "I Want You (She's So Heavy)" just a few weeks after the *Get Back* sessions, still featuring Billy Preston. The rest of the album was recorded months later, when Preston was no longer available. Given that this album would not be performed live without overdubs in the studio like *Let It Be*, he was not needed in any event.

The medley originally included "Her Majesty" between "Mean Mr. Mustard" and "Polythene Pam" but they realized it just didn't fit. It slowed down the medley and sounded out of place. It was spliced out and taped to the end of the reel. You can still hear the final note of "Mean Mr. Mustard" at the start of "Her Majesty" which The Beatles decided to leave at the very end as a surprise bonus song after "The End." (Original album covers didn't even list it, making this the first "hidden track" that lots of bands tend to do on CDs these days.)

"The End" is unique in that all four share solos: There's a drum solo (which Ringo hated doing) and then a guitar solo battle from the other three (Paul, then George, then John).

Besides the single "Something" backed with "Come Together," the album also gives us George's "Here Comes the Sun" which is the most-downloaded Beatles song ever. Ringo's "Octopus' Garden" also appears on the *1967–1970* blue album, and Paul is sure to play "Golden Slumbers / Carry That Weight / The End" on almost every tour.

The cover itself is iconic. The cover photo was taken at a crossroads near the recording studio, which has now become a mecca for fans who bother traffic by trying to take pictures of themselves crossing it. It's been copied and parodied so many times, it's now a part of the world's consciousness. The EMI studio they used even changed its name years later to "Abbey Road Studios" because, well, that's what everyone was calling it anyway.

The album stayed at #1 for eleven weeks, stayed in the Top 10 for twenty-seven weeks, and was on the chart for a total of eighty-three weeks. It then popped up again from time to time and, in the last few years, has not left the chart at all. As of this writing at the end of 2021, it is still on the chart and has been on for 435 non-consecutive weeks. That's more than eight years.

It was the best-selling album of 1969 and was even the fourth best-selling album of 1970.

A well-deserved spot on our countdown.

Alternate Countdowns

Another way to examine the data is by highest position on the chart, and how many weeks it stayed there. So, just in case you're wondering what that countdown would look like, here it is (with lots of ties).

The number in the parentheses is the highest position reached. If something was at that position for more than one week, then it breaks the tie and the number of weeks at that position is listed afterwards. For instance, the single "Please Please Me" is followed by (3:2), meaning it hit #3, and was at #3 for two weeks.

Albums

110. *Gimme Some Truth* [2010]; *Long Tall Sally* (196)
109. *Standing Stone* (194)
108. *Electronic Music* (191)
107. *Gimme Some Truth* [2020] (186)
106. *With The Beatles*; *Zoom In* (179)
105. *Liverpool Oratorio* (177)
104. *Wedding Album* (176)
103. *Past Masters 1* (174)
102. *Life with the Lions* (174:2)
101. *Bootleg Recordings 63* (172)
100. *In the Beginning* (172:2)
99. *The Apple Years* (167)
98. *Ringo the 4th* (162)
97. *The McCartney Interview* (158)
96. *Please Please Me* (155)
95. *Signature Box* (148)
94. *Ocean's Kingdom* (143)
93. *The Beatles vs. The Four Seasons* (142)
92. *Tripping the Live Fantastic Highlights* (141)
91. *The Best of Dark Horse* (132)
90. *Photograph* (130)
89. *Give More Love* (128)
88. *What's My Name* (127)
87. *Menlove Avenue* (127:2)
86. *Live in Japan* (126)
85. *Two Virgins* (124)
84. *Past Masters 2* (121)
83. *Ringo Rama* (113)
82. *Live at the Star Club* (111)
81. *Chopa B CCCP* (109)
80. *Gone Troppo* (108)
79. *Jolly What!* (104)
78. *Postcards from Paradise* (99)
77. *Stop and Smell the Roses* (98)
76. *Heartplay* (94)
75. *Ringo 2012* (80)
74. *Paul Is Live* (78)
73. *The Beatles and Guests* (68)
72. *Beaucoups of Blues*; *Lennon Legend* (65)
71. *Songs, Pictures and Stories* (63)
70. *All the Best* (62)
69. *Vertical Man* (61)
68. *Y Not* (58)
67. *20 Greatest Hits* (50)
66. *Wonderwall Music* (49)
65. *The US Albums* (48)
64. *Sometime in New York City* (48:2)
63. *The Capitol Albums Volume 2* (46)
62. *Remember* (44)
61. *The Early Beatles* (43)
60. *Live in New York* (41)
59. *The Beatles in Mono* (40)

58. *The Capitol Albums Volume 1* (35)
57. *The Lennon Collection* (33)
56. *Acoustic*; *Imagine: John Lennon*; *Tripping the Live Fantastic* (31)
55. *The Best of George Harrison* (31:3)
54. *Blast from Your Past*; *Press to Play* (30)
53. *Wings Greatest Hits* (29)
52. *Ringo's Rotogravure* (28)
51. *Driving Rain*; *Run Devil Run* (26)
50. *Let It Roll*; *Power to the People*; *Tomorrow Never Knows* (24)
49. *Love Songs* (24:2)
48. *Sentimental Journey* (22)
47. *Rarities* (21)
46. *Give My Regards to Broad Street* (21:2)
45. *Flowers in the Dirt* (21:3)
44. *Early Takes Volume 1* (20)
43. *McCartney III Imagined* (19)
42. *Reel Music* (19:3)
41. *Brainwashed* (18)
40. *Off the Ground* (17)
39. *Good Evening New York City* (16)
38. *Pipes of Peace*; *Pure McCartney*; *The Beatles in Stereo*; *Yellow Submarine Songtrack* (15)
37. *George Harrison*; *Unplugged* (14)
36. *Shaved Fish* (12)
35. *Milk and Honey* (11)
34. *Somewhere in England*; *Thirty Three and ⅓* (11:2)
33. *Traveling Wilburys Volume 3* (11:5)
32. *Live Peace in Toronto*; *Wild Life* (10)
31. *Traveling Wilburys Collection* (9)
30. *Mind Games* (9:3)
29. *Back in the U.S.*; *Cloud 9* (8)
28. *Back to the Egg*; *Goodnight Vienna* (8:2)
27. *Extra Texture* (8:3)
26. *Live at the BBC 2* (7)
25. *The Beatles' Story* (7:4)
24. *Chaos and Creation in the Backyard*; *John Lennon / Plastic Ono Band*; *Rock 'n' Roll* (6)
23. *Kisses on the Bottom*; *Let It Be…. Naked* (5)
22. *Dark Horse*; *Love* (4)
21. *Beatles at the BBC*; *New* (3)
20. *1962–1966*; *Memory Almost Full* (3:2)
19. *McCartney II* (3:5)
18. *Traveling Wilburys* (3:6)
17. *Flaming Pie*; *McCartney III*; *Wingspan*; *Yellow Submarine* (2)
16. *At the Hollywood Bowl*; *Ram*; *Ringo*; *Rock 'n' Roll Music* (2:2)
15. *Hey Jude* (2:4)
14. *London Town*; *The Concert for Bangla Desh* (2:6)
13. *Introducing The Beatles*; *Something New* (2:9)
12. *1967–1970*; *Anthology 2*; *Anthology 3*; *Egypt Station*; *Imagine*; *Venus and Mars*; *Walls and Bridges*; *Wings Over America* (1)
11. *Band on the Run* (1:2)
10. *Anthology 1*; *McCartney*; *Red Rose Speedway*; *Tug of War* (1:3)
9. *Let It Be* (1:4)
8. *Living in the Material World*; *The Beatles' Second Album*; *Yesterday and Today* (1:5)
7. *Revolver*; *Rubber Soul*; *The Beatles VI* (1:6)
6. *All Things Must Pass*; *At the Speed of Sound* (1:7)
5. *I*; *Double Fantasy*; *Magical Mystery Tour* (1:8)
4. *Help!*; *The Beatles*; *The Beatles '65* (1:9)
3. *Abbey Road*; *Meet The Beatles!* (1:11)
2. *A Hard Day's Night* (1:14)
1. *Sergeant Pepper's Lonely Hearts Club Band* (1:15)

Singles

97. "Sie Liebt Dich" (97)
96. "Freedom" (97:2)
95. "The Inner Light" (96)
94. "I'm Happy Just to Dance with You" (95)
93. "This One" (94)

Alternate Countdowns

92. "Figure of Eight"; "Four by The Beatles" (92)
91. "Why" (88)
90. "Beaucoups of Blues" (87)
89. "Hope of Deliverance" (83)
88. "What Goes On" (81)
87. "Stranglehold" (81:2)
86. "Jealous Guy" (80)
85. "Hey Baby"; "There's a Place" (74)
84. "Sgt. Pepper's Lonely Hearts Club Band" / "With a Little Help from My Friends" (71)
83. "Dance Tonight" (69)
82. "Four by The Beatles"; "Roll Over Beethoven" (68)
81. "Baby It's You" (67)
80. "The World Tonight" (64)
79. "End of the Line" (63)
78. "Seaside Woman" (59)
77. "Woman Is the Nigger of the World" (57)
76. "I Am the Walrus" (56)
75. "I'm Stepping Out" (55)
74. "I Should Have Known Better"; "If I Fell"; "Tug of War" (53)
73. "Wake Up My Love" (53:2)
72. "Ob-La-Di, Ob-La-Da" (49)
71. "Sgt. Pepper's Lonely Hearts Club Band"; "You Can't Do That" (48)
70. "Act Naturally" (47)
69. "Yes It Is" (46)
68. "All My Loving"; "Handle with Care" (45)
67. "Mother" (43)
66. "Happy Xmas (War Is Over)" (42)
65. "From Me to You" (41)
64. "I Don't Want to Spoil the Party" (39)
63. "Letting Go"; "London Town" (39:2)
62. "Wrack My Brain" (38)
61. "Ding Dong; Ding Dong" (36)
60. "Don't Let Me Down"; "Thank You Girl" (35)
59. "Baby You're a Rich Man" (34)
58. "Girls School" (33)
57. "Goodnight Vienna" (31)
56. "Cold Turkey" (30)
55. "Arrow Through Me" (29)
54. "Mary Had a Little Lamb"; "Wonderful Christmastime" (28)
53. "My Bonnie" (26)
52. "A Dose of Rock and Roll" (26:2)
51. "I'll Cry Instead"; "My Brave Face"; "Slow Down" (25)
50. "I've Had Enough"; "This Song" (25:2)
49. "When We Was Fab" (23)
48. "Bangla Desh"; "Rain"; "So Bad" (23:2)
47. "Give Ireland Back to the Irish" (21)
46. "Press" (21:2)
45. "Getting Closer"; "Stand by Me"; "You" (20)
44. "Ain't She Sweet"; "Crackerbox Palace" (19)
43. "Mind Games" (18)
42. "Matchbox" (17)
41. "Blow Away" (16)
40. "Dark Horse" (15)
39. "I Saw Her Standing There" (14)
38. "Venus and Mars Rock Show" (12)
37. "And I Love Her" (12:2)
36. "Movie Medley"; "Revolution" (12:3)
35. "Real Love" (11)
34. "Eleanor Rigby"; "Power to the People" (11:2)
33. "Helen Wheels"; "Hi Hi Hi"; "Maybe I'm Amazed"; "P.S. I Love You"; "What Is Life" (10)
32. "Watching the Wheels" (10:2)
31. "Take It Away" (10:5)
30. "#9 Dream" (9)
29. "Back Off Boogaloo" (9:2)
28. "Strawberry Fields Forever" (8)
27. "The Ballad of John and Yoko" (8:3)
26. "Jet"; "Spies Like Us" (7)
25. "Got to Get You Into My Life" (7:3)
24. "Free as a Bird"; "Only You" (6)
23. "No More Lonely Nights" (6:2)
22. "Day Tripper"; "Nobody Told Me"; "Oh My My" (5)

21. "Another Day" (5:2)
20. "Goodnight Tonight" (5:3)
19. "FourFiveSeconds" (4)
18. "It Don't Come Easy"; "She's a Woman" (4:2)
17. "Lady Madonna" (4:4)
16. "Junior's Farm"; "Nowhere Man" (3)
15. "Please Please Me" (3:2)
14. "Imagine"; "Instant Karma"; "No No Song" (3:3)
13. "Let 'Em In" (3:4)
12. "Come Together"; "Do You Want to Know a Secret?"; "The Girl Is Mine"; "Yellow Submarine" (2)
11. "Woman" (2:2)
10. "All Those Years Ago"; "Live and Let Die" (2:3)
9. "Twist and Shout" (2:4)
8. "All You Need Is Love"; "Band on the Run"; "Give Me Love (Give Me Peace on Earth)"; "Got My Mind Set on You"; "Listen to What the Man Said"; "Love Me Do"; "Penny Lane"; "Photograph"; "Something"; "Ticket to Ride"; "Uncle Albert / Admiral Halsey"; "Whatever Gets You Thru the Night"; "You're Sixteen" (1)
7. "A Hard Day's Night"; "Eight Days a Week"; "Let It Be"; "Paperback Writer"; "She Loves You"; "The Long and Winding Road"; "With a Little Luck" (1:2)
6. "Coming Up"; "Hello Goodbye"; "Help!"; "We Can Work It Out"; "I Feel Fine" (1:3)
5. "My Love"; "My Sweet Lord"; "Yesterday" (1:4)
4. "Can't Buy Me Love"; "Get Back"; "(Just Like) Starting Over"; "Silly Love Songs" (1:5)
3. "Say Say Say" (1:6)
2. "Ebony and Ivory"; "I Want to Hold Your Hand" (1:7)
1. "Hey Jude" (1:9)

As pointed out in the "About the Charts" chapter, comparing the charts over half a century is somewhat meaningless, as the methodology of creating the charts has changed many times. However, if you look only to The Beatles' singles—the vast majority of which were released in the 1960s—you can get a better comparison. Here's the list, not in countdown form:

"Hey Jude"
"Twist and Shout"
"Something"
"Come Together"
"I Want to Hold Your Hand"
"She Loves You"
"Let It Be"
"A Hard Day's Night"
"Help!"
"Get Back"
"Got to Get You Into My Life"
"Love Me Do"
"We Can Work It Out"
"Please Please Me"
"I Feel Fine"
"Hello Goodbye"
"Yesterday"
"Lady Madonna"
"Ticket to Ride"
"All You Need Is Love"
"Revolution"
"Can't Buy Me Love"
"The Long and Winding Road"
"Do You Want to Know a Secret?"
"Paperback Writer"
"Eight Days a Week"
"Penny Lane"
"Nowhere Man"
"Yellow Submarine"
"Day Tripper"
"Movie Medley"
"I Saw Her Standing There"

Alternate Countdowns

"She's a Woman"
"The Ballad of John and Yoko"
"Strawberry Fields Forever"
"And I Love Her"
"P.S. I Love You"
"Eleanor Rigby"
"Ain't She Sweet"
"Matchbox"
"Free as a Bird"
"Rain"
"I'll Cry Instead"
"Real Love"
"Slow Down"
"Thank You Girl"
"My Bonnie"
"If I Fell"
"Act Naturally"
"I Don't Want to Spoil the Party"
"Baby You're a Rich Man"

"All My Loving"
"Ob-La-Di, Ob-La-Da"
"Don't Let Me Down"
"From Me to You"
"Yes It Is"
"You Can't Do That"
"I Am the Walrus"
"I Should Have Known Better"
"Sergeant Pepper's Lonely Hearts Club Band" / "With a Little Help from My Friends"
"Roll Over Beethoven"
"Baby It's You"
"What Goes On"
"There's a Place"
"I'm Happy Just to Dance with You"
"The Inner Light"
"Sie Leibt Dich"

The Beatles Challenge

Within a period of seven years, The Beatles produced more great songs than any other musical act. Below is a list of 100 of their greatest songs. Even the most jaded person will recognize most of these. Got any friends who say The Beatles aren't that great? Challenge them to name any other act that comes close to giving us so many memorable songs in such a short period of time. They won't be able to do it.

Ideally, these should be made available in a box set (are you listening, Apple?). Instead of an album called *1*, we can have *100*. Here's my list and how they can fit on standard CDs:

CD One
"Love Me Do"
"Please Please Me"
"I Saw Her Standing There"
"Do You Want to Know a Secret?"
"From Me to You"
"She Loves You"
"It Won't Be Long"
"All My Loving"
"I Want to Hold Your Hand"
"This Boy"
"Can't Buy Me Love"
"You Can't Do That"
"A Hard Day's Night"
"I Should Have Known Better"
"If I Fell"
"I'll Cry Instead"
"And I Love Her"
"Any Time at All"
"Things We Said Today"
"I Feel Fine"
"She's a Woman"
"Eight Days a Week"
"I'll Follow the Sun"
"No Reply"
"Baby's in Black"
"Ticket to Ride"
"Yes It Is"
"Help!"
"You've Got to Hide Your Love Away"
"I've Just Seen a Face"
"Yesterday"

CD Two
"Drive My Car"
"Norwegian Wood (This Bird Has Flown)"
"You Won't See Me"
"In My Life"
"Nowhere Man"
"Michelle"
"Girl"
"Day Tripper"
"We Can Work It Out"
"Rain"
"Paperback Writer"
"Here, There, and Everywhere"
"Taxman"
"Yellow Submarine"
"She Said She Said"
"Good Day Sunshine"
"And Your Bird Can Sing"
"Got to Get You Into My Life"
"Eleanor Rigby"
"Tomorrow Never Knows"
"Penny Lane"
"Strawberry Fields Forever"
"Sgt. Pepper's Lonely Hearts Club Band"

"With a Little Help from My Friends"
"Lucy in the Sky with Diamonds"
"Getting Better"
"When I'm Sixty Four"
"Lovely Rita"
"A Day in the Life"

CD Three

"All You Need Is Love"
"Baby You're a Rich Man"
"Hello Goodbye"
"I Am the Walrus"
"Magical Mystery Tour"
"The Fool on the Hill"
"Lady Madonna"
"All Together Now"
"Hey Bulldog"
"Hey Jude"
"Revolution"
"Martha My Dear"
"Back in the USSR"
"Ob-La-Di, Ob-La-Da"
"While My Guitar Gently Weeps"
"Happiness Is a Warm Gun"
"Blackbird"
"Rocky Raccoon"
"Birthday"

"Mother Nature's Son"
"Helter Skelter"

CD Four

"Get Back"
"Across the Universe"
"Don't Let Me Down"
"Let It Be"
"Two of Us"
"I've Got a Feeling"
"The Long and Winding Road"
"The Ballad of John and Yoko"
"Old Brown Shoe"
"Come Together"
"Something"
"Maxwell's Silver Hammer"
"Oh! Darling"
"Octopus' Garden"
"Here Comes the Sun"
"You Never Give Me Your Money"
"Golden Slumbers"
"Carry That Weight"
"The End"
Bonus tracks:
"Free as a Bird"
"Real Love"

The Beatles Discography

Believe it or not, there were some records released by The Beatles that never made the charts (especially in the later solo years). Here's a list of all the records they have released in the United States, noting the highest chart position (if applicable). If the B-side charted, it's listed as well.

1963
2: "Please Please Me"
5: "From Me to You"
9: "She Loves You"
12: "I Want to Hold Your Hand" (1) / "I Saw Her Standing There" (14)

1964
1: *Introducing the Beatles* (2)
   Meet The Beatles! (1)
   "Please Please Me" (3) / "From Me to You" (41)
   "My Bonnie" (26)
   "She Loves You" (1)
3: *The Beatles* (EP)
   "Twist and Shout" (2) / "There's a Place" (74)
   "Do You Want to Know a Secret?" (2) / "Thank You Girl" (35)
   "Can't Buy Me Love" (1) / "You Can't Do That" (48)
4: *The Beatles' Second Album* (1)
   "Love Me Do" (1) / w"P.S. I Love You" (10)
   "Why" (88)
5: *Four by The Beatles* (EP) (92)
   "Sie Liebt Dich" (97)
6: *A Hard Day's Night* (1)
7: "Something New" (2)
   "A Hard Day's Night" (1) / "I Should Have Known Better" (53)
   "Ain't She Sweet" (19)
   "I'll Cry Instead" (25)
   "And I Love Her" (12) / "If I Fell" (53)
8: "Matchbox" (17) / "Slow Down" (25)
11: *The Beatles' Story* (7)
    "I Feel Fine" (1) / "She's a Woman" (4)
12: *Beatles '65* (1)

1965
2: *Four by The Beatles* (EP) (68)
   "Eight Days a Week" (1) / "I Don't Want to Spoil the Party" (39)
3: *The Early Beatles* (43)
4: "Ticket to Ride" (1) / "Yes It Is" (71)
6: *The Beatles VI* (1)
7: "Help!" (1)
8: *Help!* (1)
9: "Yesterday" (1) / "Act Naturally" (47)
12: *Rubber Soul* (1)
    "We Can Work It Out" (1) / "Day Tripper" (5)

1966
2: "Nowhere Man" (3) / "What Goes On" (81)
5: "Paperback Writer" (1) / "Rain" (23)
6: *Yesterday and Today* (1)
8: "Yellow Submarine" (2) / "Eleanor Rigby" (11)
   Revolver (1)

1967

- **1:** *The Family Way* (P)
- **2:** "Penny Lane" (**1**) / "Strawberry Fields Forever" (**8**)
- **6:** *Sgt. Pepper's Lonely Hearts Club Band* (**1**)
- **7:** "All You Need Is Love" (**1**) / "Baby You're a Rich Man" (**34**)
- **11:** *Magical Mystery Tour* (**1**)
  "Hello Goodbye" (**1**) / "I Am the Walrus" (**56**)

1968

- **3:** "Lady Madonna" (**4**) / "The Inner Light" (**96**)
- **8:** "Hey Jude" (**1**) / "Revolution" (**12**)
- **11:** *The Beatles* (**1**)
  Two Virgins (J) (**124**)
- **12:** *Wonderwall Music* (G) (**49**)

1969

- **1:** *Yellow Submarine* (**2**)
- **5:** "Get Back" (**1**) / "Don't Let Me Down" (**35**)
  Life with the Lions (J) (**174**)
  Electronic Sound (G) (**191**)
- **6:** "The Ballad of John and Yoko" (**8**)
- **7:** "Give Peace a Chance" (J) (**14**)
- **10:** *Abbey Road* (**1**)
  "Something" (**1**) / "Come Together" (**2**)
  "Cold Turkey" (J) (**30**)
- **11:** *Wedding Album* (J) (**178**)
- **12:** *Live Peace in Toronto* (J) (**10**)

1970

- **2:** *Hey Jude* (**2**)
  "Instant Karma" (J) (**3**)
- **3:** "Let It Be" (**1**)
  Sentimental Journey (R) (**22**)
- **4:** *McCartney* (P) (**1**)
- **5:** *Let It Be* (**1**)
  "The Long and Winding Road" (**1**)
  In the Beginning (**117**)
- **9:** *Beaucoups of Blues* (R) (**65**)
- **10:** "Beaucoups of Blues" (R) (**87**)
- **11:** *All Things Must Pass* (G) (**1**)
  "My Sweet Lord" (G) (**1**)
- **12:** *Plastic Ono Band* (J) (**6**)
  "Mother" (J) (**43**)

1971

- **2:** "What Is Life" (G) (**10**)
  "Another Day" (P) (**5**)
- **3:** "Power to the People" (J) (**11**)
- **4:** "It Don't Come Easy" (R) (**4**)
- **5:** *Ram* (P) (**2**)
- **8:** "Uncle Albert / Admiral Halsey" (P) (**1**)
- **10:** *Imagine* (J) (**1**)
  "Imagine" (J) (**3**)
- **12:** *Wild Life* (P) (**10**)
  "Happy Xmas" (J) (**42**)
  The Concert for Bangla Desh (G) (**1**)

1972

- **2:** "Give Ireland Back to the Irish" (P) (**21**)
- **3:** "Back Off Boogaloo" (R) (**9**)
  "Mary Had a Little Lamb" (P) (**28**)
- **4:** "Woman Is the Nigger of the World" (J) (**57**)
- **6:** "Sometime in New York City" (J) (**48**)
- **12:** "Hi Hi Hi" (P) (**10**)

1973

- **3:** "My Love" (P) (**1**)
- **4:** *1962–1966* (**3**)
  1967–1970 (**1**)
  Red Rose Speedway (P) (**1**)
- **5:** "Give Me Love (Give Me Peace on Earth)" (G) (**1**)
  Living in the Material World (G) (**1**)
- **6:** "Live and Let Die" (P) (**2**)

10: "Mind Games" (J) **(18)**
"Photograph" (R) **(1)**
10: "Helen Wheels" (P) **(10)**
11: *Mind Games* (J) **(9)**
Ringo (R) **(2)**
12: "You're Sixteen" (R) **(1)**
Band on the Run (P) **(1)**

1974

1: "Jet" (P) **(7)**
2: "Oh My My" (R) **(5)**
4: "Band on the Run" (P) **(1)**
9: "Whatever Gets You Thru the Night" (J) **(1)**
10: *Walls and Bridges* (J) **(1)**
"Junior's Farm" (P) **(3)**
11: *Goodnight Vienna* (R) **(8)**
"Only You (And You Alone)" (R) **(6)**
"Dark Horse" (G) **(15)**
12: "#9 Dream" (J) **(9)**
Dark Horse (G) **(4)**
"Ding Dong; Ding Dong" (G) **(36)**

1975

1: "No No Song" (R) **(3)**
2: *Rock 'n' Roll* (J) **(6)**
3: "Stand by Me" (J) **(20)**
5: *Venus and Mars* (P) **(1)**
"Listen to What the Man Said" (P) **(1)**
6: "Goodnight Vienna" (R) **(31)**
9: *Extra Texture* (G) **(8)**
"You" (G) **(20)**
10: *Shaved Fish* (J) **(12)**
"Letting Go" (P) **(39)**
11: "Venus and Mars Rock Show" (P) **(12)**
Blast from Your Past (R) **(30)**
12: "This Guitar (Can't Keep from Crying)" (G)

1976

3: *The Speed of Sound* (P) **(1)**
4: "Silly Love Songs" (P) **(1)**

5: "Got to Get You Into My Life" **(7)**
7: *Rock 'n' Roll Music* **(2)**
"Let 'Em In" (P) **(3)**
9: *Ringo's Rotogravure* (R) **(28)**
"A Dose of Rock 'n' Roll" (R) **(26)**
Thirty Three and 1/3 (G) **(11)**
11: "Hey Baby" (R) **(74)**
The Best of George Harrison (G) **(31)**
"This Song" (G) **(25)**
12: *Wings Over America* (P) **(1)**

1977

1: "Crackerbox Palace" (G) **(19)**
2: "Maybe I'm Amazed" (P) **(10)**
4: *Thrillington* (P)
5: "At the Hollywood Bowl" **(2)**
"Seaside Woman" (P) **(59)**
6: *Live at the Star Club* **(111)**
9: *Ringo the 4th* (R) **(162)**
"Drowning in the Sea of Love" (R)
10: *Love Songs* **(24)**
11: "Wings" (R)
"Girls School" (P) **(33)**

1978

3: *London Town* (P) **(2)**
"With a Little Luck" (P) **(1)**
4: *Bad Boy* (R) **(129)**
6: "I've Had Enough" (P) **(25)**
8: "London Town" (P) **(39)**
11: *Wings Greatest* (P) **(29)**

1979

2: *George Harrison* (G) **(14)**
"Blow Away" (G) **(16)**
3: "Goodnight Tonight" (P) **(5)**
5: "Love Comes to Everyone" (G)
6: *Back to the Egg* (P) **(8)**
"Getting Closer" (P) **(20)**
8: "Arrow Through Me" (P) **(29)**
11: "Wonderful Christmastime" (P) **(28)**

1980

3: *Rarities* **(21)**
4: "Coming Up" **(1)**
5: *McCartney II* (P) **(3)**
6: "Waterfalls" (P)
8: "Temporary Secretary" (P)
10: "(Just Like) Starting Over" (J) **(1)**
11: *Double Fantasy* (J) **(1)**
12: *McCartney Interview* (P) **(158)**

1981

1: "Woman" (J) **(2)**
3: "Watching the Wheels" (J) **(10)**
5: "All Those Years Ago" (G) **(2)**
6: *Somewhere in England* (G) **(11)**
7: "Teardrops" (G)
10: *Stop and Smell the Roses* (R) **(98)**
   "Wrack My Brain" (R) **(38)**

1982

3: *Reel Music* **(19)**
   "Ebony and Ivory" (P) **(1)**
4: *Tug of War* (P) **(1)**
7: "Take It Away" (P) **(10)**
9: "Tug of War" (P) **(53)**
10: *20 Greatest Hits* **(50)**
   "The Girl Is Mine" (P) **(2)**
11: *Lennon Collection* (J) **(33)**
   "Wake Up My Love" (G) **(53)**
   Gone Troppo (G) **(108)**

1983

2: "I Really Love You" (G)
6: "In My Car" (R)
10: "Say Say Say" (P) **(1)**
11: *Pipes of Peace* **(15)**

1984

1: *Milk and Honey* (J) **(11)**
   "Nobody Told Me" (J) **(5)**
3: "I'm Stepping Out" (J) **(55)**
5: "Borrowed Time" (J)
9: "No More Lonely Nights" (P) **(6)**
10: *Give My Regards To Broad Street* (P) **(21)**

1985

4: "I Don't Want to Do It" (G)
11: "Spies Like Us "(P) **(7)**

1986

2: *Live in New York City* (J) **(41)**
7: "Press" (P) **(21)**
8: *Press to Play* (P) **(30)**
10: "Stranglehold" (P) **(81)**
   Menlove Avenue (J) **(127)**

1987

10: "Got My Mind Set on You" (G) **(1)**
11: *Cloud Nine* (G) **(8)**
   All the Best (P) **(62)**

1988

1: "When We Was Fab" (G) **(23)**
3: *Past Masters 1* **(149)**
   Past Masters 2 **(121)**
6: "This Is Love" (G)
10: *Imagine: John Lennon* (J) **(31)**
   "Jealous Guy" (J) **(80)**
   Traveling Wilburys (G) **(3)**
   "Handle with Care" (G) **(45)**

1989

1: "End of the Line" (G) **(63)**
2: *Starr Struck: The Best of Ringo* (R)
5: "My Brave Face" (P) **(25)**
6: *Flowers in the Dirt* (P) **(21)**
7: "This One" (P) **(94)**
8: "Cheer Down" (G)
10: *The Best of Dark Horse* (G) **(132)**
11: "Figure of Eight" (P) **(92)**

1990

- 6: "Nobody's Child" (G)
- 10: *Lennon* (J)
  - *Ringo and the All-Starr Band* (R)
  - *Traveling Wilburys 3* (G) **(11)**
  - "Birthday" (P)
- 11: "She's My Baby" (G)
  - *Tripping the Live Fantastic* (P) **(26)**
  - *Tripping the Live Fantastic Highlights* (P) **(141)**

1991

- 3: "Wilbury Twist" (G)
- 5: *Unplugged* (P) **(14)**
- 10: *Liverpool Oratorio* (P) **(177)**
  - *Choba B Cccp* (P) **(109)**

1992

- 5: *Time Takes Time* (R)
  - "Weight of the World" (R)
- 7: *Live in Japan* (G) **(126)**
- 12: "Hope of Deliverance" (P) **(83)**

1993

- 2: *Off the Ground* (P) **(17)**
- 9: *Live from Montreux* (R)
- 11: *Strawberries Oceans Ships Forest* (P)
  - *Paul Is Live* (P) **(78)**

1994

- 12: *Beatles at the BBC* **(3)**

1995

- 4: "Baby It's You" **(67)**
- 11: *Anthology 1* **(1)**
- 12: "Free as a Bird" **(6)**

1996

- 3: *Anthology 2* **(1)**
  - "Real Love" **(11)**
- 10: *Anthology 3* **(1)**

1997

- 4: "The World Tonight" (P) **(64)**
- 5: *Flaming Pie* (P) **(2)**
- 8: *Ringo's All-Starr Band Volume 1* (R)
- 9: *Standing Stone* (P) **(194)**

1998

- 1: *Lennon Legend* (J) **(65)**
- 6: *Vertical Man* (R) **(61)**
- 9: *Rushes* (P)
- 10: *Storytellers* (R)
- 11: *Wonsaponatime* (J)
  - *Lennon Anthology* (J)

1999

- 9: *Yellow Submarine Songtrack* **(15)**
- 10: *I Wanna Be Santa Claus* (R)
  - *Run Devil Run* (P) **(26)**
- 11: *Working Classical* (P)

2000

- 11: *1* **(1)**

2001

- 2: *Anthology So Far* (R)
- 5: *Wingspan* (P) **(2)**
- 11: *Driving Rain* (P) **(26)**
  - "Freedom" (P) **(97)**

2002

- 2: *Instant Karma* (J)
- 8: *King Biscuit Presents* (R)
- 11: *Brainwashed* (G) **(18)**
  - *Back in the U.S.* (P) **(8)**

2003

- 3: *Ringo Rama* (R) **(113)**
- 4: *Extended Versions* (R)
- 11: *Let It Be…. Naked* **(5)**

2004

- **2:** *The Dark Horse Years* (G)
- **3:** *Tour 2003* (R)
- **11:** *Acoustic* (J) **(31)**
  The Capitol Albums Vol. 1 **(35)**

2005

- **6:** *Choose Love* (R)
  Twin Freaks (P)
- **7:** "Sgt. Pepper's Lonely Hearts Club Band" (P) **(48)**
- **8:** "Fine Line" (P)
- **9:** *Chaos & Creation in the Back Yard* (P) **(6)**
- **10:** *Working Class Hero* (J) **(135)**

2006

- **8:** *Ringo Starr and Friends* (R)
- **9:** *The US vs. John Lennon* (J)
  Ecce Cor Meum (P)
- **11:** *Love* **(4)**

2007

- **2:** *Remember* (J) **(44)**
- **4:** *The Capitol Albums Vol. 2* **(46)**
- **5:** "Ever Present Past" (P)
- **6:** *Traveling Wilburys Collection* (G) **(9)**
  "Dance Tonight" (P) **(69)**
  Memory Almost Full (P) **(3)**
- **8:** *Photograph* (R) **(130)**
- **10:** *Live at Soundstage* (R)

2008

- **1:** *Liverpool 8* (R) **(94)**
- **3:** *Ringo 5.1: Surround Sound* (R)
- **7:** *Live 2006* (R)
- **11:** *Electric Arguments* (P)

2009

- **6:** *Let It Roll* (G) **(24)**
- **9:** *The Beatles in Stereo* **(15)**
  The Beatles in Mono **(40)**
- **11:** *Good Evening NYC* (P) **(16)**

2010

- **1:** *Y Not* (R) **(58)**
- **7:** *Live at the Greek* (R)
- **10:** *Remember* **(44)**
  Power to the People (J) **(24)**
  Gimme Some Truth (J) **(196)**
  Signature Box (J) **(148)**

2011

- **10:** *Ocean's Kingdom* (P) **(143)**

2012

- **1:** *Ringo 2012* (R) **(80)**
- **2:** *Kisses on the Bottom* (P) **(5)**
- **5:** *Early Takes* (G) **(20)**
- **8:** *Tomorrow Never Knows* **(24)**

2013

- **10:** *New* (P) **(3)**
  "New" (P)
- **11:** *On Air: Live at the BBC 2* **(7)**
- **12:** *Bootleg Recordings 63* **(172)**

2014

- **1:** *The U.S. Albums* **(48)**
- **9:** *Icon* (J)
  The Apple Years (G) **(167)**

2015

- **1:** "FourFiveSeconds" (P) **(4)**
- **3:** *Postcards from Paradise* (R) **(99)**

2016

- **6:** *Pure McCartney* (P) **(15)**

2017
9: "Give More Love" (R) **(128)**

2018
6: "Come on to Me" (P)
8: "Fuh You" (P)
9: *Egypt Station* (P) **(1)**

2019
1: "Get Enough" (P)
7: *Amoeba Gig* (P)
10: *What's My Name* (R) **(127)**

2020
9: *Gimme Some Truth* (J) **(186)**
12: *McCartney III* (P) **(2)**

2021
3: *Zoom In* (R) **(179)**
4: *McCartney III Imagined* (P) **(19)**
9: *Change the World* (R)

The Charts

Now that we've finished our countdowns and have analyzed everything to death, let's look at the actual charts themselves that were used to compile the countdowns.

As I pointed out as we began, the charts have not been compiled in the same way over the years, so you'll see lots of B-sides on there up until late 1969. Because the charts back then were based primarily on radio play, songs would zoom up the chart and then zoom back down again. By the '70s, sales meant more, so the songs would stay on the chart longer. And these days, streaming and YouTube plays count as well.

So keep in mind one of the themes of this book: Despite how much fun it is to look at this countdown, it is far from scientifically valid, since the methods of creating the charts has changed so much.

So here's how you read these charts: Billboard did its charts weekly and the date of the chart is at the top, with the placement of the song or album listed appropriately. Albums are all in capital letters. Solo records are listed by the initial of the Beatle responsible (even if a group effort, such as the Traveling Wilburys or Wings). The top singles chart goes from 1 to 100 and the top album chart goes up to 200.

What is fascinating about examining the charts this way is that it becomes clearer how often The Beatles were on the charts, how close together some of the songs and albums were released, and how they competed against each other in their solo years. Since I've listed every single week—even when there was no Beatles album or single on the charts—it's also interesting to note how infrequent was their absence from the charts.

And, if you don't like the countdown because you think a song hitting #1 should get extra points or something, well, the data is here for you to make your own chart(s)!

1964	1/4	1/11	1/18	1/25	2/1	2/8	2/15	2/22	2/29	3/7
I Want to Hold Your Hand			45	3	1	1	1	1	1	1
She Loves You				69	21	7	2	2	2	2
Please Please Me				68	57	45	29	6	4	
I Saw Her Standing There						68	54	35	28	18
My Bonnie							67	54	42	31
From Me to You										86
MEET THE BEATLES!				92	3	1	1	1	1	
INTRODUCING THE BEATLES					59	22	3	2	2	
BEATLES W/ TONY SHERIDAN						147	147	142	128	

1964	3/14	3/21	3/28	4/4	4/11	4/18	4/25	5/2	5/9	5/16
I Want to Hold Your Hand	1	2	2	4	7	19	24			
She Loves You	2	1	1	3	4	8	19	36		
Please Please Me	3	3	4	5	9	16	29			
I Saw Her Standing There	15	14	26	31	38	45				
My Bonnie	26	42								
From Me to You	73	58	50	41	52					
Twist and Shout	55	7	3	2	2	2	2	7	11	20
Roll Over Beethoven		79	75	68	78					
Can't Buy Me Love			27	1	1	1	1	1	5	11
All My Loving			71	58	50	48	45	59		
Do You Want to Know a Secret			78	46	14	5	3	3	2	5
You Can't Do That				65	48	55	60			
Thank You Girl				79	61	49	37	40	35	49
There's a Place					74					
Love Me Do					81	73	67	32	12	3
Why						88				
P.S. I Love You									64	33
MEET THE BEATLES!	1	1	1	1	1	1	1	2	2	3
INTRODUCING THE BEATLES	2	2	2	2	2	2	2	4	7	7
BEATLES W/ TONY SHERIDAN	121	103	87	77	70	68	68	83	106	146
JOLLY WHAT!				135	112	104	105	113	119	
THE BEATLES' 2ND ALBUM							16	1	1	1

1964	5/23	5/30	6/6	6/13	6/20	6/27	7/4	7/11	7/18	7/25
Twist and Shout	41									
Can't Buy Me Love	23	42								
Do You Want to Know a Secret	12	19	36							
Love Me Do	2	1	2	4	7	11	19	24		
P.S. I Love You	15	11	10	15	22	37				
Four By The Beatles				97	97	92				
Sie Liebt Dich					97					
A Hard Day's Night									21	2
Ain't She Sweet									90	67
I Should Have Known Better										75
And I Love Her										80
MEET THE BEATLES!	5	5	6	7	9	9	14	14	18	25
INTRODUCING THE BEATLES	8	10	11	12	14	17	17	20	26	31
THE BEATLES' 2ND ALBUM	1	1	4	4	4	4	4	5	7	9
A HARD DAY'S NIGHT									12	1

The Charts

1964	8/1	8/8	8/15	8/22	8/29	95	9/12	9/19	9/26	10/3
A Hard Day's Night	1	1	3	3	4	8	8	12	19	24
Ain't She Sweet	40	25	22	19	24	30	37			
I Should Have Known Better	66	59	53							
And I Love Her	65	40	27	17	13	12	12	28		
I'll Cry Instead	62	44	34	29	25	34	36			
If I Fell	92	87	72	57	54	53	59	55	59	
Matchbox						81	42	32	23	18
Slow Down						99	67	55	32	27
MEET THE BEATLES!	31	32	43	46	48	49	56	54	46	44
INTRODUCING THE BEATLES	33	37	48	56	61	73	72	75	70	67
THE BEATLES' 2ND ALBUM	9	9	11	17	20	25	26	35	30	29
A HARD DAY'S NIGHT	1	1	1	1	1	1	1	1	1	1
SOMETHING NEW		125	6	2	2	2	2	2	2	2

1964	10/10	10/17	10/24	10/31	11/7	11/14	11/21	11/28	12/5	12/12
A Hard Day's Night	50									
Matchbox	18	17	52							
Slow Down	25	39								
I Feel Fine									22	5
She's a Woman									46	29
MEET THE BEATLES!	52	53	57	57	56	55	60	64	65	62
INTRODUCING THE BEATLES	78	82	93	96	97	99	104	107	111	112
THE BEATLES 2ND ALBUM	37	39	42	48	61	63	69	73	75	71
A HARD DAY'S NIGHT	1	1	1	3	3	3	3	4	4	8
SOMETHING NEW	2	2	4	4	4	5	6	6	7	10
BEATLES VS. FOUR SEASONS	147	142	145							
SONGS PICTURES STORIES				121	115	87	76	71	63	66
THE BEATLES' STORY										97

1964 / 1965	12/19	12/26	1/2	1/9	1/16	1/23	1/30	2/6	2/13	2/20
I Feel Fine	2	1	1	1	2	4	11	22	40	
She's a Woman	14	4	4	11	12	14	37			
Eight Days a Week										53
I Don't Want to Spoil the Party										81
MEET THE BEATLES!	73	69	65	57	56	52	51	49	50	66
INTRODUCING THE BEATLES	141	146								
THE BEATLES 2ND ALBUM	70	70	72	69	64	62	62	63	69	72
A HARD DAY'S NIGHT	6	6	5	5	6	11	11	13	14	18

The Charts

SOMETHING NEW	14	13	17	21	23	27	27	31	41	44
SONGS PICTURES STORIES	117	138								
THE BEATLES' STORY	7	7	7	7	16	16	29	46	62	86
BEATLES '65	98	1	1	1	1	1	1	1	1	1

1965	2/27	3/6	3/13	3/20	3/27	4/3	4/10	4/17	4/24	5/1
Eight Days a Week	19	5	1	1	4	7	11	17	38	
I Don't Want to Spoil the Party	59	47	44	39	44					
4 By The Beatles	81	77	73	70	68					
Ticket to Ride									59	18
Yes It Is										71
MEET THE BEATLES!	50	66	67	71	81	83	100	104	109	118
THE BEATLES 2ND ALBUM	69	72	80	85	89	91	94	96	100	105
A HARD DAY'S NIGHT	14	18	21	21	23	28	37	40	44	51
SOMETHING NEW	41	44	44	47	49	54	61	74	87	90
THE BEATLES' STORY	62	86	86	91	102	108				
BEATLES '65	1	1	3	3	3	3	3	7	9	12
THE EARLY BEATLES									132	110

1965	5/8	5/15	5/22	5/29	6/5	6/12	6/19	6/26	7/3	7/10
Ticket to Ride	3	3	1	2	5	9	11	20	47	
MEET THE BEATLES!	120	116	114	114	121					
THE BEATLES 2ND ALBUM	112									
A HARD DAY'S NIGHT	49	48	48	50	64	74	100	124	134	
SOMETHING NEW	117	121								
BEATLES '65	13	12	13	17	21	22	30	33	29	25
THE EARLY BEATLES	91	76	58	54	46	43	45	56	55	53
BEATLES VI								149	48	1

1965	7/24	7/31	8/7	8/14	8/21	8/28	9/4	9/11	9/18	9/25
Help!			41	14	3	2	1	1	1	5
Yesterday										45
Act Naturally										87
BEATLES '65	28	28	33	35	38	38	39	37	36	39
THE EARLY BEATLES	69	83	90	109	113	124	130	130	136	142
BEATLES VI	1	1	1	1	2	2	4	8	9	10
HELP!					148	61	1	1	1	

The Charts

1965	10/2	10/9	10/16	10/23	10/30	11/6	11/13	11/20	11/27	12/4
Help!	11	15	22	29	32					
Yesterday	3	1	1	1	1	3	11	13	26	45
Act Naturally	72	51	49	47	47	54				
BEATLES '65	43	48	51	56	59	61	76	86	87	104
THE EARLY BEATLES	145	147	148	144	137	134	121	121	118	125
BEATLES VI	10	18	19	21	21	19	25	26	32	51
HELP!	1	1	1	1	1	1	2	3	4	4

1965 / 1966	12/11	12/18	12/25	1/1	1/8	1/15	1/22	1/29	2/5	2/12
We Can Work It Out		36	11	2	1	1	2	1	4	5
Day Tripper		56	28	18	10	6	5	13	22	36
BEATLES '65	110	110	113	98	96	145	147	147	143	136
THE EARLY BEATLES	128									
BEATLES VI	48	52	54	57	66	70	72	74	79	84
HELP!	7	9	11	15	17	18	16	11	14	17
RUBBER SOUL			106	60	1	1	1	1	1	1

1966	2/19	2/26	3/5	3/12	3/19	3/26	4/2	4/9	4/16	4/24
We Can Work It Out	13	24	48							
Day Tripper	47									
Nowhere Man			25	7	4	3	6	6	11	13
What Goes On				89	81					
BEATLES '65	131	121	101	104	104	106	110	113	113	110
BEATLES VI	80	78	75	70	84	86	123			
HELP!	22	26	28	30	31	28	27	28	29	31
RUBBER SOUL	2	2	3	4	4	5	7	7	12	14

1966	4/30	5/7	5/14	5/21	5/28	6/4	6/11	6/18	6/25	7/2
Nowhere Man	28									
Paperback Writer							28	15	1	2
Rain							72	42	29	24
BEATLES '65	133	146								
HELP!	42	45	57	78	80	91	93	95	128	
RUBBER SOUL	18	19	16	18	18	18	17	16	17	24

1966	7/9	7/16	7/23	7/30	8/6	8/13	8/20	8/27	9/3	9/10
Paperback Writer	1	5	6	12	18	37				
Rain	23	23	34							
Yellow Submarine							52	8	5	3
Eleanor Rigby								65	47	26
RUBBER SOUL	24	27	31	34	36	36	31	29	31	31
YESTERDAY AND TODAY			2	1	1	1	1	1	2	7
REVOLVER									45	1

1966	9/17	9/24	10/1	10/8	10/15	10/22	10/29	11/5	11/12	11/19
Yellow Submarine	2	4	8	16	32					
Eleanor Rigby	14	11	11	21	37					
RUBBER SOUL	33	36	35	58	82	88	95	105	106	101
YESTERDAY AND TODAY	8	15	19	30	39	39	42	48	45	49
REVOLVER	1	1	1	1	1	2	2	5	8	7

1966 / 1967	11/26	12/3	12/10	12/17	12/24	12/31	1/7	1/14	1/21	1/28
RUBBER SOUL	110	113	119							
YESTERDAY AND TODAY	51	56	63	72	108	118	130	132	134	138
REVOLVER	8	6	9	13	13	12	17	18	20	23

1967	2/4	2/11	2/18	2/25	3/4	3/11	3/18	3/25	4/1	4/8
Penny Lane				83	36	5	1	3	3	6
Strawberry Fields Forever				85	45	16	11	11	8	15
YESTERDAY AND TODAY	136									
REVOLVER	24	27	29	48	51	52	72	78	77	69

1967	4/15	4/22	4/29	5/6	5/13	5/20	5/27	6/3	6/10	6/17
Penny Lane	12	21	25							
Strawberry Fields Forever	21	28								
REVOLVER	65	60	60	65	90	135	135	130	128	123

1967	6/24	7/1	7/8	7/15	7/22	7/29	8/5	8/12	8/19	8/26
All You Need is Love				71	29	3	2	1	2	
Baby You're a Rich Man					64	41	34	38	41	
REVOLVER	123	135	138	138	159	160	157	156	155	153
SERGEANT PEPPER	8	1	1	1	1	1	1	1	1	1

The Charts

1967	9/2	9/9	9/16	9/23	9/30	10/7	10/14	10/21	10/28	11/4
All You Need Is Love	2	6	8	24	48					
REVOLVER	146	143	134	137	136	136	131	128	123	121
SERGEANT PEPPER	1	1	1	1	1	1	2	3	2	2

1967 / 1968	11/11	11/18	11/25	12/2	12/9	12/16	12/23	12/30	1/6	1/13
Hello Goodbye				45	8	3	3	1	1	1
I Am the Walrus					64	57	56	75		
REVOLVER	122	135	136	142	143	146	151	153	153	153
SERGEANT PEPPER	2	2	2	4	4	3	3	3	5	5
MAGICAL MYSTERY TOUR							157	4	1	1

1968	1/20	1/27	2/3	2/10	2/17	2/24	3/2	3/9	3/16	3/23
Hello Goodbye	3	6	12	31						
Lady Madonna										23
REVOLVER	152	154	157	161	163	159				
SERGEANT PEPPER	6	6	6	13	12	17	17	16	16	14
MAGICAL MYSTERY TOUR	1	1	1	1	1	1	3	4	4	6

1968	3/30	4/6	4/13	4/20	4/27	5/4	5/11	5/18	5/25	6/1
Lady Madonna	9	7	6	4	4	4	10	15	31	44
The Inner Light	96									
SERGEANT PEPPER	14	28	29	35	33	42	51	52	47	45
MAGICAL MYSTERY TOUR	6	15	15	20	21	19	19	17	15	25

1968	6/8	6/15	6/22	6/29	7/6	7/13	7/20	7/27	8/3	8/10
SERGEANT PEPPER	43	38	34	33	31	29	27	33	34	37
MAGICAL MYSTERY TOUR	25	30	32	32	33	34	36	75	79	82

1968	8/17	8/24	8/31	9/7	9/14	9/21	9/28	10/5	10/12	10/19
Hey Jude					10	3	1	1	1	1
Revolution					38	12	12	12	15	17
SERGEANT PEPPER	37	39	45	52	47	46	42	41	55	64
MAGICAL MYSTERY TOUR	80	92	95	95	93	92	82	71	91	92

1968	10/26	11/2	11/9	11/16	11/23	11/30	12/7	12/14	12/21	12/28
Hey Jude	1	1	1	1	1	2	2	6	11	15
Revolution	17	19	19	20	29					
SERGEANT PEPPER	51	59	59	70	71	73	74	71	62	63
MAGICAL MYSTERY TOUR	100	100	101	101	99	98	91	91	85	85
THE BEATLES								11	2	1

1969	1/4	1/11	1/18	1/25	2/1	2/8	2/15	2/22	3/1	3/8
Hey Jude	23	30	38							
SERGEANT PEPPER	66	56	65	65	81	113	131	166		
MAGICAL MYSTERY TOUR	71	75	109	112	132					
THE BEATLES	1	1	1	1	1	2	1	1	1	2
WONDERWALL MUSIC (G)		197	189	149	72	58	56	51	49	49
YELLOW SUBMARINE						86	6	3	2	4
TWO VIRGINS (J)										158

1969	3/15	3/22	3/29	4/5	4/12	4/19	4/26	5/3	5/10	5/17
Get Back									10	3
Don't Let Me Down									40	36
THE BEATLES	3	3	5	17	17	18	18	18	22	34
WONDERWALL MUSIC (G)	62	65	70	72	86	104	158			
YELLOW SUBMARINE	6	7	12	22	19	19	24	34	48	46
TWO VIRGINS (J)	149	147	147	126	126	124	125			

1969	5/24	5/31	6/7	6/14	6/21	6/28	7/5	7/12	7/19	7/26
Get Back	1	1	1	1	1	3	6	12	16	27
Don't Let Me Down	35	42								
The Ballad of John and Yoko				71	24	11	11	8	8	8
Give Peace a Chance (J)										62
THE BEATLES	34	39	52	49	45	58	58	57	65	72
YELLOW SUBMARINE	54	54	77	75	78	83	107	112	122	
LIFE WITH THE LIONS (J)						197	194	190	179	184
ELECTRONIC SOUND (G)						192	191			

1969	8/2	8/9	8/16	8/23	8/30	9/6	9/13	9/20	9/27	10/4
The Ballad of John and Yoko	10	29								
Give Peace a Chance (J)	43	23	20	15	15	14	29	34		

THE BEATLES	72	70	66	66	67	67	69	80	89	97
LIFE WITH THE LIONS (J)	174	174	179							

1969	10/11	10/18	10/25	11/1	11/8	11/15	11/22	11/29	12/6	12/13
Something		20	11	11	9	3	3			
Come Together		23	13	10	3	2	7			
Something / Come Together								1	3	4
Cold Turkey (J)						86	74	47	44	39
THE BEATLES	93	90	96	102	95	101	97	96	86	87
ABBEY ROAD		178	4	1	1	1	1	1	1	1
SERGEANT PEPPER						124	118	111	110	110
MAGICAL MYSTERY TOUR						146	134	129	129	127
WEDDING ALBUM (J)										182

1969 / 1970	12/20	12/27	1/3	1/10	1/17	1/24	1/31	2/7	2/14	2/21
Something / Come Together	6	7	12	16	20	22	29			
Cold Turkey (J)	35	33	33	33	30	32	46			
THE BEATLES	84	79	85	101	117	133	133	151	177	178
ABBEY ROAD	1	2	1	1	2	1	2	2	2	2
SERGEANT PEPPER	107	104	101	115	120	118	117	115	129	129
MAGICAL MYSTERY TOUR	120	113	109	123	127	127	127	126	124	124
WEDDING ALBUM (J)	180	178								
LIVE PEACE IN TORONTO (J)				136	71	17	14	10	10	16

1970	2/28	3/7	3/14	3/21	3/28	4/4	4/11	4/18	4/25	5/2
Instant Karma (J)	85	33	15	4	3	3	3	4	4	5
Let It Be				6	2	2	1	1	2	2
THE BEATLES	169	172								
ABBEY ROAD	2	3	3	6	7	7	7	8	9	15
SERGEANT PEPPER	133	160	148	150	165	166				
MAGICAL MYSTERY TOUR	190	187								
LIVE PEACE IN TORONTO (J)	20	22	18	18	17	24	24	29	41	42
HEY JUDE				3	2	2	2	2	3	3

1970	5/9	5/16	5/23	5/30	6/6	6/13	6/20	6/27	7/4	7/11
Instant Karma (J)	8	18	27							
Let It Be	3	4	6	10	21	23	44			
The Long and Winding Road			35	12	10	1	1	4	4	8

ABBEY ROAD	20	29	30	34	51	50	50	53	53	49
LIVE PEACE IN TORONTO (J)	54	87	90	90	89	92	99	119	174	174
HEY JUDE	3	4	6	7	35	32	25	34	32	38
McCARTNEY (P)	14	3	1	1	1	2	2	2	2	3
SENTIMENTAL JOURNEY (R)		51	26	25	28	28	22	34	58	89
IN THE BEGINNING		145	142	142	154	117	117	149		
LET IT BE					104	2	1	1	1	2

1970	7/18	7/25	8/1	8/8	8/15	8/22	8/29	9/5	9/12	9/19
The Long and Winding Road	20	21								
ABBEY ROAD	54	52	52	55	68	71	76	80	93	108
LIVE PEACE IN TORONTO (J)	171	167	168	175	179					
HEY JUDE	53	57	77	76	78	78	75	90	110	112
McCARTNEY (P)	3	3	5	5	12	13	16	19	18	25
SENTIMENTAL JOURNEY (R)	120	128	130	142	144					
LET IT BE	2	2	6	4	11	11	12	14	26	24
SERGEANT PEPPER		159	160	163	161					
MAGICAL MYSTERY TOUR		194	192							

1970	9/26	10/3	10/10	10/17	10/24	10/31	11/7	11/14	11/21	11/28
Beaucoups of Blues (R)							100	96	94	87
My Sweet Lord (G)										72
ABBEY ROAD	105	122	123	122	119	134	126	123	127	131
HEY JUDE	107	143	147	144	151	160				
McCARTNEY (P)	48	48	68	61	68	70	83	88	88	99
LET IT BE	33	37	40	40	50	46	57	56	82	79
BEAUCOUPS OF BLUES (R)				141	92	75	73	71	65	76
ALL THINGS MUST PASS (G)										
JOHN LENNON (J)										

1970 / 1971	12/5	12/12	12/19	12/26	1/2	1/9	1/16	1/23	1/30	2/6
Beaucoups of Blues (R)	87									
My Sweet Lord (G)	13	6	2	1	1	1	1	2	2	3
Mother (J)					87	60	45	43	43	
ABBEY ROAD	131	138	140	136	136	137	131	124	122	122
McCARTNEY (P)	103	110	111	105	101	100	100	101	105	104
LET IT BE	75	74	86	83	90	94	99	93	93	94
BEAUCOUPS OF BLUES (R)	84	99	99	112	164	182	184	189		

ALL THINGS MUST PASS (G)		5	2	1	1	1	1	1	1
JOHN LENNON (J)			14	12	9	9	8	6	12

1971	2/13	2/20	2/27	3/6	3/13	3/20	3/27	4/3	4/10	4/17
My Sweet Lord (G)	6	16	36							
Mother (J)	55									
What Is Life (G)			66	27	19	15	10	14	14	18
Another Day (P)				55	36	20	14	10	8	5
Power to the People (J)								73	40	28
ABBEY ROAD	126	136	138	142	142	152	151	166	174	169
McCARTNEY (P)	112	121	131	123	119	120	124			
LET IT BE	98	115	111	107	112	117	122	124	132	142
ALL THINGS MUST PASS (G)	1	3	6	7	11	9	9	13	15	19
JOHN LENNON (J)	12	12	29	32	36	44	42	60	63	93

1971	4/24	5/1	5/8	5/15	5/22	5/29	6/5	6/12	6/19	6/26
What Is Life (G)	33									
Another Day (P)	5	8	8	5	5	8	14	20	39	
Power to the People (J)	15	11	11	15	31	37				
It Don't Come Easy (R)		49	24	13	8	5	4	4	5	7
ABBEY ROAD	175	174	171	176						
LET IT BE	168	170	160	166	162	160	155	164		
ALL THINGS MUST PASS (G)	24	37	40	38	45	56	53	73	87	119
JOHN LENNON (J)	88	106	109	112	131					
RAM (P)							6	4	3	3

1971	7/3	7/10	7/17	7/24	7/31	8/7	8/14	8/21	8/28	9/4
It Don't Come Easy (R)	10	12	28							
Uncle Albert Admiral Halsey (P)							65	21	12	1
Bangla Desh (G)							67	43	31	24
ALL THINGS MUST PASS (G)	132	130	152	152	165	160	160	154	180	176
RAM (P)	4	4	5	5	4	3	4	2	2	3

1971	9/11	9/18	9/25	10/2	10/9	10/16	10/23	10/30	11/6	11/13
Uncle Albert Admiral Halsey (P)	5	5	6	6	7	7	13	18	26	
Bangla Desh (G)	23	23	31							
Imagine (J)						20	6	4	3	

RAM (P)	5	5	4	5	6	7	9	9	9	9
IMAGINE (J)		163	134	10	3	2	2	1	4	4
WILD LIFE (P)										

1971 / 1972	11/20	11/27	12/4	12/11	12/18	12/25	1/1	1/8	1/15	1/22
Imagine (J)	3	6	10	13	23					
RAM (P)	19	19	22	28	53	56	69	89	84	93
IMAGINE (J)	4	4	6	7	9	18	22	29	35	39
WILD LIFE (P)					25	13	11	11	10	
CONCERT BANGLA DESH (G)							14	4	2	

1972	1/29	2/5	2/12	2/19	2/26	3/4	3/11	3/18	3/25	4/1
Give Ireland Back to Irish (P)							78	63	37	22
Back Off Boogaloo (R)										88
RAM (P)	104	128	144							
IMAGINE (J)	48	54	61	73	86	84	92	89	101	128
WILD LIFE (P)	10	19	22	25	34	51	51	53	59	58
CONCERT BANGLA DESH (G)	2	2	2	2	3	2	3	9	11	11

1972	4/8	4/15	4/22	4/29	5/6	5/13	5/20	5/27	6/3	6/10
Give Ireland Back to Irish (P)	21	30	30	35						
Back Off Boogaloo (R)	42	31	19	11	10	9	9	23	47	
Woman Is the Nigger ... (J)							76	65	61	57
IMAGINE (J)	175									
WILD LIFE (P)	81	101	148							
CONCERT BANGLA DESH (G)	18	20	20	19	19	17	24	21	25	33

1972	6/17	6/24	7/1	7/8	7/15	7/22	7/29	8/5	8/12	8/19
Woman Is the Nigger ... (J)	71									
Mary Had a Little Lamb (P)	85	58	43	38	29	28	35			
CONCERT BANGLA DESH (G)	42	43	45	58	57	70	84	101	106	107
SOMETIME IN NYC (J)			190	90	65	58	50	49	48	48

1972	8/26	9/2	9/9	9/16	9/23	9/30	10/7	10/14	10/21	10/28
CONCERT BANGLA DESH (G)	107	112	112	113	123	141	150	171		
SOMETIME IN NYC (J)	56	61	88	88	91	103	117	132	142	

The Charts

1972 / 1973	11/4	11/11	11/18	11/25	12/2	12/9	12/16	12/23	12/30	1/6
Hi Hi Hi (P)							100	42	27	22

1973	1/13	1/20	1/27	2/3	2/10	2/17	2/24	3/3	3/10	3/17
Hi Hi Hi (P)	18	12	11	10	17	24	38			

1973	3/24	3/31	4/7	4/14	4/21	4/28	5/5	5/12	5/19	5/26
My Love (P)				73	62	36	26	13	6	2
Give Me Love (G)									59	34
1962–1966				94	23	9	6	4	3	3
1967–1970				97	24	10	7	5	2	1
RED ROSE SPEEDWAY (P)								127	32	13

1973	6/2	6/9	6/16	6/23	6/30	7/7	7/14	7/21	7/28	8/4
My Love (P)	1	1	1	1	2	3	9	21	31	40
Give Me Love (G)	14	13	8	5	1	4	5	6	10	31
Live and Let Die (P)						69	44	29	21	3
1962–1966	5	5	5	11	13	17	17	20	21	24
1967–1970	3	2	2	5	6	8	11	14	17	21
RED ROSE SPEEDWAY (P)	1	1	1	2	2	3	5	5	10	19
MATERIAL WORLD (G)			11	1	1	1	1	1	3	4

1973	8/11	8/18	8/25	9/1	9/8	9/15	9/22	9/29	10/6	10/13
My Love (P)	59									
Give Me Love (G)	45	57								
Live and Let Die (P)	2	2	2	5	7	9	17	27	36	
Photograph (R)									74	60
1962–1966	29	39	49	47	49	52	57	60	64	68
1967–1970	24	26	35	35	39	42	54	57	61	62
RED ROSE SPEEDWAY (P)	21	22	31	32	48	48	63	66	84	85
MATERIAL WORLD (G)	14	17	21	31	36	38	39	38	69	72

1973	10/20	10/27	11/3	11/10	11/17	11/24	12/1	12/8	12/15	12/22
Photograph (R)	29	18	11	6	4	1	2	5	8	13
Mind Games (J)				76	60	41	30	24	20	19
Helen Wheels (P)						56	42	31	24	20
You're Sixteen (R)									75	50

1962–1966	72	84	86	88	111	111	110	124	123	120
1967–1970	68	75	82	87	86	88	88	89	89	87
RED ROSE SPEEDWAY (P)	94	98	112	140	167	163	191	188		
MATERIAL WORLD (G)	73	94	100	134	136	143	149	184		
RINGO (R)					15	3	2	2	4	3
MIND GAMES (J)					16	11	9	9	9	
BAND ON THE RUN (P)										33

1973 / 1974	12/29	1/5	1/12	1/19	1/26	2/2	2/9	2/16	2/23	3/2
Photograph (R)	28	32	45	74						
Mind Games (J)	18	25	29	34	44	60				
Helen Wheels (P)	16	12	10	12	17	20	37	58		
You're Sixteen (R)	27	16	6	5	1	2	3	3	9	11
Jet (P)							69	47	27	20
1962–1966	115	113	109	108	119	122	124	126	129	129
1967–1970	85	81	79	81	87	96	98	108	109	112
RINGO (R)	6	8	9	13	13	15	15	15	20	22
MIND GAMES (J)	10	18	19	24	29	34	41	49	72	85
BAND ON THE RUN (P)	21	14	13	9	8	7	9	8	9	9

1974	3/9	3/16	3/23	3/30	4/6	4/13	4/20	4/27	5/4	5/11
You're Sixteen (R)	20	34	47							
Jet (P)	14	10	8	7	11	14	27	38	47	48
Oh My My (R)	65	44	28	19	12	9	6	5	13	17
Band on the Run (P)							68	41	22	14
1962–1966	134	137	131	125	119	111	116	123	120	128
1967–1970	114	115	109	102	101	95	97	101	104	119
RINGO (R)	25	29	40	42	44	44	45	49	49	50
MIND GAMES (J)	118	149	187							
BAND ON THE RUN (P)	8	8	7	5	2	1	2	4	7	7

1974	5/18	5/25	6/1	6/8	6/15	6/22	6/29	7/6	7/13	7/20
Oh My My (R)	26	31	38	52						
Band on the Run (P)	7	5	2	1	5	6	8	17	15	26
1962–1966	144	140	132	134	130	126	128	124	118	123
1967–1970	128	125	119	119	115	117	111	104	98	105
RINGO (R)	51	52	62	66	76	94	117	150	160	171
BAND ON THE RUN (P)	6	4	2	1	1	2	2	1	4	4

The Charts

1974	7/27	8/3	8/10	8/17	8/24	8/31	9/7	9/14	9/21	9/28
Band on the Run (P)	40	60	70	95						
Whatever Gets You Thru (J)										53
1962–1966	132	136	129	126	137	147	154	181	193	200
1967–1970	107	110	120	124	129	140	146	162	172	195
RINGO (R)	193									
BAND ON THE RUN (P)	7	8	10	10	10	13	14	24	38	48

1974	10/5	10/12	10/19	10/26	11/2	11/9	11/16	11/23	11/30	12/7
Whatever Gets You Thru (J)	33	24	18	12	6	3	1	12	21	40
Junior's Farm (P)						59	43	28	15	12
Only You (R)						63	53	34	25	
Dark Horse (G)							69	53	43	
BAND ON THE RUN (P)	45	42	61	70	82	103	126	141	134	159
WALLS AND BRIDGES (J)		72	21	12	4	2	1	6	4	4
GOODNIGHT VIENNA (R)									70	29

1974 / 1975	12/14	12/21	12/28	1/4	1/11	1/18	1/25	2/1	2/8	2/15
Whatever Gets You Thru (J)	40	56	64	79						
Junior's Farm / Sally G (P)	10	8	6	4	3	7	17	66	50	45
Only You (R)	18	14	9	7	6	12	27	35	56	
Dark Horse (G)	32	24	20	16	15	33	49			
#9 Dream (J)		68	58	47	35	29	21	17	13	10
Ding Dong; Ding Dong (G)					81	59	46	38	36	49
No No Song (R)									78	58
BAND ON THE RUN (P)	164	178	183	191	186	196	199	200	200	195
WALLS AND BRIDGES (J)	10	20	29	42	62	73	97	97	93	98
GOODNIGHT VIENNA (R)	21	13	10	9	8	8	10	22	36	40
DARK HORSE (G)			58	21	13	5	4	7	6	5

1975	2/22	3/1	3/8	3/15	3/22	3/29	4/5	4/12	4/19	4/26
Junior's Farm / Sally G (P)	39	64								
#9 Dream (J)	9	13	47							
No No Song (R)	40	31	25	14	9	6	3	3	4	24
Stand By Me (J)				78	67	52	36	30	24	20
BAND ON THE RUN (P)	194	185	195	198	196	199	196	197	199	196
WALLS AND BRIDGES (J)	89	81	119	130	164	189	186	186		
GOODNIGHT VIENNA (R)	38	45	44	60	56	50	65	90	103	104

DARK HORSE (G)	11	22	45	50	79	101	122	147	158
ROCK AND ROLL (J)			47	18	12	10	8	7	6	9

1975	5/3	5/10	5/17	5/24	5/31	6/7	6/14	6/21	6/28	7/5
No No Song (R)	51	67								
Stand By Me (J)	20	49								
Listen to What the Man Said (P)					65	35	22	9	7	3
Goodnight Vienna (R)							82	36	52	39
BAND ON THE RUN (P)	199	197	199							
GOODNIGHT VIENNA (R)	118	144	170							
ROCK AND ROLL (J)	14	37	32	64	84	105	128			
VENUS AND MARS (P)							25	2	2	2

1975	7/12	7/19	7/26	8/2	8/9	8/16	8/23	8/30	9/6	9/13
Listen to What the Man Said (P)	3	1	5	8	12	17	44	57		
Goodnight Vienna (R)	31	31	63							
VENUS AND MARS (P)	2	1	2	5	6	11	15	18	26	37

1975	9/20	9/27	10/4	10/11	10/18	10/25	11/1	11/8	11/15	11/22
You (G)	75	49	41	33	25	23	20	20	39	91
Letting Go (P)			74	54	42	39	39	64		
Venus and Mars Rock Show (P)							82	60	36	27
VENUS AND MARS (P)	45	63	99	99	95	93	87	80	76	59
EXTRA TEXTURE (G)				34	10	8	8	8	9	12
SHAVED FISH (J)								97	37	21

1975 / 1976	11/29	12/6	12/13	12/20	12/27	1/3	1/10	1/17	1/24	1/31
Venus and Mars Rock Show (P)	17	14	12	36	97					
VENUS AND MARS (P)	47	35	32	32	48	76	74	80	92	126
EXTRA TEXTURE (G)	59	106	176	178						
SHAVED FISH (J)	16	13	12	29	47	73	73	79	125	135
BLAST FROM YOUR PAST (R)		176	59	48	39	35	32	30	30	48

1976	2/7	2/14	2/21	2/28	3/6	3/13	3/20	3/27	4/3	4/10
Silly Love Songs (P)										58
VENUS AND MARS (P)	180	191	197	196	200	198	192	188	192	188
SHAVED FISH (J)	183									

The Charts

BLAST FROM YOUR PAST (R)	91	149
AT THE SPEED OF SOUND (P)			32

1976	4/17	4/24	5/1	5/8	5/15	5/22	5/29	6/5	6/12	6/19
Silly Love Songs (P)	35	24	12	5	3	1	2	2	1	1
Got to Get You Into My Life									54	29
VENUS AND MARS (P)	186	165	160	138	110	100	92	78	68	55
AT THE SPEED OF SOUND (P)	3	1	2	2	2	2	1	2	2	1
THE BEATLES						171	130	118	93	83
BAND ON THE RUN (P)						183	164	153	138	124
1967–1970								177	98	88
1962–1966								179	97	87

1976	6/26	7/3	7/10	7/17	7/24	7/31	8/7	8/14	8/21	8/28
Silly Love Songs (P)	1	1	6	9	34	53	63	95		
Got to Get You Into My Life	18	12	10	8	7	7	7	19	23	38
Let 'Em In (P)		59	43	22	19	10	4	3	3	3
VENUS AND MARS (P)	53	50	55	69	69	69	76	94	90	90
AT THE SPEED OF SOUND (P)	1	1	1	1	2	3	6	8	7	6
THE BEATLES	68	57	57	70	85	82	82	75	73	87
BAND ON THE RUN (P)	120	110	108	105	112	110	117	118	162	166
1967–1970	74	64	54	53	58	60	60	54	54	59
1962–1966	73	63	56	56	64	72	70	64	62	75
ROCK 'N' ROLL MUSIC	8	5	2	2	8	8	8	7	6	13

1976	9/4	9/11	9/18	9/25	10/2	10/9	10/16	10/23	10/30	11/6
Got to Get You Into My Life	53	60	59	99						
Let 'Em In (P)	3	8	24	29	49	56	94			
A Dose of Rock 'n' Roll (R)					58	44	35	31	28	26
VENUS AND MARS (P)	106	153	155	152	199	197	195			
AT THE SPEED OF SOUND (P)	7	12	18	19	25	31	73	73	83	89
THE BEATLES	101	98	97	100	153	153	160	160	160	154
BAND ON THE RUN (P)	195	190	192	191	192	192	199	192	198	198
1967–1970	96	95	95	94	123	139	139	139	137	130
1962–1966	74	72	83	83	110	116	115	115	112	113
ROCK 'N' ROLL MUSIC	29	29	29	58	61	68	84	106	106	104
RINGO'S ROTOGRAVURE							57	37	33	30
SERGEANT PEPPER								174	164	161
ABBEY ROAD									170	165

1976 / 1977	11/13	11/20	11/27	12/4	12/11	12/18	12/25	1/1	1/8	1/15
A Dose of Rock 'n' Roll (R)	26	38	93							
Ob-La-Di, Ob-La-Da		79	69	59	49	49	71	71		
This Song (G)		82	63	53	38	33	27	27	25	25
AT THE SPEED OF SOUND (P)	116	158	158	158	178	198	194	194	189	176
THE BEATLES	150	179	180	176	176	178	178	178	178	180
BAND ON THE RUN (P)	198	199	198	198	195	194	190	190	180	175
1967–1970	187	187	186	185	185	191	198	198		
1962–1966	179	198	197	197			194			
ROCK 'N' ROLL MUSIC	168	195	195	195	193	192	199	198		
RINGO'S ROTOGRAVURE	28	28	28	57	161					
SERGEANT PEPPER	199				172	172	172	171	173	
ABBEY ROAD	165	194								
BEST GEORGE HARRISON (G)			67	56	34	32	31	31	52	50
THIRTY THREE & 1/3 (G)				69	17	15	15	13	11	
WINGS OVER AMERICA (P)					7	7	4	3		

1977	1/22	1/29	2/5	2/12	2/19	2/26	3/5	3/12	3/19	3/26
This Song (G)	32	64								
Crackerbox Palace (G)		66	49	39	34	30	26	24	20	19
Hey Baby (R)		90	80	74						
Maybe I'm Amazed (P)			59	37	26	20	15	13	11	
AT THE SPEED OF SOUND (P)	165	155	155	151	147	136	134	165	164	159
THE BEATLES	186									
BAND ON THE RUN (P)	175	168	178	183	173	152	152			
BEST GEORGE HARRISON (G)	111	130	141	147	143	145	143			
THIRTY THREE & 1/3 (G)	11	12	38	47	45	50	51	50	60	62
WINGS OVER AMERICA (P)	1	2	4	4	4	4	10	15	15	20
VENUS AND MARS (P)		190	183	193	183	181	199			

1977	4/2	4/9	4/16	4/23	4/30	5/7	5/14	5/21	5/28	6/4
Crackerbox Palace (G)	41	62								
Maybe I'm Amazed (P)	10	12	18	24	40	99				
33⅓ (G)	62	65	84	105	161					
WINGS OVER AMERICA (P)	15	13	12	31	54	54	54	54	61	103
MAGICAL MYSTERY TOUR		184	184	180	181					
AT THE HOLLYWOOD BOWL								13	5	3
1962–1966										176
1967–1970										177

1977	6/11	6/18	6/25	7/2	7/9	7/16	7/23	7/30	8/6	8/13
Seaside Woman (P)		83	72	62	62	59				
WINGS OVER AMERICA (P)	102	100	100	114	139	136	200	200	200	194
AT THE HOLLYWOOD BOWL	2	2	11	15	36	48	48	60	62	65
1962–1966	164	153	142	139	137	198	198			
1967–1970	154	144	131	129	129	137	139	142	146	174
LIVE AT THE STAR CLUB				171	161	123	113	111	150	191

1977	8/20	8/27	9/3	9/10	9/17	9/24	10/1	10/8	10/15	10/22
WINGS OVER AMERICA (P)	199	199	194	198	200	200	200	200	199	193
AT THE HOLLYWOOD BOWL	95	136	172	194						
RINGO THE 4TH (R)									179	169

1977	10/29	11/5	11/12	11/19	11/26	12/3	12/10	12/17	12/24	12/31
Girls School (P)				83	71	60	46	41	37	37
WINGS OVER AMERICA (P)	200	199	200	200	200	199	198	196	200	200
RINGO THE 4TH (R)	165	164	162	182						
LOVE SONGS			52	36	30	26	24	24	31	31

1978	1/7	1/14	1/21	1/28	2/4	2/11	2/18	2/25	3/4	3/11
Girls School (P)	34	33	59	95						
WINGS OVER AMERICA (P)	192	199	198	197	196	193	193	193	198	200
LOVE SONGS	61	61	60	66	86	114	128	128	163	198

1978	3/18	3/25	4/1	4/8	4/15	4/22	4/29	5/6	5/13	5/20
With a Little Luck (P)		70	57	17	12	7	5	5	3	1
WINGS OVER AMERICA (P)	200				189	166	165	199	198	195
LOVE SONGS	188	178	170	170	170	196				
LONDON TOWN (P)					20	8	3	2	2	2
BAD BOY (R)										159

1978	5/27	6/3	6/10	6/17	6/24	7/1	7/8	7/15	7/22	7/29
With a Little Luck (P)	1	4	9	17	26	56	61	71	96	
I've Had Enough (P)				81	71	61	48	40	30	27
WINGS OVER AMERICA (P)	195	195	192	192	200	200	199	200	191	200
LONDON TOWN (P)	2	2	2	3	4	13	18	25	24	31
BAD BOY (R)	149	139	129	129	192					

The Charts

1978	8/5	8/12	8/19	8/26	9/2	9/9	9/16	9/23	9/30	10/7
I've Had Enough (P)	25	25	53	90						
London Town (P)						75	65	55	48	42
Sgt Pepper / With a Little Help							87	83	71	71
WINGS OVER AMERICA (P)	198	200	200	200	196					
LONDON TOWN (P)	43	43	43	104	104	153	153	198	196	186
SERGEANT PEPPER		104	52	32	28	22	21	20	20	37
1967–1970			102	92	88	78	78	75	75	84
1962–1966				142	130	110	110	107	107	120
THE BEATLES					130	107	96	94	94	

1978	10/14	10/21	10/28	11/4	11/11	11/18	11/25	12/2	12/9	12/16
London Town (P)	39	39	89							
Sgt Pepper / With a Little Help	75	94	91							
LONDON TOWN (P)	186	196								
SERGEANT PEPPER	47	55	103	118	118	118	111	110	149	149
1967–1970	94	104	194							
1962–1966	117	127	124	188	188	188	199			
THE BEATLES	93	91	89	127	127	145	150	197		
WINGS GREATEST (P)									85	55

1978 / 1979	12/23	12/30	1/6	1/13	1/20	1/27	2/3	2/10	2/17	2/24
SERGEANT PEPPER	140	158	140	158	158	198	195			
WINGS GREATEST (P)	37	30	37	30	29	38	38	65	65	73

1979	3/3	3/10	3/17	3/24	3/31	4/7	4/14	4/21	4/28	5/5
Blow Away (G)	79	69	55	45	32	26	24	22	17	16
Goodnight Tonight (P)					38	16	13	11	9	8
WINGS GREATEST (P)	91	109	146	167	180	193				
GEORGE HARRISON (G)			28	17	15	15	15	15	14	17

1979	5/12	5/19	5/26	6/2	6/9	6/16	6/23	6/30	7/7	7/14
Blow Away (G)	16	37	91	91						
Goodnight Tonight (P)	6	5	5	5	13	17	33	43	80	99
Getting Closer (P)					64	51	37	31	25	
GEORGE HARRISON (G)	29	53	53	60	79	102	124	155	186	196
BACK TO THE EGG (P)							45	17	9	

The Charts

1979	7/21	7/28	8/4	8/11	8/18	8/25	9/1	9/8	9/15	9/22
Getting Closer (P)	23	20	20	74	75					
Arrow Through Me (P)						83	73	63	56	39
BACK TO THE EGG (P)	8	8	10	10	13	16	34	34	33	52

1979	9/29	10/6	10/13	10/20	10/27	11/3	11/10	11/17	11/24	12/1
Arrow Through Me (P)	33	30	29	46	93					
BACK TO THE EGG (P)	69	81	84	100	111	142	142	146	177	177

1979 / 1980	12/8	12/15	12/22	12/29	1/5	1/12	1/19	1/26	2/2	2/9
BACK TO THE EGG (P)	191									

1980	2/16	2/23	3/1	3/8	3/15	3/22	3/29	4/5	4/12	4/19
RARITIES									113	40

1980	4/26	5/3	5/10	5/17	5/24	5/31	6/7	6/14	6/21	6/28
Coming Up (P)	73	53	27	19	14	3	2	2	2	1
RARITIES	33	26	24	22	22	21	36	40	68	113
McCARTNEY II (P)								16	3	3

1980	7/5	7/12	7/19	7/26	8/2	8/9	8/16	8/23	8/30	9/6
Coming Up (P)	1	1	2	6	7	9	12	34	47	82
RARITIES	129	167	177							
McCARTNEY II (P)	3	3	3	10	10	18	19	31	40	48

1980	9/13	9/20	9/27	10/4	10/11	10/18	10/25	11/1	11/8	11/15
Coming Up (P)	93									
(Just Like) Starting Over (J)								38	32	10
McCARTNEY II (P)	103	103	109	139	159	192				

1980 / 1981	11/22	11/29	12/6	12/13	12/20	12/27	1/3	1/10	1/17	1/24
(Just Like) Starting Over (J)	9	8	6	4	3	1	1	1	1	1
Woman (J)									36	27
DOUBLE FANTASY (J)			25	12	11	1	1	1	1	1
1962–1966									82	71
1967–1970									83	70

SHAVED FISH (J)	84	69
SERGEANT PEPPER	86	75
IMAGINE (J)	92	77
RUBBER SOUL	96	86
MIND GAMES (J)	100	88
THE BEATLES		82

1981	1/31	2/7	2/14	2/21	2/28	3/7	3/14	3/21	3/28	4/4
(Just Like) Starting Over (J)	2	6	7	13	16	38	43	49	95	
Woman (J)	17	8	6	4	3	3	3	2	2	2
Watching the Wheels (J)									77	52
DOUBLE FANTASY (J)	1	1	1	2	2	2	4	4	4	5
1962–1966	65	63	62	71	82	85	87	95	105	112
1967–1970	64	59	58	66	66	83	79	87	85	101
SHAVED FISH (J)	62	60	57	60	59	80	78	104	108	127
SERGEANT PEPPER	75	73	81	107	114	115	119	133	150	150
IMAGINE (J)	67	66	63	72	84	84	84	103	107	119
RUBBER SOUL	86	86	83	114	124	124				
MIND GAMES (J)	88	88	86	86	100	100	108	126	132	147
THE BEATLES	72	72	69	67	68	76	77	106	120	126
ABBEY ROAD	117	107	97	95	93	96	104	107	113	114
WALLS AND BRIDGES (J)	151	140	130	130	130	132	199	199		
LOVE SONGS	154	154	149	163	165	169	174			
JOHN LENNON (J)	160	160	156	169	169	167				
McCARTNEY INTERVIEW (P)	169	158	158							

1981	4/11	4/18	4/25	5/2	5/9	5/16	5/23	5/30	6/6	6/13
Woman (J)	4	5	8	16	34	51	65	96		
Watching the Wheels (J)	38	33	25	17	13	11	10	10	17	25
All Those Years Ago (G)						33	16	11	7	
DOUBLE FANTASY (J)	6	9	9	9	9	9	9	20	20	43
1962–1966	115	133	133	133	143	161	160	184	197	
1967–1970	107	129	129	130	141	141	147	167		
SHAVED FISH (J)	144	177	177	174	172	199				
SERGEANT PEPPER	173									
IMAGINE (J)	143	194	198							
MIND GAMES (J)	170									
THE BEATLES	130	143	159	159	159	165	175	185	198	
ABBEY ROAD	125	136	137	145	146	158	153	164	182	

The Charts

1981	6/20	6/27	7/4	7/11	7/18	7/25	8/1	8/8	8/15	8/22
Watching the Wheels (J)	41	56	76	95	98					
All Those Years Ago (G)	5	5	2	2	2	11	21	42	51	81
DOUBLE FANTASY (J)	42	44	44	43	41	57	75	74	74	110
SOMEWHERE ENGLAND (G)	33	16	12	11	11	17	33	73	73	80

1981	8/29	9/5	9/12	9/26	10/3	10/10	10/17	10/24	10/31	11/7
All Those Years Ago (G)	87	95								
Wrack My Brain (R)										79
DOUBLE FANTASY (J)	116	131	131	128	149	194	192	196	195	194
SOMEWHERE ENGLAND (G)	108	123	163							

1981 / 1982	11/14	11/28	12/5	12/12	12/19	12/26	1/2	1/9	1/16	1/23
Wrack My Brain (R)	65	43	39	38	43	52	52	63	97	
DOUBLE FANTASY (J)	194	197	197	193	194	184	184	182	180	178
STOP & SMELL ROSES (R)	150	112	100	98	111	111	111	124	129	131

1982	1/30	2/6	2/13	2/20	2/27	3/6	3/13	3/20	3/27	4/3
Movie Medley									70	50
DOUBLE FANTASY (J)	177	172	199	199	194	196	173	150	140	140
STOP & SMELL ROSES (R)	184									

1982	4/10	4/17	4/24	5/1	5/8	5/15	5/22	5/29	6/5	6/12
Movie Medley	34	22	17	14	12	12	12	20	92	
Ebony and Ivory (P)	29	21	6	3	2	1	1	1	1	1
DOUBLE FANTASY (J)	164	177	177	182						
REEL MUSIC	40	33	27	22	19	19	19	35	78	96
1967–1970				181	169	155	148	146	156	186
1962–1966				184	174	161	153	153	155	182
TUG OF WAR (P)					15	3	1	1	1	1

1982	6/19	6/26	7/3	7/10	7/17	7/24	7/31	8/7	8/14	8/21
Ebony and Ivory (P)	1	1	3	8	27	48	55	92	99	
Take It Away (P)				55	31	23	18	14	12	10

REEL MUSIC	140	193							
1967–1970	193								
1962–1966	185	194							
TUG OF WAR (P)	2	2	2	6	9	12	20	29	29	29

1982	**8/28**	**9/4**	**9/11**	**9/18**	**9/25**	**10/2**	**10/9**	**10/16**	**10/23**	**10/30**
Take It Away (P)	10	10	10	10	11	66	88	98	98	
Tug of War (P)						75	64	58	53	53
TUG OF WAR (P)	28	30	30	41	41	41	55	63	99	99
20 GREATEST HITS										

1982 / 1983	**11/6**	**11/13**	**11/20**	**11/27**	**12/4**	**12/11**	**12/18**	**12/25**	**1/1**	**1/8**
Tug of War (P)	85	94	95							
The Girl is Mine (P)	45	36	14	9	8	5	4	3	3	2
Wake Up My Love (G)			68	60	53	53	100			
TUG OF WAR (P)	119	138	159	197						
20 GREATEST HITS		108	93	83	73	67	61	57	57	54
GONE TROPPO (G)				119	114	108	108	176	176	194
LENNON COLLECTION (J)					45	40	35	35	35	33

1983	**1/15**	**1/22**	**1/29**	**2/5**	**2/12**	**2/19**	**2/26**	**3/5**	**3/12**	**3/19**
The Girl is Mine (P)	2	2	5	16	34	82	91	97		
20 GREATEST HITS	50	50	62	65	75	106	138	159		
LENNON COLLECTION (J)	33	33	33	52	65	81	123	164	173	186

1983	**3/26**	**4/2**	**4/9**	**4/16**	**4/23**	**4/30**	**5/7**	**5/14**	**5/21**	**5/28**

1983	**6/4**	**6/11**	**6/18**	**6/25**	**7/2**	**7/9**	**7/15**	**7/23**	**7/30**	**8/6**

1983	**8/13**	**8/20**	**8/27**	**9/3**	**9/10**	**9/17**	**9/24**	**10/1**	**10/8**	**10/15**
Say Say Say (P)										26

1983	**10/22**	**10/29**	**11/5**	**11/12**	**11/19**	**11/26**	**12/3**	**12/10**	**12/17**	**12/24**
Say Say Say (P)	19	11	6	4	2	2	2	1	1	1
So Bad (P)										49
PIPES OF PEACE (P)					20	17	16	15	19	

The Charts

1983 / 1984	12/31	1/7	1/14	1/21	1/28	2/4	2/11	2/18	2/25	3/3
Say Say Say (P)	1	1	1	2	7	13	24	41	56	76
So Bad (P)	49	34	31	28	25	24	23	23	37	51
Nobody Told Me (J)				36	27	22	17	12	7	5
PIPES OF PEACE (P)	19	19	20	19	23	30	35	39	43	46
HEARTPLAY (J)			185	181	176	163	102	95	94	97
MILK AND HONEY (J)							39	17	13	12
1962–1966									179	163
1967–1970									188	165
ABBEY ROAD									195	180
THE BEATLES									198	168
SERGEANT PEPPER										179
MAGICAL MYSTERY TOUR										185
20 GREATEST HITS										186

1984	3/10	3/17	3/24	3/31	4/7	4/14	4/21	4/28	5/5	5/12
Say Say Say (P)	99									
So Bad (P)	61	84	98							
Nobody Told Me (J)	6	9	19	33	55	75	98			
I'm Steppin' Out (J)				82	64	57	55	88	100	
PIPES OF PEACE (P)	55	65	99	98	120	136	140	197		
HEARTPLAY (J)	109	113	157	189						
MILK AND HONEY (J)	11	13	14	18	24	31	51	67	76	76
1962–1966	139	136	143	141	144	145				
1967–1970	140	133	137	140	149	151	167			
ABBEY ROAD	150	144	149	147	173	175	181	179		
THE BEATLES	143	139	153	148	192	186	183	186		
SERGEANT PEPPER	161	159	164	166	186	179				
MAGICAL MYSTERY TOUR	178	186	183	199						
20 GREATEST HITS	165	146	142	158	155	157	158	172	200	197

1984	5/19	5/26	6/2	6/9	6/16	6/23	6/30	7/7	7/14	7/20
MILK AND HONEY (J)	93	98	134	156	188					

1984	7/28	8/4	8/11	8/18	8/25	9/1	9/8	9/15	9/22	9/29

1984	10/6	10/13	10/20	10/27	11/3	11/10	11/17	11/24	12/1	12/8
No More Lonely Nights (P)		48	38	30	25	19	14	11	10	6
BROAD STREET (P)					40	22	21	21	28	

The Charts

1984 / 1985	12/15	12/22	12/29	1/5	1/12	1/19	1/26	2/2	2/9	2/16
No More Lonely Nights (P)	6	8	8	15	23	35	66	86	97	
BROAD STREET (P)	36	35	35	37	36	45	56	69	92	102

1985	2/23	3/2	3/9	3/16	3/23	3/30	4/6	4/13	4/20	4/27
BROAD STREET (P)	134	141	187							

1985	5/4	5/11	5/18	5/25	6/1	6/8	6/15	6/22	6/29	7/6

1985	7/13	7/20	7/27	8/3	8/10	8/17	8/24	8/31	9/7	9/14

1985	9/21	9/28	10/5	10/12	10/19	10/26	11/2	11/9	11/16	11/23

1985 / 1986	11/30	12/7	12/14	12/21	12/28	1/4	1/11	1/18	1/25	2/1
Spies Like Us (P)	47	41	31	28	24	24	19	13	10	8

1986	2/8	2/15	2/22	3/1	3/8	3/15	3/22	3/29	4/5	4/12
Spies Like Us (P)	7	14	30	42	58	85				
LIVE IN NEW YORK CITY (J)							77	43	41	41

1986	4/19	4/26	5/3	5/10	5/17	5/24	5/31	6/7	6/14	6/21
LIVE IN NEW YORK CITY (J)	57	55	84	110	115	164	200			

1986	6/28	7/5	7/12	7/19	7/26	8/2	8/9	8/16	8/23	8/30
Press (P)						66	51	47	39	28
Twist and Shout							89	65	55	39

1986	9/6	9/13	9/20	9/27	10/4	10/11	10/18	10/25	11/1	11/8
Press (P)	26	21	21	32	50	72				
Twist and Shout	32	29	25	23	26	36	47	56	71	75
PRESS TO PLAY (P)		123	52	40	31	30	30	36	45	55

1986 / 1987	11/15	11/22	11/29	12/6	12/13	12/20	12/27	1/3	1/10	1/17
Twist and Shout	99									
Stranglehold (P)	97	84	81	81	95	100				
PRESS TO PLAY (P)	76	80	84	87	92	125	137	137	139	173
MENLOVE AVENUE (J)		193	127	127	175					

The Charts

1987	1/24	1/31	2/7	2/14	2/21	2/28	3/7	3/14	3/21	3/28
PRESS TO PLAY (P)	186	174	197							

1987	4/4	4/11	4/18	4/25	5/2	5/9	5/16	5/23	5/30	6/6

1987	6/13	6/20	6/27	7/4	7/11	7/18	7/25	8/1	8/8	8/15

1987	8/22	8/29	9/5	9/12	9/19	9/26	10/3	10/10	10/17	10/24
Got My Mind Set on You (G)										66
SERGEANT PEPPER		171	141	141	157	157	146	182		
THE BEATLES				179	141	96	87	87	134	145
YELLOW SUBMARINE						180				
MAGICAL MYSTERY TOUR									163	177

1987 / 1988	10/31	11/7	11/14	11/21	11/28	12/5	12/12	12/19	12/26	1/2
Got My Mind Set on You (G)	54	44	38	26	19	11	10	5	4	4
THE BEATLES	168	156	164	174						
MAGICAL MYSTERY TOUR	165	181								
ABBEY ROAD			69	69	99	123	142	128	166	166
LET IT BE			88	94	149	185				
CLOUD NINE (G)			77	23	18	15	12	11	11	
ALL THE BEST (P)								120	72	72

1988	1/9	1/16	1/23	1/30	2/6	2/13	2/20	2/27	3/5	3/12
Got My Mind Set on You (G)	2	1	4	7	18	25	36	51	65	93
When We Was Fab (G)					63	58	44	34	31	25
ABBEY ROAD	160	156	159	158	173					
CLOUD NINE (G)	9	10	8	9	9	10	9	10	10	14
ALL THE BEST (P)	62	62	62	68	72	82	95	99	109	110

1988	3/19	3/26	4/2	4/9	4/16	4/23	4/30	5/7	5/14	5/21
Got My Mind Set on You (G)	99									
When We Was Fab (G)	24	23	33	59	100					
CLOUD NINE (G)	19	24	28	34	37	38	51	62	73	79
ALL THE BEST (P)	129	140	167	163						
PAST MASTERS 2			150	147	121	121	129	179	181	
PAST MASTERS 1			160	149	149	174	192	200		

The Charts

1988	5/28	6/4	6/11	6/18	6/25	7/2	7/9	7/16	7/23	7/30
CLOUD NINE (G)	88	129	139	188						

1988	8/6	8/13	8/20	8/27	9/3	9/10	9/17	9/24	10/1	10/8

1988	10/15	10/22	10/29	11/5	11/12	11/19	11/26	12/3	12/10	12/17
Jealous Guy (J)	84	80	81	91						
Handle with Care (G)			83	66	62	56	48	47	45	46
IMAGINE: JOHN LENNON (J)		144	45	32	32	31	32	40	46	62
TRAVELING WILBURYS (G)				57	23	12	9	8	8	

1988 / 1989	12/24	12/31	1/7	1/14	1/21	1/28	2/4	2/11	2/18	2/25
Handle with Care (G)	59	59	63	72	83	100				
End of the Line (G)								83	69	63
IMAGINE: JOHN LENNON (J)	76	76	72	81	94	112	143	178	187	
TRAVELING WILBURYS (G)	8	8	5	8	7	3	3	3	3	3

1989	3/4	3/11	3/18	3/25	4/1	4/8	4/15	4/22	4/29	5/6
End of the Line (G)	63	66	79	78	90	95				
TRAVELING WILBURYS (G)	4	4	4	5	3	4	7	10	10	14

1989	5/13	5/20	5/27	6/3	6/10	6/17	6/24	7/1	7/8	7/15
My Brave Face (P)			72	54	45	36	33	26	25	26
TRAVELING WILBURYS (G)	13	14	17	21	23	28	38	49	58	66
FLOWERS IN THE DIRT (P)						66	21	21	21	

1989	7/22	7/29	8/5	8/12	8/19	8/26	9/2	9/9	9/16	9/23
My Brave Face (P)	57	80								
This One (P)								95	94	95
TRAVELING WILBURYS (G)	82	90	105	112	127	149	148	147	155	191
FLOWERS IN THE DIRT (P)	26	29	35	44	45	58	71	69	75	80

1989	9/30	10/7	10/14	10/21	10/28	11/4	11/11	11/18	11/25	12/2
TRAVELING WILBURYS (G)	199									
FLOWERS IN THE DIRT (P)	101	118	133	155	149	166	193	160	140	129
BEST OF DARK HORSE (G)					132	132		146	152	

The Charts

1989 / 1990	12/9	12/16	12/23	12/30	1/6	1/13	1/20	1/27	2/3	2/10
Figure of Eight (P)						92	95	95	96	99
FLOWERS IN THE DIRT (P)	98	87	84	83	83	89	97	100	97	83

1990	2/17	2/24	3/3	3/10	3/17	3/24	3/31	4/7	4/14	4/21
FLOWERS IN THE DIRT (P)	76	77	62	64	68	71	78	91	98	98

1990	4/28	5/5	5/12	5/19	5/26	6/2	6/9	6/16	6/23	6/30
FLOWERS IN THE DIRT (P)	110	128	154	187	197					

1990	7/7	7/14	7/21	7/28	8/4	8/11	8/18	8/25	9/1	9/8

1990	9/15	9/22	9/29	10/6	10/13	10/20	10/27	11/3	11/10	11/17
TRAVELING WILBURYS 3 (G)										40

1990 / 1991	11/24	12/1	12/8	12/15	12/22	12/29	1/5	1/12	1/19	1/26
TRAVELING WILBURYS 3 (G)	12	11	11	11	11	11	15	17	26	33
TRIPPING THE LIVE ... (P)	52	26	31	32	34	34	40	44	55	63
TRIPPING HIGHLIGHTS (P)				157	157	163	141	143	166	153

1991	2/2	2/9	2/16	2/23	3/2	3/9	3/16	3/23	3/30	4/6
TRAVELING WILBURYS 3 (G)	35	44	49	55	60	72	84	95	106	108
TRIPPING THE LIVE ... (P)	75	96	109	145	151	198				
TRIPPING HIGHLIGHTS (P)	183	194								

1991	4/13	4/20	4/27	5/4	5/11	5/18	5/25	6/1	6/8	6/15
TRAVELING WILBURYS 3 (G)	172									

1991	6/22	6/29	7/6	7/13	7/20	7/27	8/3	8/10	8/17	8/24
UNPLUGGED (P)	14	19	19	56	62	93	133	189		

1991	8/31	9/7	9/14	9/21	9/28	10/5	10/12	10/19	10/26	11/2

1991 / 1992	11/9	11/16	11/23	11/30	12/7	12/14	12/21	12/28	1/4	1/11
CHOBA B CCCP (P)		109	137	175						
LIVERPOOL ORATORIO (P)		193			188	189	177	177	199	

1992	1/4	1/11	1/18	1/25	2/1	2/8	2/15	2/22	2/29	3/7
LIVERPOOL ORATORIO (P)	199									

1992	3/14	3/21	3/28	4/4	4/11	4/18	4/25	5/2	5/9	5/16

The Charts

1992	5/23	5/29	6/6	6/13	6/20	6/27	7/4	7/22	7/25

1992	8/1	8/8	8/15	8/22	8/29	9/5	9/12	9/19	9/26	10/3
LIVE IN JAPAN (G)	126									

1992	10/10	10/17	10/24	10/31	11/7	11/14	11/21	11/28	12/5	12/12

1992 / 1993	12/19	12/26	1/2	1/9	1/16	1/23	1/30	2/6	2/13	2/20
Hope of Deliverance (P)										88

1993	2/27	3/6	3/13	3/20	3/27	4/3	4/10	4/17	4/24	5/1
Hope of Deliverance (P)	84	87	83	87	89					
OFF THE GROUND (P)	17	28	52	56	69	84	105	106	104	110

1993	5/8	5/15	5/22	5/29	6/5	6/12	6/19	6/26	7/3	7/10
OFF THE GROUND (P)	115	125	105	133	143	135	128	151	100	149

1993	7/17	7/24	7/31	8/7	8/14	8/21	8/28	9/4	9/11	9/18

1993	9/25	10/2	10/9	10/16	10/23	10/30	11/6	11/13	11/20	11/27

1993 / 1994	12/4	12/11	12/18	12/25	1/1	1/8	1/15	1/22	1/29	2/5
PAUL IS LIVE (P)	78	147	151	200						

1994	2/12	2/19	2/26	3/5	3/12	3/19	3/26	4/2	4/9	4/16

1994	4/24	4/30	5/7	5/14	5/21	5/28	6/4	6/11	6/18	6/25

1994	7/2	7/9	7/16	7/23	7/30	8/6	8/13	8/20	8/27	9/3

1994	9/10	9/17	9/24	10/1	10/8	10/15	10/22	10/29	11/5	11/12

1994 / 1995	11/19	11/26	12/3	12/10	12/17	12/24	12/31	1/7	1/14	1/21
BEATLES AT THE BBC					3	7	10	30	33	

1995	1/28	2/4	2/11	2/18	2/25	3/4	3/11	3/18	3/25	4/1
BEATLES AT THE BBC	34	38	51	65	59	56	89	93	117	122

1995	4/8	4/15	4/22	4/29	5/6	5/13	5/20	5/27	6/3	6/10
Baby It's You			67	79	89	99				
BEATLES AT THE BBC	120	138	143	137	164	181	197	172		

1995	6/17	6/24	7/1	7/8	7/15	7/22	7/29	8/5	8/12	8/19

1995	8/26	9/2	9/9	9/16	9/23	9/30	10/7	10/14	10/21	10/28

1995 / 1996	11/4	11/11	11/18	11/25	12/2	12/9	12/16	12/23	12/30	1/6
Free as a Bird									10	6
ANTHOLOGY 1						1	1	1	2	3

1996	1/13	1/20	1/27	2/3	2/10	2/17	2/24	3/2	3/9	3/16
Free as a Bird	15	32	57	63	77	91	98	93	99	
ANTHOLOGY 1	9	11	21	30	45	60	67	59	93	104

1996	3/23	3/30	4/6	4/13	4/20	4/27	5/4	5/11	5/18	5/25
Real Love	11	26	21	54	60	70	88			
ANTHOLOGY 1	95	83	44	63	77	100	131	151	181	152
ANTHOLOGY 2			1	2	4	8	17	23	29	27

1996	6/1	6/8	6/15	6/22	6/29	7/6	7/13	7/20	7/27	8/3
ANTHOLOGY 1										
ANTHOLOGY 2	42	56	66	77	54	71	119	137	128	148

1996	8/10	8/17	8/24	8/31	9/7	9/14	9/21	9/28	10/5	10/12
ANTHOLOGY 2	164	174	193	188						

1996	10/26	11/2	11/9	11/16	11/23	11/30	12/7	12/14	12/21	12/28
ANTHOLOGY 1									192	168
ANTHOLOGY 2				138	161	148	146	127	111	96
ANTHOLOGY 3				1	5	12	24	21	16	17

1997	1/4	1/11	1/18	1/25	2/1	2/8	2/15	2/22	3/1	3/8
ANTHOLOGY 1	156	197								
ANTHOLOGY 2	97	111	177	194						
ANTHOLOGY 3	17	28	57	74	97	121	145	160	151	

1997	3/15	3/22	3/29	4/5	4/12	4/19	4/26	5/3	5/10	5/17

1997	5/24	5/31	6/7	6/14	6/21	6/28	7/5	7/12	7/19	7/26
The World Tonight (P)	64	64	68	73	74	74	77	76	92	93
FLAMING PIE (P)				2	8	12	25	38	47	44

1997	8/2	8/9	8/16	8/23	8/30	9/6	9/13	9/20	9/27	10/4
FLAMING PIE (P)	47	60	75	90	110	125	144	163	187	200

1997	10/11	10/18	10/25	11/1	11/8	11/15	11/22	11/29	12/6	12/13
STANDING STONE (P)				194						

1997 / 1998	12/20	12/27	1/3	1/10	1/17	1/24	1/31	2/7	2/14	2/21

1998	2/28	3/7	3/14	3/21	3/28	4/4	4/11	4/18	4/25	5/2
LENNON LEGEND (J)			76	65	72	99	120	132	124	164

1998	5/9	5/16	5/23	5/29	6/6	6/13	6/20	6/27	7/4	7/22
LENNON LEGEND (J)	179									
VERTICAL MAN (R)									61	117

1998	7/28	7/25	8/1	8/8	8/15	8/22	8/29	9/5	9/12	9/19
VERTICAL MAN (R)	110	151								

1998	9/26	10/3	10/10	10/17	10/24	10/31	11/7	11/14	11/21	11/28

1998 / 1999	12/5	12/12	12/19	12/26	1/2	1/9	1/16	1/23	1/30	2/6

1999	2/13	2/20	2/27	3/6	3/13	3/20	3/27	4/3	4/10	4/17

1999	4/24	5/1	5/6	5/13	5/20	5/27	6/3	6/10	6/17	6/24

1999	7/1	7/8	7/15	7/22	7/29	8/5	8/12	8/19	8/26	9/2

1999	9/11	9/18	9/25	10/2	10/9	10/16	10/23	10/30	11/6	11/13
YELLOW SUBMARINE SONG…				15	26	45	59	71	84	108
RUN DEVIL RUN (P)							26	50	71	114

1999 / 2000	11/20	11/27	12/4	12/11	12/18	12/25	1/1	1/8	1/15	1/22
YELLOW SUBMARINE SONG…	134	153	178	187	161	162	154	146		
RUN DEVIL RUN (P)	163	196								

2000	1/29	2/5	2/12	2/19	2/26	3/4	3/11	3/18	3/25	4/1

2000	4/8	4/15	4/22	4/29	5/6	5/13	5/20	5/27	6/3	6/10

2000	6/17	6/24	7/1	7/8	7/15	7/22	7/29	8/5	8/12	8/19

The Charts

2000	8/26	9/2	9/9	9/16	9/23	9/30	10/7	10/14	10/21	10/29

2000 / 2001	11/4	11/11	11/18	11/25	12/2	12/9	12/16	12/23	12/30	1/6
1					1	2	2	1	1	1

2001	1/13	1/20	1/27	2/3	2/10	2/17	2/24	3/3	3/10	3/17
1	1	1	1	1	4	4	2	2	3	6

2001	3/24	3/31	4/7	4/14	4/21	4/28	5/5	5/12	5/19	5/26
1	7	12	13	26	26	23	33	35	38	24
WINGSPAN (P)										2

2001	6/2	6/9	6/16	6/23	6/30	7/7	7/14	7/21	7/28	8/4
1	36	51	49	60	43	70	80	75	87	86
WINGSPAN (P)	9	12	15	27	25	51	70	76	110	122

2001	8/11	8/18	8/25	9/1	9/8	9/15	9/22	9/29	10/6	10/13
1	85	91	93	105	109	128	108	124	137	138
WINGSPAN (P)	140	154	186							

2001	10/20	10/27	11/3	11/10	11/17	11/24	12/1	12/8	12/15	12/22
Freedom (P)									97	97
1	131	136	143	132	149	138	141	146	73	57
DRIVING RAIN (P)							26	65	68	78

2001 / 2002	12/29	1/5	1/12	1/19	1/26	2/2	2/9	2/16	2/23	3/2
My Sweet Lord (G)						94				
1	58	63	73	68	94	107	104	120	110	102
DRIVING RAIN (P)	102	112	152	171	200					

2002	3/9	3/16	3/23	3/30	4/6	4/13	4/20	4/27	5/4	5/11
1	120	136	144	153	148	154	140	146	140	132

2002	5/18	5/25	6/1	6/8	6/15	6/22	6/29	7/6	7/13	7/20
1	131	120	149	156	125	143	121	143	149	125

2002	7/27	8/3	8/10	8/17	8/24	8/31	9/7	9/14	9/21	9/28
1	146	149	142	113	134	102	98	112	114	110

The Charts

2002	10/5	10/12	10/19	10/26	11/2	11/9	11/16	11/23	11/30	12/7
1	126	110	112	111	105	120	131	156		
BRAINWASHED (G)										18

2002 / 2003	12/14	12/21	12/28	1/4	1/11	1/18	1/25	2/1	2/8	2/15
BRAINWASHED (G)	57	63	80	97	120	144	153	178		
BACK IN THE US (P)	8	16	22	26	30	31	36	47	58	79

2003	2/22	3/1	3/8	3/15	3/22	3/29	4/5	4/12	4/19	4/26
BACK IN THE US (P)	106	117	159	170	200					
RINGO RAMA (R)									113	186

2003	5/3	5/10	5/17	5/24	5/31	6/7	6/14	6/21	6/28	7/5

2003	7/12	7/19	7/26	8/2	8/9	8/16	8/23	8/30	9/6	9/13

2003	9/20	9/27	10/4	10/11	10/18	10/25	11/1	11/8	11/15	11/22

2003 / 2004	11/29	12/6	12/13	12/20	12/27	1/3	1/10	1/17	1/24	1/31
LET IT BE ... NAKED		5	17	16	20	17	26	56	56	85

2004	2/7	2/14	2/21	2/28	3/6	3/13	3/20	3/27	4/3	4/10
LET IT BE ... NAKED	102	130	132	137	172					

2004	4/17	4/24	5/1	5/6	5/15	5/22	5/29	6/5	6/12	6/19

2004	6/26	7/3	7/10	7/17	7/24	7/31	8/7	8/14	8/21	8/28

2004	9/4	9/11	9/18	9/25	10/2	10/9	10/16	10/23	10/30	11/6

2004 / 2005	11/13	11/20	11/27	12/4	12/11	12/18	12/25	1/1	1/8	1/15
ACOUSTIC (J)		31	76	116	163	173				
THE CAPITOL ALBUMS VOL. 1			35	104	103	104	110	128		

2005	1/22	1/29	2/5	2/12	2/19	2/26	3/5	3/12	3/19	3/26

2005	4/2	4/9	4/16	4/24	4/30	5/7	5/14	5/21	5/28	6/4

2005	6/11	6/18	6/25	7/2	7/9	7/16	7/23	7/30	8/6	8/13
Sgt. Pepper's Lonely Hearts... (P)						48				

The Charts

2005	8/20	8/27	9/3	9/10	9/17	9/24	10/1	10/8	10/15	10/22
CHAOS AND CREATION... (P)							6	16	32	38
WORKING CLASS HERO (J)										135

2005	10/29	11/5	11/12	11/19	11/26	12/3	12/10	12/17	12/24	12/31
CHAOS AND CREATION... (P)	54	44	44	66	83	74	62	67	106	105
WORKING CLASS HERO (J)	147	197								

2006	1/7	1/14	1/21	1/28	2/4	2/11	2/18	2/25	3/4	3/11
CHAOS AND CREATION... (P)	112	200								

2006	3/18	3/25	4/1	4/8	4/15	4/22	4/29	5/6	5/13	5/20
THE CAPITOL ALBUMS VOL. 2							46	129		

2006	5/27	6/3	6/10	6/17	6/24	7/1	7/8	7/15	7/22	7/29

2006	8/5	8/12	8/19	8/26	9/2	9/9	9/16	9/23	9/30	10/7

2006	10/14	10/21	10/28	11/4	11/11	11/18	11/25	12/2	12/9	12/16
LOVE									4	5

2006 / 2007	12/23	12/30	1/6	1/13	1/20	1/27	2/3	2/10	2/17	2/24
LOVE	8	8	5	13	9	8	15	22	35	41

2007	3/3	3/10	3/17	3/24	3/31	4/7	4/14	4/21	4/28	5/5
LOVE	36	56	57	63	74	104	90	129	84	98

2007	5/12	5/19	5/26	6/2	6/9	6/16	6/23	6/30	7/7	7/14
Dance Tonight (P)									69	72
LOVE	132	108	90	99	129	66	83	103	97	77
MEMORY ALMOST FULL (P)							3	3	5	9
WILBURYS COLLECTION (G)								9	27	38

2007	7/21	7/28	8/4	8/11	8/18	8/25	9/1	9/8	9/15	9/22
LOVE	83	94	96	127	103	101	101	129	113	101
MEMORY ALMOST FULL (P)	19	26	34	43	55	94	104	118	172	132
WILBURYS COLLECTION (G)	49	64	78	94	73	103	106	124	153	173
PHOTOGRAPH (R)									130	189

224 The Charts

2007	9/29	10/6	10/13	10/20	10/27	11/3	11/10	11/17	11/24	12/1
LOVE	102	109	160	129	117	126	153	175	168	167
MEMORY ALMOST FULL (P)									165	

2007 / 2008	12/8	12/15	12/22	12/29	1/5	1/12	1/19	1/26	2/2	2/9
LOVE		151		192	145	173				170
LIVERPOOL 8 (R)									94	113

2008	2/16	2/23	3/1	3/8	3/15	3/22	3/29	4/5	4/12	4/19
LOVE	171	155	104	127	139	190	121	102	123	142

2008	4/26	5/3	5/10	5/17	5/24	5/31	6/7	6/14	6/21	6/28
LOVE	180	198	103	157	153	158				

2008	7/5	7/12	7/19	7/26	8/2	8/9	8/16	8/23	8/30	9/6

2008	9/13	9/20	9/27	10/4	10/11	10/18	10/25	11/1	11/8	11/15

2008 / 2009	11/22	11/29	12/6	12/13	12/20	12/27	1/3	1/10	1/17	1/24

2009	1/31	2/7	2/14	2/21	2/28	3/7	3/14	3/21	3/28	4/4

2009	4/11	4/18	4/26	5/2	5/9	5/16	5/23	5/29	6/6	6/13

2009	6/20	6/27	7/4	7/11	7/18	7/25	8/1	8/8	8/15	8/22
LET IT ROLL (G)		24	41	66	88	117	150	150	166	

2009	8/29	9/5	9/12	9/19	9/26	10/3	10/10	10/17	10/24	10/31
LET IT ROLL (G)	114	168	194	163	155					
THE BEATLES IN STEREO					15			86	34	92
THE BEATLES IN MONO					40	199				

2009 / 2010	11/7	11/14	11/21	11/28	12/5	12/12	12/19	12/26	1/2	1/9
THE BEATLES IN STEREO		143	48	53	151	197	89	102	99	131
THE BEATLES IN MONO	45	113								
GOOD EVENING NYC (P)					16	31	42	50	43	48
ABBEY ROAD					118	108	104	98	82	73
THE BEATLES					152	164	138	109	85	83
SERGEANT PEPPER					189	196	170	160	130	114
1						179	163	126	130	
RUBBER SOUL									163	138
REVOLVER									170	140

The Charts

PAST MASTERS								177	154
LOVE								184	158
LET IT BE									182
A HARD DAY'S NIGHT									199

2010	1/16	1/23	1/30	2/6	2/13	2/20	2/27	3/6	3/13	3/20
GOOD EVENING NYC (P)	92	93	98	117						
ABBEY ROAD	99	110	132	137	163	165	191	188	199	190
THE BEATLES	119	129	164	172	200					
SERGEANT PEPPER	148	170	193							
1			173	173		196				
RUBBER SOUL	163	187								
REVOLVER	181									
LOVE		192								
Y NOT (R)			58	136						

2010	3/27	4/3	4/10	4/17	4/24	5/1	5/6	5/13	5/20	5/27
THE BEATLES			164	191						
ABBEY ROAD			184	183	173					

2010	6/3	6/10	6/17	6/24	7/1	7/8	7/15	7/22	7/29	8/5

2010	8/12	8/19	8/26	9/2	9/11	9/18	9/25	10/2	10/9	10/16
REMEMBER (J)								44	57	79

2010	10/23	10/30	11/6	11/13	11/20	11/27	12/4	12/11	12/18	12/25
REMEMBER (J)	66	78								
POWER TO THE PEOPLE (J)	24	45	82	156	178			107		
DOUBLE FANTASY (J)	34	123	194							
IMAGINE (J)	88									
SIGNATURE BOX (J)	148									
GIMME SOME TRUTH (J)	196									
1967–1970			29	86	143		67	150	119	139
1962–1966			32	114	171		75	172	130	166
BAND ON THE RUN (P)					29	81	147			
ABBEY ROAD							48	117	133	140
THE BEATLES							61	176	168	188
THE BEATLES IN STEREO							64	181	188	
SERGEANT PEPPER							66		182	
RUBBER SOUL							86			
REVOLVER							103			
MAGICAL MYSTERY TOUR							110			

LET IT BE	120
A HARD DAY'S NIGHT	130
PLEASE PLEASE ME	155
HELP!	160
WITH THE BEATLES	179

2011	1/1	1/8	1/15	1/22	1/29	2/5	2/12	2/19	2/26	3/5
1967–1970	137	131	141	167						
1962–1966	159	153	184							
BAND ON THE RUN (P)	198									
ABBEY ROAD	133	118	97	130	115	127	182			
THE BEATLES	172	157	176	180	187					
1	174									
THE BEATLES IN STEREO		181								
LOVE								37	79	91

2011	3/12	3/19	3/26	4/2	4/9	4/16	4/24	4/30	5/7	5/14
LOVE	147	186								
ABBEY ROAD										173

2011	5/21	5/28	6/4	6/11	6/18	6/25	7/2	7/9	7/16	7/23
LOVE						160				
McCARTNEY (P)								50	115	
McCARTNEY II (P)								82	194	

2011	8/6	8/13	8/20	8/27	9/3	9/10	9/17	9/24	10/1	10/8
1								4	6	17
ABBEY ROAD								183		

2011	10/15	10/22	10/29	11/5	11/12	11/19	11/26	12/3	12/10	12/17
1	30	55	72	82	122	158	178			
OCEAN'S KINGDOM (P)		143								

2011 / 2012	11/19	11/26	12/3	12/10	12/17	12/24	12/31	1/7	1/14	1/21
1	158	178					177	72	55	76
ABBEY ROAD								148	142	185

2012	1/28	2/4	2/11	2/18	2/25	3/3	3/10	3/17	3/24	3/31
1	159	198	199	97	91	51	102			
RINGO 2012 (R)				80	192					
KISSES ON THE BOTTOM (P)			5	7	20	46	40	63		

The Charts

2012	4/7	4/14	4/21	4/28	5/5	5/12	5/19	5/26	6/2	6/9
KISSES ON THE BOTTOM (P)	85	60	92	150	188					
EARLY TAKES VOL. I (G)							20	70	123	
RAM (P)										24

2012	6/16	6/23	6/30	7/7	7/14	7/21	7/28	8/4	8/11	8/18
RAM (P)	58	124	177	187						
YELLOW SUBMARINE SONG…		55								
LET IT ROLL (G)					80					
TOMORROW NEVER KNOWS									24	200
1									96	

2012	8/25	9/1	9/8	9/15	9/22	9/29	10/6	10/13	10/20	10/27
KISSES ON THE BOTTOM (P)					121	105	132			
MAGICAL MYSTERY TOUR										57
THE BEATLES IN STEREO										

2012 / 2013	11/3	11/10	11/17	11/24	12/1	12/8	12/15	12/22	12/29	1/5
THE BEATLES IN STEREO					161					
1										117
ABBEY ROAD										172

2013	1/12	1/19	1/26	2/2	2/9	2/16	2/23	3/2	3/9	3/16
1	95	88	109							
ABBEY ROAD	151	153								
KISSES ON THE BOTTOM (P)	192									

2013	3/23	3/30	4/6	4/13	4/20	4/27	5/4	5/11	5/18	5/25
1			165		153					
LET IT BE … NAKED					32	92				

2013	6/1	6/8	6/15	6/22	6/29	7/6	7/13	7/20	7/27	8/3
WINGS OVER AMERICA (P)		22	86	93	122					
1							37	61	115	121
HELP!							83			

2013	8/10	8/17	8/24	8/31	9/7	9/14	9/21	9/28	10/5	10/12
1	157	194	151	160	178					90

2013	10/19	10/26	11/2	11/9	11/16	11/23	11/30	12/7	12/14	12/21
1	157	184								

NEW (P)		3	11	17	40	63	94	120	106
LIVE AT THE BBC 2						7	29	88	64
LIVE AT THE BBC						34	136		

2014	12/28	1/4	1/11	1/18	1/25	2/1	2/8	2/15	2/22	3/1
NEW (P)	98	60	92	163	170			189		
LIVE AT THE BBC 2	64	55	84	141	123	197				145
BOOTLEG RECORDINGS 63		172								
1			187	174	135	149	84	74	37	20
ABBEY ROAD					199				119	82
THE U.S. ALBUMS							48			
HEY JUDE							72	191		186
YESTERDAY AND TODAY							74			
A HARD DAY'S NIGHT							102		189	150
REVOLVER							143			156
RUBBER SOUL							170		134	103
MEET THE BEATLES!							171		192	170
SERGEANT PEPPER									132	98
THE BEATLES									159	119
LOVE									191	62
1967–1970										137
1962–1966										154

2014	3/8	3/15	3/22	3/29	4/5	4/12	4/19	4/26	5/3	5/10
1	44	64	93	95	120	143	157	151	185	177
ABBEY ROAD	103	141	191	200						
RUBBER SOUL	172									
SERGEANT PEPPER	132	183								
THE BEATLES	155									

2014	5/17	5/24	5/31	6/7	6/14	6/21	6/28	7/5	7/12	7/19
1	181	186			177		167	190	186	
REVOLVER							193			

2014	7/26	8/2	8/9	8/16	8/23	8/30	9/6	9/13	9/20	9/27
1	179	186	199		194	164				
ABBEY ROAD					165	196				
SERGEANT PEPPER										108
THE BEATLES										147
REVOLVER										159
THE BEATLES IN MONO										166
RUBBER SOUL										176

The Charts

2014	10/4	10/11	10/18	10/25	11/1	11/8	11/15	11/22	11/29	12/6
SERGEANT PEPPER	172									
THE APPLE YEARS (G)	167									
POWER TO THE PEOPLE (J)				133						
VENUS AND MARS (P)								31	114	
AT THE SPEED OF SOUND (P)								45	175	

2014 / 2015	12/13	12/20	12/27	1/3	1/10	1/17	1/24	1/31	2/7	2/14
FourFiveSeconds (P)									54	15
LONG TALL SALLY	196									
ABBEY ROAD			196	199						
1				195	154	137	140	200	184	187

2015	2/21	2/28	3/7	3/14	3/21	3/28	4/4	4/11	4/18	4/26
FourFiveSeconds (P)	6	4	6	5	5	5	5	8	9	13
1	186	154	177			200	192			
POSTCARDS … (R)									99	

2015	5/2	5/9	5/16	5/23	5/29	6/6	6/13	6/20	6/27	7/4
FourFiveSeconds (P)	16	26	36	45	56	66	75	76		
1			195			200				

2015	7/11	7/18	7/25	8/1	8/8	8/15	8/22	8/29	9/5	9/12
1	193									
1967–1970				84						

2015	9/19	9/26	10/3	10/10	10/17	10/24	10/31	11/7	11/14	11/21
TUG OF WAR (P)						56				
PIPES OF PEACE (P)						70				

2015 /2016	11/28	12/5	12/12	12/19	12/26	1/2	1/9	1/16	1/23	1/30
1	6	35	61	76	70	58	41	16	33	37
ABBEY ROAD					147	135	77	96	110	
SERGEANT PEPPER								121	181	
RUBBER SOUL								158		

2016	2/6	2/13	2/20	2/27	3/5	3/12	3/19	3/26	4/2	4/9
1	56	64	70	87	85	98	95	84	85	97
ABBEY ROAD	183								195	

2016	4/16	4/23	4/30	5/7	5/14	5/21	5/28	6/4	6/11	6/18
1	106	114	108	106	121	112	107	116	120	116

2016	6/25	7/2	7/9	7/16	7/23	7/30	8/6	8/13	8/20	8/27
1	117	41	101	135	128	146	154	127	122	173
PURE McCARTNEY (P)		15	62	143	196					
ABBEY ROAD										189

2016	9/3	9/10	9/17	9/24	10/1	10/8	10/15	10/22	10/29	11/5
1	113	129	136	121	156	112	119	120	180	123
HOLLYWOOD BOWL					7	37	99	136		
ABBEY ROAD										196

2016 / 2017	11/12	11/19	11/26	12/3	12/10	12/17	12/24	12/31	1/7	1/14
1	175		186	176		188			124	95
HOLLYWOOD BOWL					152					
ABBEY ROAD				179		176	153	128	119	164

2017	1/21	1/28	2/4	2/11	2/18	2/25	3/4	3/11	3/18	3/25
1	113	123	147	153	157	155	151	150	159	152
ABBEY ROAD	118	122	152	156	175	180	158	158	169	164

2017	3/18	3/25	4/1	4/8	4/15	4/22	4/29	5/6	5/13	5/20
1	159	152	153	142	141	156	157	158	153	169
ABBEY ROAD	169	164	167	159	147	163	166	166	156	155
FLOWERS IN THE DIRT (P)				33						

2017	5/27	6/3	6/10	6/17	6/24	7/1	7/8	7/15	7/22	7/29
1	158	145	141	119	115	131	143	146	149	134
ABBEY ROAD	170	166	159	130	125	138	138	147	148	148
SERGEANT PEPPER			3	4	11	21	45	51	58	

2017	8/5	8/12	8/19	8/26	9/2	9/9	9/16	9/23	9/30	10/7
1	153	147	150	165	147	157	162	162	176	175
ABBEY ROAD	130	157	161	167	149	133	170	161	180	186
SERGEANT PEPPER	73	104	118	124	125	164	182	153	178	
GIVE MORE LOVE (R)										128

2017	10/14	10/21	10/28	11/4	11/11	11/18	11/25	12/2	12/9	12/16
1	173	176	182	193						
ABBEY ROAD	134	162	184	199	193	191	185	194	174	138
SERGEANT PEPPER	199									187

The Charts

2017 / 2018	12/23	12/30	1/6	1/13	1/20	1/27	2/3	2/10	2/17	2/24
1			142	149	106	114	168	160	169	153
ABBEY ROAD	131	97	112	140			186	171	175	140
SERGEANT PEPPER	190	158	89	155	181	182				

2018	3/3	3/10	3/17	3/24	3/31	4/7	4/14	4/21	4/28	5/5
1	149	125	95	137	107	110	99	118	106	129
ABBEY ROAD	145	138								
SERGEANT PEPPER		69	101	162						

2018	5/12	5/19	5/26	6/2	6/9	6/16	6/23	6/30	7/7	7/14
1	162	162	150	165	159	174	156	157	38	75
ABBEY ROAD	165	163	153	170	155	172	149	151	156	

2018	7/21	7/28	8/4	8/11	8/18	8/25	9/1	9/8	9/15	9/22
1	81	139	133	148	142	142	131	144	155	161
ABBEY ROAD		155	143	159	153	148	160	162	163	177
EGYPT STATION (P)										1

2018	9/29	10/6	10/13	10/20	10/27	11/3	11/10	11/17	11/24	12/1
1	151	177	163	178	154	174	184	177	185	196
ABBEY ROAD	178	194	190	189	184	183	188	183	164	85
EGYPT STATION (P)	8	55	72	146						
IMAGINE (J)					83					
THE BEATLES									6	30

2018 / 2019	12/8	12/15	12/22	12/29	1/5	1/12	1/19	1/26	2/2	2/9
Happy Xmas (War is Over) (J)				45	42					
Wonderful Christmastime (P)				47						
1	199		200	180	163	128	135	164	185	179
ABBEY ROAD	101	127	117	97	117	126	138	155	173	159
EGYPT STATION (P)			57	34						
IMAGINE (J)					68	81	117	143	161	173
THE BEATLES	33	43	57	48	86					
POWER TO THE PEOPLE (J)		188	167	140						
RED ROSE SPEEDWAY (P)			149							
McCARTNEY II (P)			182	157	94					
WILD LIFE (P)			199							
SERGEANT PEPPER			191	181						

2019	2/16	2/23	3/2	3/9	3/16	3/23	3/30	4/6	4/13	4/20
1	186	145	131	160	173	167	166	155	159	156
ABBEY ROAD	165	140	138	153	156	156	158	156	147	155
EGYPT STATION (P)							86			
THE BEATLES	181	181	188							

2019	4/27	5/4	5/11	5/18	5/25	6/1	6/8	6/15	6/22	6/29
1	169	136	171	162	144	144	98	80	79	81
ABBEY ROAD	155	152	167	160	140	154	105	102	93	85
THE BEATLES										198

2019	7/6	7/13	7/20	7/27	8/3	8/10	8/17	8/24	8/31	9/7
1	60	43	41	50	58	71	74	73	74	87
ABBEY ROAD	96	67	65	60	65	90	92	69	80	97
THE BEATLES	190	154	151	152	177	198	168			

2019	9/14	9/21	9/28	10/5	10/12	10/19	10/26	11/2	11/9	11/16
1	88	89	71	66	48	59	61	61	73	73
ABBEY ROAD	100	95	100	71	3	13	24	28	40	43
THE BEATLES					165	180				
WHAT'S MY NAME (R)									127	

2019 / 2020	11/23	11/30	12/7	12/14	12/21	12/28	1/4	1/11	1/18	1/25
1	80	83	88	99	97	100	109	63	68	77
ABBEY ROAD	46	45	16	17	31	29	29	36	56	74
THE BEATLES						172	176	163		
SERGEANT PEPPER				173	169	126	126	189		
POWER TO THE PEOPLE (J)				181	152	159				
McCARTNEY II (P)							144			

2020	2/1	2/8	2/15	2/22	2/29	3/7	3/14	3/21	3/28	4/4
1	79	83	90	76	85	83	85	79	69	61
ABBEY ROAD	82	97	88	80	86	93	92	91	102	106
THE BEATLES									199	197

2020	4/11	4/18	4/25	5/2	5/9	5/16	5/23	5/29	6/6	6/13
1	66	69	60	64	69	73	70	75	80	93
ABBEY ROAD	109	111	95	98	89	82	84	93	88	106

2020	6/20	6/27	7/4	7/11	7/18	7/25	8/1	8/8	8/15	8/22
1	84	78	78	86	74	84	86	86	89	87

ABBEY ROAD	98	96	88	111	103	83	85	113	105	102
FLAMING PIE (P)									74	

2020	8/29	9/5	9/12	9/19	9/26	10/3	10/10	10/17	10/24	10/31
1	92	93	102	90	85	101	112	116	97	95
ABBEY ROAD	95	108	111	102	110	119	132	132	116	104
McCARTNEY (P)							151			

2020 / 2021	11/7	11/14	11/21	11/28	12/5	12/12	12/19	12/26	1/2	1/9
Wonderful Christmastime (P)							45	46	28	
1	106	107	91	89	121	122	117	106	93	89
ABBEY ROAD	131	137	104	79	91	67	57	59	54	68
McCARTNEY II (P)					180	168	160	114		
GIMME SOME TRUTH 2020 (J)						189	186			
SERGEANT PEPPER							139	117	169	
McCARTNEY III (P)									2	37

2021	1/16	1/23	1/30	2/6	2/13	2/20	2/27	3/6	3/13	3/20
1	74	76	79	79	90	75	48	80	88	88
ABBEY ROAD	75	79	80	94	118	116		119	123	118
SERGEANT PEPPER	178									
McCARTNEY III (P)	90	200								

2021	3/27	4/3	4/10	4/17	4/24	5/1	5/6	5/15	5/22	5/29
1	80	81	56	53	88	96	106	106	98	135
ABBEY ROAD	107	107			141	146	148	142	126	132
ZOOM IN (R)		179								

2021	6/5	6/12	6/19	6/26	7/3	7/10	7/17	7/24	7/31	8/7
1	154	107	113	126	115	127	96	107	101	102
ABBEY ROAD	142	110	106	109	89	123	105	116	113	105
McCARTNEY III IMAGINED (P)										19

2021	8/14	8/21	8/28	9/4	9/11	9/18	9/25	10/2	10/9	10/16
1	144	106	106	116	111	99	104	111	111	112
ABBEY ROAD	124	125	120	137	125	118	131	134	134	138
ALL THINGS MUST PASS (G)		7	85							

2021	10/23	10/30	11/6	11/13	11/20	11/27	12/4	12/11	12/18	12/25
Wonderful Christmastime										41
1	101	164	168	190	162	175	154	152	168	180
ABBEY ROAD	128	115	130	129	114	111	71	36	40	34
LET IT BE		5	42	84	116	137	80	19	26	31
GIMME SOME TRUTH (2020)(J)									182	163

INDEX

Abbey Road 170
Acoustic 109
"Act Naturally" 30
"Ain't She Sweet" 38
"All My Loving" 27
All the Best 120
All Things Must Pass 151
"All Those Years Ago" 71
"All You Need Is Love" 57
"And I Love Her" 41
"Another Day" 61
Anthology 1 141
Anthology 2 141
Anthology 3 131
The Apple Years 1968–75 92
"Arrow Through Me" 34

"Baby It's You" 19
"Baby You're a Rich Man" 28
Back in the U.S. 125
"Back Off Boogaloo" 47
Back to the Egg 138
Bad Boy 105
"The Ballad of John and Yoko" 47
"Band on the Run" 79
Band on the Run 164
"Bangla Desh" 34
The Beatles at the Hollywood Bowl 136
The Beatles Bootleg Recordings 1963 92
The Beatles in Mono 108
The Beatles in Stereo 121
The Beatles' Second Album 160
Beatles '65 162
The Beatles' Story 135
The Beatles vs. The Four Seasons 101
The Beatles (White Album) 167
The Beatles with Tony Sheridan and Guests 118
"Beaucoups of Blues" 17
Beaucoups of Blues 117
The Best of Dark Horse 1976–1989 105
The Best of George Harrison 122
Blast from Your Past 119
"Blow Away" 51
Brainwashed 113

"Can't Buy Me Love" 56
The Capitol Albums Volume 1 111
The Capitol Albums Volume 2 104

Chaos and Creation in the Backyard 129
Choba B CCCP 102
Cloud Nine 149
"Cold Turkey" 45
"Come Together" 80
"Coming Up" 84
The Concert for Bangla Desh 152
"Crackerbox Palace" 46

"Dance Tonight" 18
"Dark Horse" 44
Dark Horse 134
"Day Tripper" 49
"Ding Dong; Ding Dong" 29
"Do You Want to Know a Secret?" 55
"Don't Let Me Down" 26
"A Dose of Rock 'n' Roll" 41
Double Fantasy 158
Driving Rain 112

The Early Beatles 140
Early Takes Volume 1 107
"Ebony and Ivory" 82
Egypt Station 116
"Eight Days a Week" 54
"Eleanor Rigby" 39
Electronic Sound 90
"End of the Line" 25
Extra Texture (Read All About It) 124

"Figure of Eight" 16
Flaming Pie 131
Flowers in the Dirt 150
Four By The Beatles 15
4 By the Beatles 20
"FourFiveSeconds" 83
"Free as a Bird" 35
"Freedom" 14
"From Me to You" 25

George Harrison 133
"Get Back" 70
"Getting Closer" 40
Gimme Some Truth 89
Gimme Some Truth: The Ultimate Mixes 99
"The Girl Is Mine" 78
"Girls School" 33
"Give Ireland Back to the Irish" 36

"Give Me Love (Give Me Peace on Earth)" 69
Give More Love 95
Give My Regards to Broad Street 132
"Give Peace a Chance" 43
Gone Troppo 108
Good Evening New York City 118
"Goodnight Tonight" 74
Goodnight Vienna 143
"Got My Mind Set on You" 82
"Got to Get You Into My Life" 68

"Handle with Care" 36
"Happy Xmas (War Is Over)" 20
A Hard Day's Night 161
"A Hard Day's Night" 72
Heartplay: Unfinished Dialogue 112
"Helen Wheels" 59
"Hello Goodbye" 61
"Help!" 70
Help! 157
"Hey Baby" 17
"Hey Jude" 86
Hey Jude 148
"Hi Hi Hi" 50
"Hope of Deliverance" 19

"I Am the Walrus" 22
"I Don't Want to Spoil The Party" 28
"I Feel Fine" 62
"I Saw Her Standing There" 48
"I Should Have Known Better" 21
"I Want to Hold Your Hand" 78
"If I Fell" 30
"I'll Cry Instead" 33
"I'm Happy Just to Dance with You" 14
"I'm Stepping Out" 22
"Imagine" 52
Imagine 153
Imagine: John Lennon 130
In the Beginning (Circa 1960) 109
"The Inner Light" 13
"Instant Karma (We All Shine On)" 67
Introducing the Beatles 156
"It Don't Come Easy" 64
"(It's All Down to) Goodnight

235

Index

Vienna" 31
"I've Had Enough" 39

"Jealous Guy" 18
"Jet" 63
The John Lennon Collection 128
John Lennon/Plastic Ono Band 142
Jolly What! The Beatles & Frank Ifield 110
"Junior's Farm" 75
"(Just Like) Starting Over" 88

Kisses on the Bottom 122

"Lady Madonna" 60
Lennon Legend 112
"Let 'Em In" 73
"Let It Be" 76
Let It Be 159
Let It Be ... Naked 129
Let It Roll 115
"Letting Go" 29
"Listen to What the Man Said" 69
"Live and Let Die" 71
Live at the BBC 136
Live at the Star Club 107
Live in Japan 96
Live in New York City 117
Live Peace in Toronto 146
Liverpool 8 103
Liverpool Oratorio 96
Living in the Material World 144
"London Town" 31
London Town 144
"The Long and Winding Road" 55
Long Tall Sally 89
Love 157
"Love Me Do" 67
Love Songs 134

Magical Mystery Tour 163
"Mary Had a Little Lamb" 33
"Matchbox" 36
"Maybe I'm Amazed" 58
McCartney 155
McCartney II 139
McCartney III 109
McCartney III Imagined 103
Meet The Beatles! 165
Memory Almost Full 128
Menlove Avenue 102
Milk and Honey 135
"Mind Games" 53
Mind Games 145
"Mother" 27
"Movie Medley" 49
"My Bonnie" 31
"My Brave Face" 38
"My Love" 79
"My Sweet Lord" 75

New 120
1962–1966 165
1967–1970 166
"No More Lonely Nights" 76
"No No Song" 62
"Nobody Told Me" 57
"Nowhere Man" 51
"#9 Dream" 53

"Ob-La-Di, Ob-La-Da" 26
Ocean's Kingdom 93
Off the Ground 127
"Oh My My" 65
On Air: Live at the BBC Volume 2 116
1 168
"Only You (And You Alone)" 59

"Paperback Writer" 54
Past Masters 94
Past Masters 1 102
Past Masters 2 106
Paul Is Live 98
"Penny Lane" 52
"Photograph" 73
Photograph 96
Pipes of Peace 142
"Please Please Me" 64
Please Please Me 93
Postcards from Paradise 97
"Power to the People" 43
Power to the People 114
"Press" 44
Press to Play 137
"P.S. I Love You" 40
Pure McCartney 107

"Rain" 34
Ram 154
Rarities 126
"Real Love" 32
Red Rose Speedway 147
Reel Music 121
Remember 111
"Revolution" 56
Revolver 161
Ringo 150
Ringo Rama 97
Ringo the 4th 103
Ringo 2012 99
Ringo's Rotogravure 115
Rock 'n' Roll 132
Rock 'n' Roll Music 140
"Roll Over Beethoven" 20
Rubber Soul 162
Run Devil Run 111

"Sally G" 75
"Say Say Say" 87
"Seaside Woman" 23
Sentimental Journey 123
"Sergeant Pepper's Lonely Hearts Club Band" 17

Sergeant Pepper's Lonely Hearts Club Band 169
"Sergeant Pepper's Lonely Hearts Club Band/With a Little Help from My Friends" 21
Shaved Fish 146
"She Loves You" 77
"She's a Woman" 48
"Sie Liebt Dich" 13
Signature Box 93
"Silly Love Songs" 81
"Slow Down" 32
"So Bad" 51
"Something" 81
Something New 155
Sometime in New York City 126
Somewhere in England 125
Songs, Pictures and Stories of the Fabulous Beatles 114
"Spies Like Us" 72
"Stand By Me" 37
Standing Stone 90
Stop and Smell the Roses 113
"Stranglehold" 18
"Strawberry Fields Forever" 45

"Take It Away" 65
"Thank You Girl" 32
"There's a Place" 16
Thirty Three & ⅓ 138
"This One" 15
"This Song" 42
"Ticket to Ride" 58
Tomorrow Never Knows 101
The Traveling Wilburys 156
The Traveling Wilburys Collection 120
Tripping the Live Fantastic 127
Tripping the Live Fantastic Highlights 105
"Tug of War" 25
Tug of War 147
20 Greatest Hits 133
"Twist and Shout" 85
Two Virgins 110

"Uncle Albert / Admiral Halsey" 68
Unfinished Music No 2: Life with the Lions 100
Unplugged 114
The U.S. Albums 100

Venus and Mars 158
"Venus and Mars Rock Show" 37
Vertical Man 106
Volume 3 139

"Wake Up My Love" 23
Walls and Bridges 145
"Watching the Wheels" 63
"We Can Work It Out" 66

Index

Wedding Album 94
"What Goes On" 16
"What Is Life" 46
"Whatever Gets You Thru the Night" 66
What's My Name 95
"When We Was Fab" 42
"Why" 15
Wild Life 137
Wings at the Speed of Sound 153
Wings Greatest 130
Wings Over America 149

Wingspan: Hits and History 124
"With a Little Luck" 77
With the Beatles 91
"Woman" 83
"Woman Is the Nigger of the World" 23
"Wonderful Christmastime" 29
Wonderwall Music 123
Working Class Hero 99
"The World Tonight" 26
"Wrack My Brain" 35

Y Not 104
"Yellow Submarine" 50
Yellow Submarine 143
Yellow Submarine Songtrack 119
"Yes It Is" 24
"Yesterday" 60
Yesterday and Today 148
"You" 40
"You Can't Do That" 24
"You're Sixteen" 74

Zoom In 91

www.ingramcontent.com/pod-product-compliance
Ingram Content Group UK Ltd.
Pitfield, Milton Keynes, MK11 3LW, UK
UKHW050532150426
5217IPUK00026B/1910